TOM BRADY

There's No Expiration Date On Dreams

By Rich Wolfe

ISBN: 0-9664912-3-8

Cover Photo: Gary Rothstein
Cover Design: Pinnacle Press
Interior Design: The Printed Page, Phoenix, AZ

DEDICATION

To wonderful Bay State guys from college days, the Cape
Cod Summer League, and the business world including but
not limited to:
Matt Storin and Kevin Collins (Springfield),
Jim Murray (Lowell),
Jack Reilly (Andover),
Jim Smith (Braintree and Martha's Vineyard),
Ken MacLean (Framingham),
Jimmy Leonard (Auburndale),
Neil McPhee (Waltham),
Joe and Ron Young (Watertown),
Shaun Fitzmaurice (Wellesley)
and Walter Crotty (Winchester)…
as well as former Gillette hotshot Will Bennett of Gig
Harbor, Washington

ACKNOWLEDGMENTS

The people who helped me put this book together could be sorted into three groups, probably. I don't know what the three groups are or why I would want to sort them, but since everything else in this book is sorted into groups, I thought this would be an appropriate place to start. I'm sure I could figure out the three groups if I had to.

My appreciation especially to Jim Nuckols, President of *Sporting News*, Carol Reddy in Phoenix, Mr. Walter B. Planner, Terry McDonell and Prem Kelliat at *Sports Illustrated*, the wonderful baseball guru Bill James in Lawrence, Kansas, *The San Mateo County Times*, Ron Kroichick at *The San Francisco Chronicle*, Kourosh Safani at Serra High School, Brian Morrey at *Patriots' Football Weekly,* Stacey James, Director of Patriots Media Relations, Cory Laslocki at NFL Films, ESPN and the *Unscripted* production staff, Marty Mule and *The New Orleans Times-Picayune*, Donna Bender at *People Magazine,* Richard Lodge and the CNC Group, Millicent Mayfield and T*he Alameda Times Star* and particularly to Dave Ablauf and Bruce Madej at the University of Michigan.

The best part was the help, encouragement, and shared laughter with old friends in Boston and the excitement of meeting new ones in New England.

I am personally responsible for all errors, misstatements, inaccuracies, ommissions, commissions, comminglings, communisms, fallacies....If it's wrong and it's in this book, it's my fault. But thanks anyway to Ingrid Woods, Mike Lynch, and Lisa Liddy for production help.

My thanks to Special K for everything, and especially, to Ellen Brewer, the most beautiful, talented and nicest woman in Edmond, Oklahoma, if not the entire state, and clearly the best typist any Sooner has seen since Troy Aikman of Henryetta (OK) High School won the state high school boys' typing championship in 1983.

CHAT ROOMS

PREFACE

Last Labor Day, you were more likely to see a left-handed female golfer than Tom Brady was to become the starting quarterback for the New England Patriots. I was more likely to be struck by lightning while honeymooning with Christie Brinkley than for Tom Brady to be the MVP of Super Bowl XXXVI.

At least I knew who he was. A very good friend of mine and neighbor in Paradise Valley, Arizona, is Gene Cervelli. Many years ago, Gene and Tom Brady, Sr. were Maryknoll seminarians together in the San Francisco area. Over the years, Gene has kept me abreast of his friend's son starring in high school sports in northern California, how he was going to go to Michigan and beat my alma mater, Notre Dame, which he ended up doing. During Brady's last two years at Michigan, we both watched him constantly on television and were proud of how well he was playing.

After his senior year, I was talking to Charlie Armey, the general manager of the St. Louis Rams. I had just finished a book on Kurt Warner, and Charlie Armey is the guy who most people credit with discovering and staying with Kurt Warner when nobody else believed in him. In discussing the quarterbacks coming out in the 2000 draft, Armey said that he liked Brady better than all the other quarterbacks, but he was not going to be taken that high because a lot of scouts had reservations about him sharing playing time his senior year with former Michigan high school phenom Drew Henson. Instead of a negative as most scouts felt, Charlie thought it was a big plus for Brady. Armey said that for Brady to play at Michigan ahead of Henson, he had to be almost twice as good; otherwise, the head football coach is not gonna irritate Michigan high school coaches by not playing their most prized high school player ever, and playing a kid from California, which is not exactly a hotbed of recruiting for the Wolverines.

However, all of us were rather surprised when Brady fell to the sixth round, the one-hundred-ninety-ninth pick overall, which is where the Patriots drafted him. Armey said he would have taken Brady no later than the second round if he didn't have Trent Green backing up Warner at the time.

Every Monday morning during Brady's rookie year, we would check the papers to see if he got in the game. In the entire year, he suited up for only two games and got in one, completing one out of three passes.

This season, while watching the Patriots upset the Steelers in the AFC Championship game, I called my friend, Gene Cervelli and said, "Gene, let's go to the Super Bowl. You root for Brady. I'll root for Warner. I'll get the game tickets and the hotel rooms. You get the airplane and rent-a-car." So, we were off to The Big Easy.

New Orleans is still as filthy as it ever was...Bourbon Street has more thugs than it ever did...Pat O'Briens still sells more booze than any single establishment in the world....There were more policemen, national guardsmen and security people than any four previous Super Bowls combined....By count, there were more than three times as many people wearing Ram paraphernalia as Patriot gear. But most of the Ram fans appeared to be 'older Yuppies.' Meanwhile, the Pats fans were easily leading the league in getting arrested on Bourbon Street.

On Friday before the Super Bowl, we met the Brady family for lunch in downtown New Orleans. They were so non-plussed by what was going on, you'd think they were having lunch at a café near their home in San Mateo, California. It was ironic that none of the Bradys and no one sitting near our table could possibly have realized the whirlwind trips that the whole family was about to embark on in the coming two weeks.

Tom Brady, Sr. is a fun, outgoing Irishman while his wife Galynn has to be the prettiest and nicest young lady ever to come out of Browerville, Minnesota. They met while working in the airline business. Galynn was a stewardess back in the days when all stewardesses and cheerleaders were beautiful. Galynn had even appeared in print ads for Northwest Orient Airlines. Their three daughters were there along with their son-in-law, Brian, and their first grandchild, Maya. Maureen, the oldest daughter, is twenty-eight and works in a San Francisco Bay area contractor's office; Julie is twenty-seven and helps run her father's insurance and ESOP Management business; Nancy, twenty six, is a management recruiter. You could immediately see the closeness and the vivaciousness of the family as we swapped jokes and stories for half of the afternoon—all of the stories were true, give or take a lie or two.

When the Dallas Cowboys Cheerleaders
started in 1972, each earned $15 per game—
the same amount they receive today.

I asked Tom Sr. why a fine young Irishman like Tommy Brady—the son of an ex-seminarian—did not go to Notre Dame? He replied that he was still so upset about Ara Parseghian settling for a 10-10 tie with Michigan State in the 1966 "Game of the Century" that he never rooted for Notre Dame again. He had refused to even send Notre Dame a video resume of young Tom prior to his senior year in high school. Earlier at their hotel's health club, his sister Nancy had told about her brother's first start for Michigan. It was at Notre Dame. Before the game, Tom drove to the Notre Dame campus so he could get a 'feel' for the stadium. He finally found an unlocked gate into the stadium where he toured the visitors' locker room, roamed the sidelines, examined the sod, etc. When he went to exit the stadium, someone had locked the gate. Young Tom had thoughts of being unable to get out of the Stadium in any fashion until he realized that he could climb to the top row of seats and yell for help. He had visions of newspaper headlines blaring, "Michigan Quarterback Arrested for Trespassing at Notre Dame Stadium." He finally escaped by climbing over a fence.

Well, it *was* funny the way Nancy told it.

Of course, by the end of that lunch, I was so smitten with the Brady family that even though I really enjoyed everything about Kurt Warner, I had to change my allegiance and root for the Patriots on Super Bowl Sunday.

Many Patriots fans were lingering outside the Superdome on Super Bowl Sunday as there was a four-hour musical extravaganza going on inside. The Pats fans had a quiet confidence about them. Not loud and boisterous, but just a quiet confidence that if the Pats played their game plan, they could beat the Rams. Most of the Ram fans were rather sedate and looked more like it was a social event to them. The real shocker was when the Patriots came onto the field, the roar in the stadium belied the number of Patriots fans there. The Patriot fans cheered much louder than the Rams fans throughout the game.

After the incredible contest was over, Gene and I had to drive to Houston since we were unable to get a return flight to Phoenix out of New Orleans. As we were wending our way through eastern Texas, well after midnight, the cell phone rang. It was Tom Brady, Sr., so exuberant, so pumped up, that he didn't even know if he would go to Disney World the next morning. He was living a sports father's dream.

Flash ahead two weeks, and we're sitting in Tom Brady Sr.'s office in San Mateo. He had just returned after two weeks of incredible trips to Disney World and Boston for the huge Patriots parade that drew over a million people. The Bradys flew back home overnight from Boston to Northern California and then took off for another week in Hawaii for Tom's Pro Bowl debut. After the Pro Bowl, young Tom stayed an extra week in Hawaii with some buddies.

Work had piled up in the nearly two weeks since Brady, Sr. had last been in his office, but he and Julie looked tanned and fit and were still living in a fantasy world. A huge stack of papers on the corner of his desk were requests from his clients for autographed balls or autographed pictures from Tommy. Tom Brady was the only player in the NFL last season to make less money than his father did.

After doing the aforementioned Kurt Warner book, which was just a great pleasure to do, I never dreamed that I'd ever see another young athlete come along with the same qualities as Kurt Warner. And lo and behold, less than two years later, here comes Tom Brady.

Real rags-to-riches stories like Kurt Warner and Tom Brady just don't seem to happen except in novels. Growing up on a farm in Iowa, I had avidly read every Horatio Alger-style book of John R. Tunis, Clair Bee's Chip Hilton series, all about Frank Merriwell, The Ozark Ike and Gil Thorpe comic strips: All preached the virtues of hard work, perseverance, obedience and sportsmanship where, sooner or later, one way or another, some forlorn underweight, underdog would succeed beyond his wildest dreams in the sports arena.

But Tom Brady was better than Horatio Alger. He was real life. He was more natural than Roy Hobbs. He was a Rudy with talent, a John Daly without a drinking problem. He was 'Manna from Heaven' to the NFL and every other beleaguered professional sports league. The Washington Redskins, a few years ago, had sold for eight hundred million dollars even though several other teams may have had a higher "street" value. More and more players were widowers by choice. Wilt Chamberlain boasted of having slept with twenty thousand women. (I'm not sure I've even peed that many times!) Some general managers were hoping that bail money didn't count against the salary cap. Baltimore Ravens' fans didn't know whether to root for the defense or the prosecution, and O. J. Simpson was down to about six commandments. (Back in the summer of 1994, when a friend of

> The B.D. character in *Doonesbury* is named after former Yale and Cleveland Browns quarterback Brian Dowling. The title character in the current sports comic strip Gil Thorpe is named for Gil Hodges and Jim Thorpe.

mine heard that a famous ex-football player had been arrested for murdering his wife, he prayed that it was Frank Gifford.)

From the age of ten, I've been a serious collector of sports books. During that time—for the sake of argument let's call it thirty years—my favorite book style is the eavesdropping type where the subject talks in his own words. In his own words, without the 'then he said,' or 'the air was so thick you could cut it with a butter knife,' waste of verbiage which makes it harder to get to the meat of the matter. Books like Lawrence Ritter's *The Glory of Their Times*, Donald Honig's *Baseball When the Grass was Real*, or any of my friend Pete Golenbock's books like *Go Gators* or *Amazin' Mets*. Thus, I adopted that style when I started compiling oral histories of the Mike Ditkas and Bobby Knights of the world.

I write sports books as a hobby, and they are great fun to do…books on Harry Caray, Mike Ditka, Bobby Knight and Dale Earnhardt, among others. The problem with doing a book on Tom Brady or a Kurt Warner versus the other guys is that not only are the other guys much older, which gives them more time to develop funny stories over many years, they also were much wilder than either Warner or Brady. They all liked to have a drink now and then. Some of them were pathological skirt-chasers—none of the things that Brady and Warner exemplify. So the bad news is, when you have someone so young and so clean, how do you get stories? The good news is when you get done writing a book on a Kurt Warner or a Tom Brady, it reaffirms your belief in sports and in the young people of America versus what we've been seeing from many athletes in recent years.

I'm a sports fan first and foremost. I don't even pretend to be an author. This book is written solely for other sports fans. I really don't care what the publisher, editors or critics think. I'm only interested in the fans having an enjoyable read and getting their money's worth. Sometimes the person being

> O. J. Simpson's cousin is Ernie Banks.
> Their grandfathers were twin brothers.

> Frank and Kathie Lee Gifford have the same birthday,
> except they're twenty-three years apart age-wise.
> They were married in 1986. Frank Gifford was a grandfather
> at the time. Cody and Cassidy are Uncle and Aunt to
> Frank Gifford's grandchildren. When told that Kathie Lee
> was pregnant, Don Meredith said, "I'll hunt the guy
> down, Frank, and I'll kill him."

interviewed will drift off the subject, but if the feeling is that sports fans would enjoy their digression, it stays in the book. So if you feel there is too much material in this book about Steve "Sudden Death" Sabol or golfing in Ireland, don't complain to the publisher…just jot your thoughts down on the back of a twenty-dollar bill and send them directly to me. I love constructive criticism.

In an effort to get more material into the book, the editor decided to merge certain paragraphs and omit some commas, which will allow for the reader to receive an additional twenty thousand words, the equivalent of fifty pages. More bang for your buck…more fodder for English teachers.

We're not here to solve world problems. When all is said and done, remember this is just a book. It's a book to entertain you. It's not a treatise. It's not a bible. So have some laughs. Learn some interesting facts. Read some fascinating tales and get a better understanding of Tom Brady.

Go now!

Rich Wolfe
Scottsdale, AZ

Introduction

T om Brady is a young man the way young men used to be in a world that is not the way it used to be. He was born August 3, 1977 to Tom and Galynn Brady in upscale San Mateo, California.

His earliest football memory occurred when he was four years old. On January 10, 1982, he went to the famous "The Catch" 49ers playoff game against the Dallas Cowboys. He cried constantly during the first half because he wanted a big foam rubber "We're #1" finger glove. Because his parents wanted to enjoy the second half (which included Joe Montana's high desperation-type, game-winning pass to Dwight Clark), they relented.

His three older sisters became outstanding softball players and young Tommy became known as the Brady sisters' tag-along little brother. Once his Little League seasons were over, he would vacation at his cousins' homes in northern Minnesota.

He attended Junipero Serra High School in San Mateo, a highly regarded parochial school of about eight hundred students. The school is known for producing outstanding athletes. Tom Brady is not even the first Super Bowl MVP to graduate Serra; that honor belongs to Lynn Swann. Swann starred at Southern Cal (USC) where another Serra grad, John Robinson, coached the Trojans to a National Title. Among the Serra baseball alumni is a guy named Barry Bonds.

After his freshman year at Serra, he attended a football camp whose organizer, quarterback guru Tom Martinez, was to have a profound effect on his football career. He also traveled to football camps at Arizona State, Arizona, UCLA and Cal-Berkeley.

At the same time, he became a coveted catching prospect in baseball and was drafted in the eighteenth round of the 1995 major league baseball draft by the Montreal Expos. Brady would have gone in the first or second round if he hadn't announced his definite intention to play college football.

After a solid junior season quarterbacking the Serra Padres, his dad put together a video recruiting tape that was sent to fifty-five Division One football schools. The tapes cost two thousand dollars but were well worth it as big-name programs started looking closer at his skills. At a Reebok camp at St. Mary's College in Moraga, California, over eighty coaches were there primarily to look at Brady. He didn't disappoint, and then his star rose further when he became MVP of the Cal camp. Terry Donahue at UCLA offered a full ride that later went to Cade McNown. Keith Gilbertson, the head coach of the California Golden Bears, told him, "You'll start as a sophomore, junior and senior at Cal." Michigan told him he would have to compete against six other quarterbacks for playing time.

Michigan got interested because of the recruiting video they received from his dad. Later, Tom and his dad were going through an NCAA book. They were sitting on their family room floor when Tom, Sr. came to Michigan's page in the book. "How about Michigan, Tommy?" (Everyone in his immediate family calls him Tommy.) Tommy said, "My God—Michigan. That would be unbelievable." He had been intrigued by Michigan's winged helmets ever since he saw them during a Rose Bowl game when he was in grade school.

Michigan doesn't recruit California heavily and got into the picture because of the relationship that Wolverine assistant Billy Harris established with the Brady family—a connection that is still very strong. Michigan head coach, Gary Moeller, was delighted to break new recruiting ground in northern California, as was Wolverine head baseball coach, Bill Freehan, the former All-Star catcher with the Detroit Tigers.

Young Brady's decision surprised the West Coast recruiters. Brady's explanation was simple: "If I'm going to be the best, then I must compete against the best." A shocked coach said, "How many kids would give up a guaranteed starting job for three years in the Pac-10 Conference, right across the Bay from his backyard, leave the mild California weather to go two thousand miles from home and freeze his butt off with no guarantees where there's so much talent at Michigan that they're backordering futures?"

Billy Harris wanted Tom to get to Ann Arbor early so they could golf together, and Tom could get acclimated to the campus. Shortly after signing the Michigan letter of intent, the shenanigans began. The Big Chill started three days later when Billy Harris called and said, "Tommy, I've got good news and bad news. The good news is that we're going to tee it up a lot sooner than expected. The bad news is I'm leaving Michigan and joining the Stanford staff." Six weeks later, Michigan head coach Gary Moeller was fired after a bizarre drunken episode at a Michigan supper club. Following that, Michigan baseball coach, Bill Freehan, was fired and new football coach Lloyd Carr prohibited his players from playing two sports. So Tom Brady goes cross-country to a Michigan campus where he doesn't know a soul....And has, no one "fighting" for him inside the Michigan coaches' room.

His father had to see a psychologist for two months. He and his son had been so close that every time he talked about Tom being in the Midwest, he cried.

Few schools have sent more quarterbacks to the NFL than Michigan and when Brady hit the practice field, he found more talent than the Betty Ford Center. Since 1987, six Michigan quarterbacks have gone on to the NFL: Jim Harbaugh, Todd Collins, Elvis Grbac, Scott Dreisbach, Brian Griese, and Tom Brady. Most NFL experts felt that if Drew Henson, Brady's backup for two years, didn't sign a seventeen million dollar contract with the New York Yankees, that he would have been the number one overall pick in the 2002 NFL Draft by the Houston Texans, rather than David Carr.

Scott Dreisbach, currently with the Cleveland Browns, was slated to be the Wolverines starting quarterback in '95 and '96 but injuries sidelined him. Brady red-shirted his first season in Ann Arbor and saw limited action his sophomore season. Brian Griese barely edged out Brady in the Wolverines 1997 National Championship year. Brady underwent surgery in October, missed two complete games but still completed 80 percent of his passes in the four games he played.

In 1998, his first as the full-time starter, he completed 61 percent of his passes and set a school record for most attempts and completions in a season.

Brady earned three letters at Michigan and recorded a 20-5 record as a starter. Only Jim Harbaugh has thrown for more yards in a season and only Elvis Grbac has thrown for more touchdowns, one more than Brady did his senior season.

In their annual grudge match against Ohio State, he established single game Michigan records for attempts and completions (31-56). Despite almost transferring to Cal during his sophomore year, he ended up having a wonderful career in Ann Arbor and cherished having matriculated there.

Little did he realize that the trials and tribulations of sitting on the bench, fighting Griese and Henson for playing time and overcoming enormous odds to succeed would prepare him for his well-documented NFL success.

Six quarterbacks were picked ahead of Tom Brady in the 2000 draft: Chad Pennington to the Jets. Giovanni Carmazzi to the 49ers. Chris Redman to the Ravens. Tee Martin to the Steelers. Marc Bulger to the Saints. Spergon Wynn to the Cleveland Browns. In Brady's first full season, he completed two hundred and sixty-four passes compared to a combined fifty-eight completions by the six quarterbacks in the 2000 draft who were picked ahead of him. By completing over seventy percent of his passes in four straight games, Tom Brady is second only to Joe Montana among quarterbacks who have completed at least seventy percent of their passes in four or more consecutive games.

Brady set an NFL record in 2001 when he completed one hundred and sixty-two passes before he was intercepted for the first time.

Only two quarterbacks other than Tom Brady have led their teams to the Super Bowl in their first year as starters. Vince Ferragamo with the Los Angeles Rams in 1980, and Kurt Warner of the Rams in 2000.

He went from Boy Wonder to The Great Unknown to Super Bowl MVP in a matter of months.

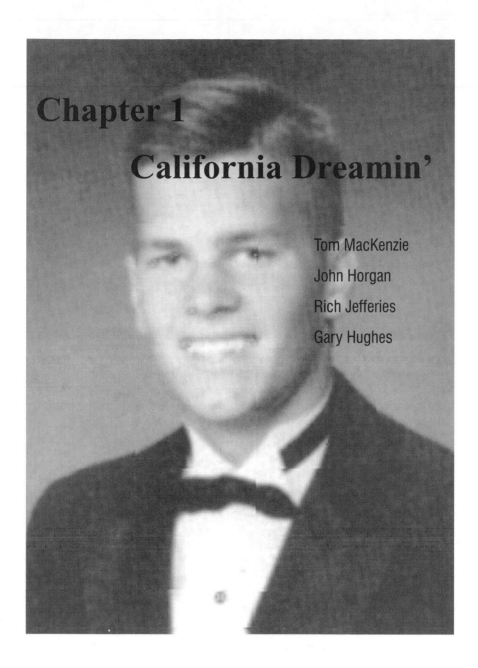

Chapter 1

California Dreamin'

Tom MacKenzie

John Horgan

Rich Jefferies

Gary Hughes

TAKE THIS JOB AND LOVE IT
TOM MACKENZIE

Tom MacKenzie dedicated 31 years of his life coaching young athletes until his recent retirement. He was Tom Brady's head football coach at Junipero Serra High School and very instrumental in his early development.

I knew Tom as a little boy because he grew up in my parish, St. Gregory's. He has older sisters, and one of his older sisters was in my son's class, who is about four years older than Tom. I knew about him as a little guy. He was like any normal little kid. He grew up in the shadow of his sisters. They were the better athletes in the family. He was a little chubby. He played all the sports. Now in Catholic grammar schools, everybody plays, everybody makes a team. Back in my generation, I got cut in fourth and fifth grade, but they don't do that anymore. He came along, and he played baseball, and he played basketball growing up. His mom played soccer for a number of years and is a very good athlete. She might be the athlete in the family. The girls were either in dance or softball. The oldest one, Maureen, went to Fresno State on a scholarship. My son was in eighth grade when Tom would have been in about fourth grade, and my son said, "This is the kid I remember trading baseball cards with in the school yard." He was just a normal, easy-going kid growing up in upper middle-class America. He got along with anybody and everybody.

It's absolutely gratifying. When Tom was going to school here, as a freshman he made the squad, but he didn't start at quarterback. To be honest with you, I can't remember who it was. In his sophomore, jayvee year, the starter at quarterback got hurt, and our jayvee head coach, Bob Vinal, knew that Tommy could throw. We put Tom in as quarterback and essentially threw the slant and the fade. Tommy was fairly accurate and could drop the ball in. He was sort of lanky—not lean and mean like he is now—and awkward

> The XFL still had more viewers than the LPGA, the NHL, or Major League Soccer.

and a little overweight. He still had a little bit of his baby fat, but you could tell he was going to be a big kid. He had big hands and he had big feet. You could see that he was going to grow. He was always a fairly decent size. But the thing is that he was a little bit awkward—sort of like a big bear cub that hasn't exactly figured out how everything works.

If I had to say that there was one thing over the last couple of years when he was in high school, is that he worked real hard trying to make himself into an athlete. By the time he was a junior, he looked more like a quarterback. The big question was in his arm. I told his father that when he was a sophomore I always thought he'd have a Division One arm, and as far as the lower body, he had a Division Five lower body. What it would take over the next year and a half would tell the tale of how competitive he would be as far as becoming a Division One quarterback—his foot quickness, being able to get back, set his feet, be able to plant, and throw the ball. He took up jumping rope, and he did all sorts of things. He made himself into the athlete that he is. I just basically told him and his father one time toward the end of the Jayvee year, this is what I think you need to do. Dad did a great job of providing all the opportunities he could for Tom, but Tom was very good about taking advantage of every opportunity that was presented him. He was the one that did all the hard work to make himself into where the college people thought he had the potential.

There were a lot of people that recruited him out of high school. Before his senior year, I met with his mom and dad, and we talked about some of the things they were going to face as far as getting their son ready to play football. They had already set up files with information coming from seventy-five to eighty colleges. All the Pac-10 schools were sending him information except for Stanford. The only reason I think they didn't is that they were looking for the more mobile, scrambling type of quarterback. Cal was very, very interested in him. They contacted him, and they contacted me as much as they could under the NCAA rules. We figured that Cal was going to be the place that Tom was going to end up at, that he would probably stay in the Bay Area, play at Cal, and his friends and family and everybody would be able to see him. Then he got offered visits from Cal, UCLA, Michigan and Illinois, and I'm not sure the fifth one. He took all five trips. San Jose, Texas A&M, New Mexico, Utah, the Oregon schools,

> To be a Division One school in football,
> your stadium must have 30,000 seats and you
> must average 17,000 in attendance. Rice is the smallest
> Division One football school, 2600 students.

the Washington schools—you could go on and on—a lot of people were very, very interested.

Then he took the Michigan trip and whatever happened back there, he fell in love with the place,because all of a sudden that jumped to the head of the list, and it was between Michigan and Cal. The head coach at Michigan at the time, Gary Moeller, came out and visited the family and visited the school. I sat down and talked with him for quite a while, and they were really interested in him. They were more into drop-back quarterbacks. Once, after they got Tom there, all of a sudden, they wanted to go with more the athlete, more the scrambler—Scott Dreisbach and Drew Henson. He was right at the end of the prototype, drop-back passer, that they had been going with for years and years.

I was not surprised that Michigan recruited him. I was surprised that Tom decided to go there, because up until that time he hadn't really expressed any great interest in Michigan. Then all of a sudden, after he went back there—I don't know what they do on their recruiting trip—but boy, they sure as heck sold him. This was the place he wanted to go to.

He loved to practice and work hard.

When Gary Moeller came out to visit, he shows up here in gray slacks and blue blazer, starched white shirt, and blue and gold tie with the "University of Michigan" on it. He came across as being very, very professional. We've had a lot of coaches on campus, but not that many head coaches— big names. They very much wanted Tom back there because when Moeller came out, he also had an appointment to meet with the family. They came across as being very professional. They sold Tom and the family on Michigan.

The nice thing about Tom was the fact that he never put us, the coaching staff, into a position where we had to say, "Knock it off." He was not a lazy kid. He always worked hard. He always did the right thing. There was never a question of whether I might have to teach him a lesson by sitting him down because he wouldn't apply himself. He loved the game of football. He loved to compete. He loved to practice and work hard. Other than just being himself, he didn't have any real competition or somebody that was going to threaten him. Whereas at Michigan everybody was maybe as good an

> Athletes, with the coach's blessing,
> have about a fifty percent better shot at
> admission to college than non-athletes.

athlete if not better than he was. Michigan is where he had to learn how to compete. In high school, Tom's struggles were being patient with himself, being patient with his teammates, because they'd drop passes that they should catch. They just weren't physically mature enough, with the hand development, to catch Tom's passes. Whereas in the college level, Tom had to compete with other great athletes for playing time and understanding the fact that "if you go on and you're not real successful moving the team, they're gonna sit you." At our place, he didn't face that kind of challenge. His challenges were more to relax, be patient, if it's real windy outside, Tom might press and put too much pressure on himself and get frustrated and impatient with himself because he's trying to do it perfectly. All of a sudden he's not getting the results that he thinks he should be. At Michigan, he's facing guys that you'd better produce, you'd better be accurate, you better have a high percentage of passes, and those kinds of things.

We're sort of an old-school kind of program, very disciplined. One thing that was very important with me is that I make everybody else see that Tom had to toe the line. A lot of times I've seen kids, and have seen quarterbacks, in our area that have been maybe not even as good a prospect as Tom, spoiled and double standards set. Tom never got spoiled here, and he never got spoiled at Michigan. He was always made to toe the line. Then when he got the chance by being drafted by the Patriots, he understood the concept that you're based on your last performance, and you're only as good as your last performance. So he's never had the opportunity to ever take anything for granted. He understands that if he doesn't do the job as well as he's supposed to, then somebody else is going to take his place, and he's going to sit down. He's understood that kind of concept, and because of it, he knew and

"Is he really that real? That sort of goody-two-shoes?"

he understood the importance of what it means to become a student of the game, pay attention to detail. If you talk to him right now, he knows that last year was last year, that he has to go in and he has to improve on what he did last year or he won't have his job.

When reporters and people have asked me, "Have I been surprised?" I haven't been surprised at what has happened. I just am surprised that it happened so soon. The character issues and fitting in—in and out of the locker room, on the field and off the field—were never a question. Tom Brady is a young man where if somebody comes up and starts a conversation with him, the conversation will end up not being about Tom Brady. It will end up being about the other person. He's got wonderful people skills. But he's always been that way. "Is he really that real? That sort of goody-two-shoes?" I say, "Hey, what you see is what you get." He's got a nice little sense of humor.

When I was e-mailing him during the season, there was a thing in New England. Something had happened with the wide receiver, Terry Glenn. It was right after Tom had started playing, right after Bledsoe had gotten hurt. There was a news conference going on, and all the reporters were with Tom Brady. Then word sprang out that Terry Glenn was in the building. Some of the reporters started to leave the room, and in a very nice way, Tom Brady called them on it. "I was always told that it wasn't polite to get up before a person was finished speaking." He said it with a smile, and he knew exactly what was going on, he knew they had heard enough of him and they were going to check out and see what was going on with Terry Glenn. Tom has a nice way of dealing with the media. He has a lot of patience. He has a real sense of what kind of a person and what kind of a teammate he's supposed to be.

> **...he holds up the car keys after getting the Cadillac Escalade and said, "Hey, team car."**

I think that's just reflected on the fact that he holds up the car keys after getting the Cadillac Escalade and said, "Hey, team car." He immediately begins to take the attention off himself and spread it around to everybody because he understands the development of that offensive line was huge as far as his success. Antowain Smith was a huge factor in the development of their offense. Their special teams made huge plays that allowed him to be successful, and the team to be successful. The defense did a great job of trying not to put the offense ever in jeopardy. He understands how all this allowed him to take his responsibility of managing the game and doing the things and being patient with his development. The coaching staff gave him the flexibility and the freedom—they did things as the season went on that allowed Tom to be a little bit more successful—shotgun, and throwing when they needed to, and by changing his launch points so they had everything working and everybody on the same page. He understands that 'okay, he did a great job himself,' but it was all these other things, and he was sort of the 'cherry on top', that all of a sudden made everything go.

The only criticism that I had on Tom I look on as being very positive. My messages were never, "You need to work harder." That was never a message that I gave to Tom. My message to Tom is that "You need to be patient, don't try to assume too much of the responsibility. You've got a cast of people around you. Let them work for you. You don't have to assume the entire burden." In a practice, he would get frustrated because say the wind's blowing or it's tough weather conditions, and he's a perfectionist. If I would say, "Relax, set your feet, throw the ball," he would sometimes become impatient. "But Coach I did that." I'd say, "Yes, you did Tom, but you've got to understand that every time you do something, I'm going to reinforce the concept because when you're in the game situation you're twenty-five to forty yards away from me on the sideline, and if I reinforce the concepts time after time after time, then it's going to become instinctive. It will be instinctive and you will automatically do it."

That last Super Bowl drive of eight plays where he had to get rid of the ball a couple of times, not taking a sack, I would love to get those eight plays, and I would use that as a textbook—as a clinic—for any young quarterback. This is what you do and this is how you achieve competitive greatness because he does things on each of those eight plays that if you were to grade out, he would grade out at, if not one hundred percent, ninety-five to a hundred of exactly what he needed to do on each one of those plays—under a situation where you can't have any more pressure than on that particular incident—that whole scenario.

He's grown up—because he struggled at Michigan. Sometimes the great athletes don't have to struggle. They get to the top levels of sport and competitive greatness and they've never had to struggle. Then how do they deal with that? Tom Brady basically struggled in high school. He struggled in college. I'm sure that he has struggled with the New England Patriots. But because of having to deal with those struggles, now he believes in setting his goals high

> **He's grown up—because he struggled at Michigan.**

and he is not afraid of shrinking from that responsibility. When the pressure's on, he loves to compete and is able to accomplish things that a lot of people say, "Well, I don't think he's got good enough feet to do this. I don't think this or that." At our assembly here at school, one of the kids asked both him and Lynn Swann, "Have you ever been afraid? Has fear ever factored into what you're facing?" Both Lynn Swann and Tom Brady said, "It's all right to fear something, or to feel it, but the big thing is that you don't allow it to control you, and you don't allow yourself to be consumed by it. It's all right, and if you do have butterflies, it just means that you care and that you want to do well and because of that you probably will in the long run." It was a very, very honest, sincere answer that he gave the kids to let them know that it's all right to sometimes have doubts as long as you don't allow those to control you and also as long as you realize that every success as well as failure that you have is only a temporary condition. It only lasts until you choose to get up and compete again. So from that standpoint, he has a real healthy sense of his own abilities. I think he really understands his own limitations. Because of that, what he does, that most teenagers don't do, is he works to get better at it. He challenges himself to be better at it as opposed to what happens with most teenagers is they go into denial and avoidance.

For example, you have the basketball player that's good right-handed but can't go with his left hand. Most often what they do is they just go right-handed and don't try to do the left. With Tommy in football, it basically had to do with foot quickness and agility. He couldn't jump rope to save his life when he started. Then he went out, and through the Pacific Athletic Club, found a couple of trainers over there that showed him a number of things in the jump-rope routine and by the start of his junior year, he was already better at jump roping than anybody I had in the program. Somewhere I still have a copy, written out by Tom, of his jump-rope routine. I took that and incorporated it into our off-season program with all our football players. Whatever he realized that he needed to work on, instead of avoiding it, he went out of his way to try to get better at it. That's why he is such a very sound fundamental quarterback with his mechanics and all because he had to be due to his lack of foot speed to begin with. Now you hear the coaches and people talk about his mobility and they look at Drew Bledsoe as being very slow-footed and the mobility that Tom Brady gives the Patriots—no coach can take credit for that.

That goes solely to Tom Brady's competitive heart and his willingness to make those kinds of improvements on his own. He was so focused that after his junior year of high school he would put down the baseball, bat and glove and then he would start getting ready for football. He did that of his own volition. He wanted to be a college prospect. I never asked him to do that. I never had to ask him to go work out. Some people have asked us what our records were. Well, we were six and four with him as a junior, and we were five and five with him as a senior. People might ask, "Why weren't you more successful?" If I could have had more of Tom Brady's teammates work as diligently as Tom did for those seasons, our records would have been better—so don't blame that on him. And we do play in an extremely tough league.

> Lombardi never said, "Winning isn't everything,
> it's the only thing." That line was originally
> said by John Wayne in the 1953 movie,
> *Trouble Along The Way*. Lombardi said,
> "Winning isn't everything, but trying to win is!"

One of the things that we have difficulty in our school is that we don't have 'game breakers'. We had a Tom Brady, but if we'd had receivers that were break-away, like a Terry Glenn or some of the other receivers, in high school that you hit them and they're gone. That didn't happen with Tom Brady. We didn't have those kinds of receivers.

When Tom was here at school last month, I introduced him to the student body, and we chatted a couple of minutes, but we had very little time to talk. He's dealing with all this notoriety and he's on a very tight schedule. I keep in contact with him through e-mail. There hasn't been much downtime. Now, he is back with the Patriots. I got an e-mail from him this week because NFL films had contacted me trying to get some materials from school and so I e-mailed Tom about some of the things I wanted to try to do to make sure it was okay. He told me that they're in quarterback meetings and camps and says he can't wait for the season to begin so things will calm down a bit.

Tom comes across as being very grounded, down to earth. He's very approachable. With him and Lynn Swann together they sort of put on a show that our student body won't long forget. They really did a nice job and you could see that they enjoyed being there and interacting with the kids. Tom was with the kids, and then with the faculty afterward, signing all kinds of things. There was a story in Sports Illustrated about when Tom was eight

> **"What makes me even more proud is the person, the young man, the human being that he's developed into."**

years old and he went up and asked Chili Davis for an autograph and Chili said no. Tom still remembers that, and he remembers how it felt to be a young kid and have someone sort of not have enough time for you. His parents did a wonderful job raising him up – all their children. He's a young man that follows a couple of different rules. I think he's been well taught by his parents. "If you don't have something nice to say, don't say anything at all. Treat other people the way you want to be treated. Make sure before you say anything. Put yourself in the other person's shoes and walk in their shoes for a mile or so and see how it feels." These are the kinds of things I see from Tom. I'm not saying he's a saint. As successful and as proud as I am for all his accomplishments, what I told our student body was, "What makes me even more proud is the person, the young man, the human being that he's developed into." That's his greatest accomplishment. I also congratulated his parents because I think they are models for parents today to see what can happen when parents do a nice job raising their children.

The students felt very privileged. I think they feel very proud of the fact that people like Tom and Lynn Swann come back and take the time, that they're not too big to return and say hello and talk about when they sat in our stands and faced the same challenges and frustrations that our kids are facing now—it was the same twenty years ago. I felt very honored by the fact that Tom would take the time to revisit, that Serra High School is important to him. He wanted to come and give something back to the school and tell them what it meant going to Serra High School and how important it was to him. And he did, he loved Serra High School. Some of the friends that he made here will be life-long friends.

> **I guess I have gotten my 'fifteen minutes' of fame.**

I've been bombarded by a lot of journalists. I've been on radio talk shows, a couple here locally and one back in Boston. I guess I have gotten my 'fifteen minutes' of fame. I've enjoyed it. What makes it even more special, and I was much more emotional about introducing Tom than I thought I would be, but it's not because of what he's accomplished, it's because of who he is and the way he's handled the whole thing.

Tom's dad made an interesting comment to me, "Who would have ever thunk?" Over the last number of months, I've thought an awful lot and have had an awful lot of time to reflect about Tom, not only to follow what he was doing and what he was saying. This is my first year in retirement after coaching thirty-one years on the high school level. Because I've reflected and thought about it so much, I said, "You know, Mr. Brady, believe it or not, the more I think about it, there were signals even when Tom was in high school as far as work ethic, as far as character, as far as people skills, as far as competitiveness. There were some signals there." It's only now when I look back and I think about them that all of a sudden it strikes me that, "You know, this isn't all that surprising." The fact that the opportunity presented itself, that's the most surprising—that all of a sudden it happened, and then, boom, he did it. The way he was talking and the belief and the self-confidence in himself, and believe me performance has a lot to do with how you feel about yourself. And the coaches at the end of last semester sent him away not only feeling good about himself, but letting him know that they felt good about him—that they were real, real pleased with his efforts and his progress and his development. Again, he's the type of guy that when you get into the huddle, he can get after you, but he can do it in a positive way where you feel bad about letting him down. On the other hand, in dealing with the defensive starters, he loves to compete so when he had to do the scout team and was going against the first team defense, he was trying to make the scout team look pretty good and really trying to challenge that starting defense. The veterans appreciate that especially when young guys come in and work hard because oftentimes that's not the case. Because of Tom's coaching, not only at our school, but at Michigan, we don't like people who are lazy, and we expect people to work hard—he just doesn't know how to do it any other way.

In high school, Tom was very durable. He never missed any playing time. When he was a senior, we based our offense on throwing the football. He was always very interested in how we were going to block things, especially pass-blocking schemes because depending on the defensive fronts and the potential blitzes and stunts that you face, you have to adjust and adapt to those kinds of things oftentimes week to week. The rule we always had for them is that you don't have to worry about your backside, we will protect that, and we will make sure that you'll never get hit from the backside. But you may have a

In high school, Tom was very durable. He never missed any playing time.

'hot read' or something, but it's coming at you, you see it, and you'll know who to get rid of the ball and how to get rid of it and in what progression. So he was very comfortable. Because we threw so much, especially his senior year, we did an awful lot of shifting, motion. The other thing we did an awful lot was quick pass series. If you have a thrower, you sit back and you play pass defense. If you have a passer, you put him on the clock and you rush him and you try to either make him throw before he wants to or you put him on his back. We knew people would try to come after him so we always tried to have 'hot reads' and we always tried to go with a quick passing game so that after a while they would stop blitzing because, "We can't get to him because he gets back quick. He's got a good release. He has good mechanics. We're better off trying to get into the pass zones than we are trying to get into his face." He's been very durable. He's physically a lot tougher than people might give him credit for. If he has to try to make a tackle, he'll try to make a tackle. If he throws a pick or something like that, or if he needs to throw a block, he understands that it's a physical game and if he's caught in that kind of a position, he's going to respond. He knows that.

As a coach, I felt very privileged, very fortunate, very lucky to have happened to be the guy who had the head coaching job when Tommy happened to go to school here. You're lucky if you have one or two kids a year that can go on and play Division One football.

From a notoriety standpoint, I feel just very blessed, very honored and privileged that I had the opportunity to work with this guy. What makes it even more special isn't because of who he is. What's important to a parent are your children—who they are and who they become. I told the Bradys they've done themselves proud.

He says, "My greatest fear is being a 'one-hit' wonder." My response to him is this, "Hey, pal, you don't have to worry about that. The fact that you had the courage and the guts to come right out and say it—you won't be a 'one-hit' wonder." He'll be able to persevere. The big thing now is not whether he can do it or not. Now he is going to have to be able to sometimes make those great plays and, at some point in his career, he's not going to have as good a supporting cast as he had this year. That's where he's going to have to grow. That's how you get to the Steve Youngs, the Joe Montanas, the Brett Favres, and the Dan Marinos. You have to play great even when your supporting cast isn't as adequate as it needs to be. Now Tom has done it with a very good supporting cast, but this will give him the confidence so that when it comes time to retool the Patriots, now he's gonna have the wherewithal to be able to allow his performance to jump to the next level or so.

It's a special moment when you have kids come back and say, "You made a difference," or "You were a special part of my life."

Lynn Swann and Tom Brady back at Serra High School.

HOME SWEET HOME...SAN MATEO
JOHN HORGAN

John Horgan was the Sports Editor of the San Mateo County Times when Tom Brady was a star athlete at Junipero Serra, the local High School

Here in San Mateo, we have 21 schools that play high school football. I saw Tom play baseball and football when he was a junior. He was a good baseball player. He was a catcher. He hit with power. He had a good arm. I thought he was a prospect in baseball. I think a lot of other people did too. In football, he didn't play on good teams, and he did not play varsity football in his sophomore year, which is a little surprising when you think about what he's accomplished since high school. Now, whether that was a combination of their style of play at Serra High School, or whatever it was, he was on the varsity only in his junior and senior years, and his combined record at the varsity level was eleven and nine, and both years, their league record was two and three. They played in the West Catholic Athletic League, and that is one of the stronger high school football leagues in the Bay area here. I remember watching him in his senior year.

When he was in high school, he definitely stood out because of his stature. He had a good throwing arm. When he threw the ball there was something on it, and he was tall. He literally stood out among a lot of the other kids. His teams were not very good. He threw for a lot of yardage. Serra's got all of his numbers, and he's in their record books. I don't think he has the career passing record. They've had quarterbacks over there—that's one thing they have had at that school. They've had some really good quarterbacks.

The other thing that struck me was—he had trouble getting away from a pass rush—now this is in high school—he did not have unusually quick feet in high school. Hence, his position in baseball was catcher. The two things that really stood out about him were his toughness and his throwing arm. But, he came up on my radar screen because my daughter played softball with his sister, Maureen Brady, back in the late eighties and very early nineties, so that's how I met the family. That's how I knew Tom Brady, Sr., and Maureen, and of course, little Tommy was always hanging around, throwing a baseball or doing something. He was on the periphery when I first knew him.

The word "varsity" is the British short form of the word "university."

I knew he could take a hit and he could throw. I was surprised he didn't go to Cal. When he was a junior in high school—you know, the junior year is really a critical year in high school—he wasn't on anybody's radar screen. He played on a team that wasn't very good. I don't think he had gone to too many camps and they looked upon him more as a baseball player anyway, but he went to a camp at UCLA or someplace between his junior and senior years, and he knocked some socks off with his arm strength and his size. He was a prototype drop-back quarterback, and people who had never heard of him or seen him went "Whoa! Who the heck is this guy?" Cal had a scholarship available for a quarterback and they wanted him. It was all kind of a last minute deal and then Michigan came in, and lo and behold, he wound up surprising everybody and went to Michigan, and staying and hanging in there. He redshirted in his first year and then "rode the pine" for two years so he waited three years for his chance. I was utterly amazed. Now, again I saw him play on TV a lot at Michigan. I saw him play against Notre Dame—saw him play in the Orange Bowl, and every time I saw him, he looked good. He was completing passes—he was moving the ball—he wasn't turning it over—he wasn't throwing a whole lot of interceptions, and he was just very efficient. So, he got in the pros and I was a little surprised. One thing that surprised was that I think he's quicker now than I've ever seen him. I think he has better footwork. I think, even though he's put on some weight, he still seems a little bit quicker to me, and boy he can take a hit. I don't know where that came from, but boy, oh boy. There are a lot of guys that had better numbers, they had more wins, they did more in high school. The whole thing has been very deceptive. A lot of us have been faked out by this guy. There were two reasons why we were all faked out: number 1—we looked at him more as a baseball player, and number 2—his high school teams weren't very good, and we're not smart enough—guys like me— we're not smart enough to see beyond wins and losses and gaudy statistics. He had good statistics, but they didn't translate into W's, so guys like me who aren't recruiters, and don't understand it as well as we might, got faked out.

All this is happening to Brady over here on this side of the Bay, while Darrell Russell is deep doo-doo in Oakland for the Raiders. Apples and oranges.

> One out of 40 high school basketball players play college basketball. One out of 15 play football.

A COACH IS A TEACHER WITH A DEATH WISH

RICH JEFFERIES

Rich Jefferies is a former major league scout who is an assistant baseball coach at Serra High School. His son, Gregg, enjoyed a long and successful major league career with the Mets, Phillies and Cardinals.

Probably his freshman and sophomore year Tom was just getting into baseball and was more of a football-type guy. His junior, senior year, he was potential unlimited. He improved so much. He was one of my top players—to this day I think he'd be an All-Star catcher, just because of his work ethic. He just does not accept middle-of-the-road work. He's a leader. That's why the New England Patriots couldn't cut him. There would have been a revolution with the other players.

Bill Freehan was the baseball coach at Michigan, and Tom went there to play baseball and football. They okayed that prior 'cause we had a long talk about Michigan. Our high school league is awfully good. I told Tom when he was going to Michigan, "Now you're stepping into a football power house. Baseball's pretty good at Michigan, but I don't think they will let you play both sports." Bill Freehan had promised him that he would be able to play both, but once he got there, Bill Freehan was fired. But Tom in the back of his mind always wanted to play football. I used to kid him and say, "You know, you're a six foot four kid, You can play baseball for twenty-five years. In football you're lucky if you play for five."

Last week, Lynn Swann and Brady came to our school to talk to the kids. I said, "Well, the old coach was wrong. You're right where you belong." But he would have been absolutely a heck of a baseball player. He was a serious guy. He had a great sense of humor and a great smile as far as funny stories. Thre were times we could kid in between drills, but he was just such a hard worker. His dream was to beat Bellarmine and St. Francis and win our league and win the CCs, and we did all that with him. We didn't have time for a lot of kids' stuff. I'm not at all surprised by how well he has done in football. There's not one person from Serra High School, and I'm sure Michigan's the same way, if you ask people, who wouldn't say you've got to know this personality. There's not a lot of kids like Tom Brady. He understands what he wants and he doesn't con himself. A lot of kids would say, 'Well, I'm working here, and I'll split time here….." Not Tom, he has a dream, and he works for it. In high school coaching, and in professional coaching, too, you get kids out there and all of a sudden they think that to be a professional baseball player, you've got to chew tobacco, scratch your crotch and look in the stands. No. You've got to get your kid's game, and you've got to go over your skills, both defensively and offensively, and you've got to look to see who's ahead of you and say, "I'm gonna beat that guy out, and I'm gonna work harder than him."

> ## In Brady's case, I think he understood the hard work.

In Brady's case, I think he understood the hard work. Again, I'm gonna go back to conning yourself, kids are great to work with, but eighty percent of them don't know what 'real' hard work is. Tommy did. My son did. I'm not sure either one of them would ever coach seriously in baseball. It's kind of ironic, eventually they'll both be good football coaches. My son wants to get into football, too 'cause it's a physical thing. But baseball, there's so much that you have to do in between the lines, without the coach, to be better. All I had to do to Tommy and to my son was to say, "Hey, there's a kid in Oakland, and I'm not sure he's better than you, but boy he's pretty good." That's all you did, and there was a spark in their eye—you could see it—'no, he's not better than me,' and they worked hard to achieve what they wanted. They didn't con. If I said, "Swing a heavy bat a hundred times." They'd swing it a hundred and twenty times, where some kids would swing it fifty and say, 'well, that's all I need.'

We had the local newspaper guy upset with us at school because here we have two Super Bowl MVPs and not one newspaper was invited. Tommy wanted it that way. They were speaking to the whole school, the whole student body. He didn't want one person outside the school to know about it. He didn't want to be interviewed. He just wanted a one-on-one, as he put it, with the students from Serra. He was unbelievable—about reaching your dream. They tape-recorded him. And Lynn Swann was great, too. Of course, Lynn Swann gave the greatest acceptance speech to the Hall of Fame I've ever heard in any sport. But they were both just 'reach your dream.' That was the whole thing. Whatever it's going to be, work hard for it. The reaction from the kids was unbelievably positive. In today's age where the athletes kind of big-time you or flip you off—they were unbelievably positive.

You ask why so many good athletes from Serra High—good coaching! I'll tell you what. The school, first of all, is very disciplined. The parents know what they're getting. I had a big argument with this good friend of mine who is a great friend with Bobby Knight, would you send your kid to Bobby Knight? Well, you know what you're getting when you go to Bobby Knight. You know what you're getting when you go to Serra High School. You're gonna get discipline. You're gonna get a great education. You're going to have a challenge. If you do your homework, you're gonna be able to qualify for most colleges in the country. If you choose to go out for a sport, you're gonna be in the toughest league in our area, and you're gonna be challenged there, too. So with all that, as a sixth, seventh, eighth grader, the parents know when they come there, you're gonna have a pretty good four years. We've got a couple of prospects this year that are the same thing—following right in their footsteps.

When I said, student body only, there were about twenty five of his friends from all over the country that came back to the school just to see him. It's really a positive place. I was a public school teacher for thirty-five years, and I coached in all areas, and scouted with the Chicago Cubs for a while, but there's nothing like the old parochial school coaching. And then running into these kids that just love to play. To see Tommy's smile on TV. How about his interviews after the Super Bowl? Whether you know Tom Brady or not, you look at that interview and go, "Wow. What a nice kid."

Tom is a tough hombre. He's an altar boy, in terms of trouble, but boy, he's got a burning desire to succeed. If it means that you have to play at the top of your game, he will get on you in a second.

Even locally, I still hear, "Well you know, his passing stats are this, and...." But he doesn't do anything to lose the game. He'll do little things to get you another first down. He understands his ability, and he doesn't have to lead the league in touchdown passes or yards. He has to lead the league in wins. That's the whole thing that we get here at Serra. It's not an individual thing of 'who leads the league.' We play the toughest schedule in the whole area. We play all the good teams, and we usually play them back-to-back when we're out of pitching, and we'll lose some games before we get into our league, but that's the test for kids. How do you come back after a loss once

> Johnny Bench named his son after Bobby Knight...In 1962, NCAA semi-final, Ohio State versus Wake Forest, Billy Packer had 17 while Knight failed to score. It was Knight's last college game as he did not play in the title game.

> ## He worked twice as hard of anybody in football prior to even getting on the field.

we get in our league? And how do you play when you're in a down situation? We could play the weaker teams around and be undefeated going into the league, but we want to lose some games 'cause the kids learn from that. I believe Tom was one of the best we've had at learning that. His attitude was "No matter the situation, who's pitching, who we're playing, I'm gonna do my filmwork. I'm gonna do my weight training." He worked twice as hard as anybody in football prior to even getting on the field.

You've got to have a short memory. If you make an error, you've got to forget that and go on. And yet, you can't have a short memory— 'cause you've got to remember the good times when you're going bad. Why was I hitting the ball well then? You've got to remember why. It's kind of funny. My son was going through some tough times in Philly, and Richie Asburn calls him over and says, "Hey Gregg, have your parents send you your scrapbook. You need to read your scrapbook again. You're not here by accident. You're a heck of a player, but it looks like you've lost your confidence." He did that, and then he went on a twenty-four game hitting streak. But it took Richie Ashburn to tell him he had to remember why he was here. You forget. You get caught up in it. Everybody goes through some down times. You just make some changes and boom—you're right back on a streak.

Brady's dream in high school was to go to Michigan and play football. He had never been away from home, and his family is very close. He would rather have gone there and competed and look what happened to him there. He had great stats, and he had to fight like heck to be a starter.

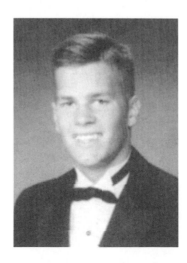

WHEN HE PLAYED, GARY WAS SLOW, BUT HE HAD BAD 'HANDS'
GARY "BOOMER" HUGHES

Gary Hughes is one of the most famous baseball scouts of the modern era. In 1995, as the Scouting Director of the Florida Marlins, he was asked to 'cross-check' one of the top catching prospects in the nation. Ironically, the prospect, a kid named Tom Brady, played for Hughes' old high school.

Hughes built the 1997 World Champion Florida Marlins following a stint with the Montreal Expos where he and his scouts discovered an astonishing sixty-three major leaguers—including several superstars—in just five years.

I only saw Tom Brady play one time in high school. I was very impressed with him. The only thing was he made it perfectly clear he was going to play football so we didn't really pursue drafting him at the time. I had no idea how good a football player he was.

He was big, strong—had great size. If you compared him to somebody, it would probably be like a Ben Davis type kid. He had some 'pop' in his bat, and let it swing from his left side, a left-handed hitting catcher, and had real good arm strength.

I'd love to say I took one look at him and said, "Gee this guy's a great leader, and all of that," but 'no' that didn't happen. I talked to some of the people at Serra High just briefly, Pete Jenson, who is the baseball coach, and of course Rich Jefferies, who's Gregg's dad, was also one of the coaches there. They said, "He's a great kid and all that, but he's gonna play football." There was just no question about it.

I was going all around the country watching guys play, and he was one of the top kids out there. I didn't even actually meet him. It seems like he's just got great makeup. You read about the family and the whole thing about how they closed down the street for the Super Bowl and all that. He wouldn't have been the best quarterback I ever signed to a professional baseball contract. I did sign John Elway.

> **He wouldn't have been the best quarterback I ever signed to a professional baseball contract. I did sign John Elway.**

History breeds history, and our high school has turned out a large percentage of great athletes. I think the fact that we've had so many people, going all the way back. I was at the first—what they call the 'new school' which is where Serra is now. I was the first freshman class to be in there. We had two big-leaguers on our high school team, Tim Cullen and Jim Fregosi, who probably combined for about twenty five years in the big leagues together. The athletes just kept coming. Danny Frisella, of the Mets who died at such a young age and now has the Serra baseball field named after him.

I was raised in the fifties on the San Francisco peninsula—there wasn't a better time in the world to be raised in a great atmosphere. We'd go down to the ball diamond in the morning. We'd pack a lunch and we go in the morning and played nine on nine. By the afternoon, guys would kind of weed themselves out. We were making up games to play three on three, or stick ball and stuff like that. There was always something. It was unbelievable. It was a wonderful time to be raised. I was the class of '59 at Serra.

The New England Patriots once played a regular-season home game in Birmingham, Alabama, in September 1968.

In the 1980s movie, Back to the Future Part II, Biff Tanner scans a sports almanac brought back from the future. Biff read aloud, "Florida's going to win the World Series in 1997. Yeah, right." The Marlins were not a team at that time, but they did win the World Series in 1997.

Chapter 2

The Big Ten, The Big House, The Big Chill

Billy Harris

Scot Loeffler

Jason Kapsner

Mike DeBord

Lloyd Carr

SAY WHAT YOU WANT ABOUT OHIO STATE...AND FRANKLY, "LOSERS" COMES TO MIND
BILLY HARRIS

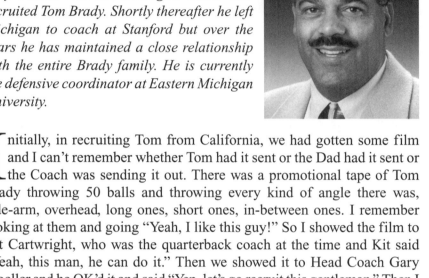

Billy Harris was the Michigan coach who recruited Tom Brady. Shortly thereafter he left Michigan to coach at Stanford but over the years he has maintained a close relationship with the entire Brady family. He is currently the defensive coordinator at Eastern Michigan University.

Initially, in recruiting Tom from California, we had gotten some film and I can't remember whether Tom had it sent or the Dad had it sent or the Coach was sending it out. There was a promotional tape of Tom Brady throwing 50 balls and throwing every kind of angle there was, side-arm, overhead, long ones, short ones, in-between ones. I remember looking at them and going "Yeah, I like this guy!" So I showed the film to Kit Cartwright, who was the quarterback coach at the time and Kit said "Yeah, this man, he can do it." Then we showed it to Head Coach Gary Moeller and he OK'd it and said "Yep, let's go recruit this gentleman." Then I had a chance to go over to the Serra High School and met the coach and met Tom and made a home visit. Then Moeller and Cartwright went out there and they followed up after I had met the family and talked to Tom. Then they went out there and said, "Hey you know, we're interested." You've got the quarterback coach and you've got the head coach and you're sitting down there, and we got rid of the recruiting coach now, because he just spots the talent. Right now we've got to go out there and figure out a way to get this man to come. So then you send the artillery in there, so to speak.

The thing that you notice about him when you first start talking to him on the phone was that he had confidence in his ability. You say, "Hey, Tom, you come to Michigan and there's going to be some competition at quarter-back." And he said "Hey, coach, I'm looking for competition. I'm not shying away. I would never not go to a place just because there's

> A quarterback needs seven seconds to call an audible and to make sure his teammates heard him.

competition." You talk to his Dad and you tell him the same thing because you don't want him to come out there and think things are going to be easy. His Dad would say, "Hey, Tommy's known competition all his life. He had to go out there and prove himself every day." So that was the thing that got me excited because bringing anybody from California, it's a long walk home and you don't want them to get here and turn around and go home. The competition is the first thing that scares you and being away from home. I was just excited to hear that he was up for that challenge.

Bring a player all the way from California, the first thing that's important is that they think that they can play and that they can play early because you don't travel that far away from home to sit on the bench. So, that's where the confidence comes from the young man and the family saying,

> **The competition is the first thing that scares you and being away from home.**

"We're going to send him that far, but he wants to go there so he can play." That is the key. I recruited Amani Toomer and that was the key with him, "hey, I'm coming in and I'm gonna play." Any of those kids that you bring from a long distance, they gotta have the ability and they've got to have the thought that "yes, I'm going to play and I'm going to play right away."

Playing at a High School like Serra really helped him. The guys who have graduated from there are some pretty prominent athletes like Lynn Swann and Barry Bonds. The competition of having athletes like that around... Tommy was a baseball player too, so he got drafted by Montreal. When I was out there recruiting him and then after he had signed, I think Montreal was in town to play San Francisco and he took batting practice at Candlestick Stadium. His Mom and Dad and sisters and myself, we all went down to watch the game, watch him hit and it was kind of neat to see him out there hitting balls. I didn't see any go out of the stadium like he told me he was going to put some out of there, but he did hit that ball pretty hard though.

I remember talking to him about coming to Michigan. I said I'm going to call you back in the middle of the week and let me know what you want to do. I called him and got him on the phone and we were talking and I just said "what do you think?" and he said, "Coach, I'm coming to Michigan. I'm going to be a Michigan man. I'm going to come out there and play quarterback for you." He was all like, I'm ready to go, and then once he had made up his mind, he was saying the right things, the things I wanted to hear, that "yes, I want to come out there and play."

I had taken the job at Stanford before Tom came onto campus, so I called up his Dad and told him, "Say, listen, I've got some good news and I've got some bad news." He said, well hit me with the bad news. I said, "The bad news is that I left Michigan. The good news is that I'm right in your neighborhood in San Mateo, right here at Stanford, so I'll be able to see the family and root with you for Tom." After I went to Stanford, a short time later, Moeller got into trouble and he left. Brady goes to school in the fall and all the people that had a hand in bringing him to Michigan, they slowly all left there. I left, and then Moeller left, and Kit Cartwright left, so all the people that were recruiting him hard and knew him the best and had had conversations with him in having him come to Michigan, in a year's time, they're all gone. You bond with those people and so if you have a problem or if you're feeling down, or if you're feeling homesick, those are the first people you're going to go to. You've had a chance to get to know them and they got to know you. If you're walking around campus and if you knew Tom, if he didn't have a smile on his face, you knew something was up. This man is always smiling. I think that bothered him some, early, when he didn't have the early success and all the people that he got to know before he got there weren't there to lean on, so to speak.

We got a chance to talk after I left Michigan and I went over to the house and had dinner with Mom and Dad and the family. Plus Tommy and his Dad and myself, we went golfing a couple of times. So we got a chance to talk about the process, how it was going to unfold, what was going to happen. I told him I was going to be there for him cause I'm going to be here. So every time he would come home in the vacation periods, after the Bowl games, or in the summertime when he came, we'd get together, him and his Dad and I. We'd always go golfing and we'd talk about Michigan. We'd talk about if he had any problems, what's the best way to go about solving these things. I remember one time he was talking about the competition and I remember Freddy Jackson was telling me, "Hey, this Brady, he's going to be right up there. He's going to be competing." I'm sure they were telling him that and then all of a sudden I think he ended up like third—I think it was Dreisbach, Griese, and then Brady. He thought he was going to be somewhere up there, number two, and didn't quite make it there, but it turned out that he stuck around and did well by anybody who was watching him.

> Michael Jordan was given his first set of golf clubs
> by fellow University of North Carolina classmate
> Davis Love, Davis Love, Davis Love.

I was able to become closer friends with the Bradys, being at Stanford, than I probably would have been able to, being at Michigan. I just remember that first year that Tom was on campus and I had come back before Thanksgiving. Michigan played Ohio State that weekend. So we had flown back to watch the game. We had a reception at the Spaghetti Bender and invited Tom and his Mom and Dad plus a couple of other people that had come to the game. So we got a chance to see him. Because I was away from it, then when we got together, he could talk about the program, talk about how he felt and the family felt about what was going on and how tough it was on him at first. But it worked out pretty well.

We stay in touch since we've moved back to Michigan. My wife e-mails them often. It was really funny because she e-mailed big Tom and said "it's great to see what Tom is doing. We talk about him just like family." Big Tom e-mailed her back and said, "What do you mean. You are family." Really makes you feel good. These people are something special.

There's a rumor that Tom's not the most talented of the Brady kids. It's really funny because each one of them have got their own niche whether it's the softball game or the soccer, but they are a competitive group. I don't care what you're competing in, whether you're competing with Tom or his sisters, they're not going to let you win. I think they probably got that from their Mom because their Mom's a good tennis player and so if you're going to play with her, you better have your game together, because she wasn't going to give you anything.

> **The thing that made Tom successful in Michigan...is that he's got a lot of confidence in himself.**

The thing that made Tom successful in Michigan and carry that into what he's done the past year is that he's got a lot of confidence in himself. I remember talking to him his rookie year. In an the exhibition game the Lions had hosted New England and Tom had engineered a last minute drive for a touchdown. After the game I saw him and gave him a big hug and asked him how things were going. I said to him, "Tom, I am just so glad that you got drafted by New England. Bledsoe's the same kind of quarterback you are that drop back, throw the ball, there's going to be a lot you can learn from Bledsoe." And he looked at me and said, "Coach, I got a lot to teach Bledsoe, too." So I'm talking about some confidence. That's the kind of person he is. He believes in himself and here he was just a rookie. This was like the first year, but he believed that not only could he learn something from

Bledsoe but that he could teach Bledsoe something about the game as well. I think he showed that he could teach anybody a little bit about the game.

He was calm and cool and had many fourth quarter comebacks at Michigan. I think growing up, watching those Joe Montanas out there in the Bay would get anybody who's a quarterback to feeling that "this is how I want to be." And if you remember Joe Montana leading people in the fourth quarter, the comebacks, as well as Elway down there in Denver, but on the West Coast he had Montana to emulate, a guy that said under pressure, "be calm, do what you know what to do and lead the team to victory." I think Tom grew up watching Joe play and perform down there and he saw himself as the same kind of player.

> **...it was just a case of "hey, give me an opportunity."**

Everybody would have to be surprised about the Super Bowl, except for Tom. If you knew Tom, like I said, what he had to say early in his career about learning from Bledsoe and him teaching Bledsoe a thing or two. For him it was just a case of "hey, give me an opportunity." For the rest of us we're happy for him and glad that he had the success, but to have it come that early, I was definitely surprised. As a coach you know that certain kids have a lot of talent and they've got a lot of things in them, but when you do something special like that, it takes a lot of individuals around you, but it takes the kind of person like Tom to have people trust him and trust in his ability. He gives you that confidence by going out there and working hard and doing the things he's supposed to do.

The one memory that I'll always have about Tom Brady would be when we came back and got a chance to see him play the last game against Ohio State. He did the thing, bringing them back for the big win and seeing him out there in front of Crisler Arena when everybody else was gone, he had all these little kids around him and asking for his autograph. And there's Tom, just standing like the average guy, sitting around there saying "I'm going to stay here until they're all gone because I know that if I was a little kid and I was trying to get that autograph, I'd hope that they'd stick around and give it to me." He is a special young man. In the last game, his Mom is there, his Dad, sisters, everybody, and to have him sit there and give those kids the autograph and the time. I remember standing there saying, "Tom, I know this is the last time so I've got to get my picture, too." So we stood there side by side, got that picture, smiling. So that's a special memory for me.

YOU CAN'T GO TO HEAVEN UNLESS YOU'RE A WOLVERINE
SCOT LOEFFLER

When Tom Brady hit the Michigan campus the one quarterback he was worried most about was Scot Loeffler, a former "Mr. Football" in Ohio prep ranks. But Loeffler suffered a severe shoulder injury that ended his career while three of his under-studies went on to become NFL QB's. He is currently the Michigan quarterbacks coach and remains close with Brady.

I watched Tommy in Freshman Camp. Obviously we were getting ready for training camp and I came in a few days early. Just watching him out there was…there was something about him even when he was a Freshman. "This guy's gonna have a chance some day."

He had natural leadership skills. He had all the quarterback intangibles. It's just that the physical skills weren't there at the time. When you first met him, I don't know what "it" is but he had "it".

He had "bad ass" hair. He had that California surfer hair.

Tom was afraid of everybody on the staff, all the quarterbacks. I was the one he was most afraid about before I was injured. Back then I knew my physical skills were gone. He had no reason to worry about me to say the least, but I felt an obligation. It's been a tradition around here that all the quarterbacks have helped younger guys. I knew my physical skills were done and I looked forward to working with him.

We have very similar personalities and we instantly hit it off—like two peas in a pod.

Tom was an overachiever. He had the ability, not only to make himself better, but he made everyone else around him better. He had natural leadership skills. He still has natural leadership skills and he's a perfectionist.

It's been tradition around here ever since we walked in the door, Brian Griese and I, that regardless of where you're at on the depth chart, you have to learn to prepare as if you were going to be the starting quarterback. So Brian basically came in and in his Freshman year he prepared like he was going to be the starter. I prepared so that when the opportunity arises, you're not going to have to prepare another guy. We passed that along to Tom. And Tom Brady, when he walked in here as a Freshman and he was the fourth string quarterback, prepared as if he was going to play on Saturday as a Freshman.

Tom is extremely inner-arrogant. You would never know his confidence, but he believes that he can't be stopped and that it is definitely one of his biggest intangibles that he uses to be successful. He comes to the line of scrimmage just

> **Tom, in practice, was exactly like he was on game day.**

wondering which receiver is going to get his next completion because he's a positive thinker, he's a guy that has no negative thoughts and it's one of the reasons why he's where he's at. It's because of how confident he is. The reason he's confident is because of his preparation. If you're prepared, there's no reason not to be confident.

Tom, in practice, was exactly like he was on game day. No difference. You've got to be a State Street (practice field) quarterback before you become a Stadium quarterback. There's not one thing different that he did in the game compared to practice. He was so good in practice that all game day really was was an extension of practice except with fans.

Tom is a solid guy. He was never a practical joke guy. He had a way. He was always intense. He had a way to motivate guys, yet not make it look as if he was their boss, but he could get people around him to do things to make them better. He would do impressions of Tony Montana from that movie *Scarface*, but he was terrible, absolutely horrible.

The competition between Brian and Tom before the 1997 season was probably just as competitive as the Drew Henson, Tommy Brady comparison, except it didn't get media attention. That's exactly what happened. But it was unbelievable and that's partly the reason why Brian was as successful as he was, is because he had a young guy that was sharp, had a strong arm, was intelligent, knew the game, that was pushing him every day. That's going to be Michigan football at the quarterback position forever here. It's going to be a constant fierce competitive atmosphere. However, they were very mature in how to handle them so that they wanted to see each other be successful.

When Tom was considering transferring, he called me that evening and said that he was going to leave. He met with Lloyd Carr the next day, called me in the afternoon and said, "I'm staying," which was probably the best thing he did. His Dad gave him some great advice with that whole thing. He came here to play at the highest level of competition, so why are you running from it? Between his Dad and Lloyd and his family, he made the right decision.

We always talked about, visualize in yourself, doing great things and that's why he went down to Notre Dame and snuck into the stadium. He's not the first player that has done that. There's other players that have done that, but obviously his story is coming out.

Between him and Brian, I've never seen better huddle presence. He had the ability…we have a quote around here…"quarterback must believe in himself. His work must convince his teammates that he can be trusted when all else fails." When he walked in that huddle, ten guys, 20 eyeballs, were looking at him and they knew that he was going to get it done. And that didn't happen overnight. Guys watched him struggle, guys watched him have to fight through adversity, and they believed in him. Through every single thing he did here at Michigan from his work ethic to fighting through adversity, his teammates bought into him.

Tom is confident and he's cool and he was always confident. There wasn't a time that he didn't believe that he wasn't going to get it done. It is amazing during the week he would visualize himself having to come back against Ohio State to win the game, to come back versus Notre Dame. So that was all based on preparation. He was prepared. He was confident and he never panicked, ever. He was a winner.

Thinking back on the Penn State game, it was funny, we got into the stadium the night before the game and I picked the wrong end zone. I go to Tommy, "You've got to prepare yourself if you're going to have to throw a touchdown pass in the back corner to win the game." It was the wrong end zone. It was actually the south side where he did, but he did take command that week. He put himself in some bad situations early in the game and he was able to keep his poise and his confidence to lead the team back, but his preparation, his confidence, is the reason why he's where he's at. We had a special play where he had to fake an injury. He practiced the limp off the field, that was Coach Carr's idea, which was pretty neat. Kap was laughing the whole time because he was faking it. Kapsner was laughing his rear end off. I will never forget it. Kapsner was a signaler that year and we could hear him on the headphones laughing. He was hysterical. Tom's not going to be an actor.

Thinking about his last home game, I remember he said on Thursday, "I can't believe this is my last game", cause Friday is the day that we do the Seniors for the last time practice. He was real emotional and couldn't believe that this was his last opportunity to play at Michigan Stadium. I remember sitting in the room with him on Friday night at the Hotel. It was past curfew actually. I snuck up there and we sat and talked for about a good two hours, just reflecting back on everything from him walking in as a Freshman, not knowing a darn thing to thinking about transferring, Drew Henson, to the Brian Griese battle, and it was just a great night sitting back and talking about his career. I'll never forget that. He left the room and was just like normal. "Hey I'm gonna go and beat Ohio State tomorrow." Confident, cool and calm. We just talked about him and about Michigan and about how much he loved Michigan and it was a great evening.

The Orange Bowl against a good Alabama team with multiple comebacks was a good way to go out. No question. He did a good job.

Tom is a student of the game, just like I am. He's an offensive coordinator out there playing quarterback. He knows the game, he knows what beats what coverages. He would come in every Monday with his own game plan, which is beautiful. His preparation was unbelievable in the fact that after he came up with his game plan, he would be in here until 11:00, 11:30 at night. He was the last one to leave the building, watching film. Every Thursday and every Monday he had his talks about Tom Brady's game plan. It was kind of comical…but look who's laughing now.

In regard to Tom's volunteerism, the Mott's Children's Hospital sticks out probably the most. I believe it started back here with I think Juwan Howard, I want to say, was one of the first ones to start doing it. It was passed to the quarterbacks and Brian and I really hit it hard and then Tommy followed in the footsteps. But Tommy did a lot of big things with the Mott's Children's Hospital.

What happened to Tom Brady during the Super Bowl didn't shock me one bit. The only thing that shocked me is about how fast it happened. I didn't believe that Tom Brady's second year in the NFL, that he'd be winning the Super Bowl. The type of person he is, the type of overachiever he is, I knew it would happen, I just didn't know that it would be Year Two in the NFL.

> When Clemson University plays in a bowl game most of their fans pay their bills with $2 bills to show their economic impact…and increasing their chances of a future invitation.

My best Tom Brady memory would probably be that night in the hotel. The Friday night in the hotel before the Ohio State game. Just the conversation that we had about quarterbacks, about quarterback play, about Michigan, about himself, about our relationship. It was a night that I will never forget. It was great conversation.

The one word I would use to describe Tom Brady is genuine.

Mike DeBord (left) and Head Coach Lloyd Carr (center)

TOM BRADY IS JUST A REGULAR GUY WHO SOMETIMES WEARS A CAPE

JASON KAPSNER

Jason Kapsner met sophomore Tom Brady during his first day on the former's first day on the Ann Arbor campus. The teammates soon grew to be close friends as they worked, studied and played together.

Tom and I were instant friends. With him being a year older, he could have been kind of an jerk, but he was really cool. When I first got there, he was very friendly and very welcoming. Coming into the quarterback crew, he gave me the inside scoop on how to handle, how to act, what coach likes, what coach doesn't like, how to handle Griese and Dreisbach and these guys. He kinda showed me the ropes initially.

I came to school early. My first day on campus, there were three of us, Lefty (Scot Loeffler), Tom and me, and we just worked out every day in the summer. Lefty was, for all practical purposes, our coach. I don't think Stan Parish, our quarterbacks coach, would like to hear that, but…Tom and I would get together and go out with Lefty at five o'clock and go through about an hour's workout. From there, we'd go out to dinner and hang out the rest of the night. That was kind of our daily routine. We get along very, very well.

When I first met Tom, I was very impressed by his demeanor, the way he carried himself. I particularly liked the way he interacted with the other teammates. The guys just had a lot of respect for him. Tom's always been the kind of guy that's fun to be around. He's just a fun, charismatic kind of guy to be around.

> **He's just a fun, charismatic kind of guy to be around.**

Probably more than anyone I've ever known in football, Tom exuded just an absolute passion and love for football, and also for the concept of 'team.' That really came through very strong with the team and that really drew in everyone across the board, regardless of your class, your race, and all that kind of stuff. Aside from personality, I think Tom just drew guys in purely because of his love for the team and the guys and for football. No one wanted to win more than he did. That just really showed through in workouts—seven on seven—all those kinds of drills. He just commanded a lot of respect because of that passion he had.

I lived with Lefty for a summer so the three of us would get together and go out at night. We went to parties or just would hang out and watch TV or we would play golf together. Tom was always pretty smooth with the ladies. But he wasn't up for commitment, that's for sure. He always had plenty of ladies liking him—probably not the stature he has with them now!

Another off-the-field thing we did sophomore year was I went with Tom once on spring break back to his family in San Mateo. That was an absolutely great trip. His family is just amazing. You hear all these things about how nice his family is and it's extremely true. His mom and dad are just the most generous, loving people as I've known. They're an amazing family. His sisters are all really cool and very fun. It was one of the best spring breaks you could have to go and spend some time with his family.

Tom is extremely Catholic and I know that his faith is very important to him, but we never really did a lot there together.

Tom and I always roomed together before games. We always had more and deeper conversations, away from just football and girls and stuff like that. One time we were sitting at the hotel getting ready for the Indiana game, an away game. We were in the middle of nowhere Indiana. This was in the midst of the Drew Henson rotation and some strange things were going on in the quarterbacking ranks to say the least. We definitely always leaned on each other when we had some football struggles or football issues. We sat and reflected about what we think this kind of experience may mean to us and how it's going to affect us as we go on through life. Some things are extremely hard about football—particularly football at Michigan. We felt it would give us a very good base to work from and how to deal with some of the issues that you deal with coming from a tough program. I'm thankful for the program because it really mentally prepares you for the real world.

> The state of Michigan has more golf courses
> than any other state in the Union.

> By winning percentage, Indiana ranks 12th in all-time Big
> Ten Football standings behind the University of Chicago.

> There are many times more sportswriters
> than there are religious reporters.

So Tom and I had a real heart-to-heart one night just discussing that. Kind of how we really feel this is going to put us that far ahead when we get out into the regular world—the real world. We should be better able to deal with tough issues. When you're playing college football, you can say, "Well, it's football." But when you're going through it, that stuff seems pretty real. Now looking at that, and as I think back to some of those conversations we had, and I look at the success Tom is having, a lot of it, I feel like, is due to some of the hardships then. He had dealt with some of the battles he had to go through mentally and struggle to get over. I think the football tradition at Michigan, the coaching style that our team had really prepared him and us to face the situations we are currently under. That's one of the reasons why I think Tom is one of the best leaders I've ever seen. He had to face adversity early on.

The expectation on the Michigan quarterback is to be the best leader on the field—to be the general—you have to be. You look at every good quarterback that we've had and he is the leader on the field. That's a role that I really believe to a large part cannot be taught. Some guys just naturally have it to a degree and some guys don't have it. That's one thing that Tom was able to just step in and he was a natural leader, as natural as they come. I think that his leadership stems from just a pure passion for the game and a love for it. The expectation is that you're the first at all drills, you're the first to be in the morning working out, the hardest working guy out there. When other guys are relaxing and not really working, be the first to get on them and get them going—and be able to do that in a way where you don't aggravate people. Tom was able to do that. He was able to motivate guys in a positive and encouraging way to get the most out of them. I think that definitely shows through. If you look at all the games we played where maybe we're down or tied with two minutes left in the game, during Tom's couple of years of playing, I think we won ninety percent of those games. I attribute that ninety percent to Tom and in the ability that he had to move the team in those critical, crucial times.

I don't really think Tom was ever trying to get his confidence to rub off on other players, but it's an unexplainable thing—part leadership and part confidence. Tom's confidence just came from—the kind of confidence that he has at that level is just purely a natural thing where he just knows that he's the best and that he's gonna get it done just because he is so passionate about getting it done and getting that win. I think that kind of natural passion and confidence just exudes out to a team. He's the kind of guy when you sit and watch him in the huddle, he comes into the huddle and gives the play and all these little intangible things, but you look in his eyes and the tone of his voice and the way he's looking at the guys. That's what inspires a team. They don't want to see a guy that's walking into the huddle, gives the play in a very mundane voice maybe. Tom stood up and would get in there excited. He'd go in the huddle and if he saw a guy was tired, he'd talk to him, not in a mean way, but just, "Come on. Get yourself up. There's a big play here." Just something to single that guy out and let him know, "Hey, you've got to carry your weight."

I guess to go back to the 'Why was Tom confident?' In a large part it had to do with his preparation. No one I know sat and watched more film and knew what the other team was going to do more than Tom did. Tom went well far beyond what the expectation would be from even the coaches as far as watching film. The thing about Tom is he knew exactly what that defense was gonna do on every play. He'd come out of the game and he'd be able to tell what he had seen as far as the defense and their blitzes and what they were doing, and on the film that would be exactly what you saw. His preparation was unbelievable, and I think that's probably really what's carried it over, part of that work ethic. He prepares himself better than anyone I've ever seen for a game, which allows him to have the confidence to go out there and succeed. I think Tom is definitely not the best athlete out there. I think Tom would probably say that, too. He's not a Michael Vick. He's not the fastest guy out there, but he is the smartest guy out there. I would put Tom's leadership ability and his intelligence of this game up against anyone in the NFL, anyone in this game right now. I would be extremely confident that he would win out on that.

> **The thing about Tom is he knew exactly what that defense was gonna do on every play.**

Tom was always goofing around to a degree. Griese does this impersonation of Al Pacino in *Scarface* as Tony Montana. Tom would always try to do the impersonation and he was just brutal. He didn't give it up though. He kept trying and trying. It was almost funny in how bad of a Tony Montana he does.

Tom was a laid-back California kid as soon as he got off the field. But as soon as he got on the field, he was yelling, hollering—sometimes the guys on the team would laugh at him—it seemed so kind of cheesy at times. He would be jumping up and down and screaming at the top of his lungs and

> Saints quarterback Aaron Brooks and Falcons quarterback Michael Vick are cousins.

guys would go, "Hey, man, it's just practice." That was just his natural expression, even though some of guys may have thought it was kind of cheesy and dorky for him to get that excited, but he was extremely intense during practice. He was a great practice quarterback. There was no joking around as soon as you got on the field.

I thought it was hilarious because, and this could be the middle of a game—say the Ohio State game, fourth quarter, if they sent in a play he didn't like, he'd roll his eyes and just be so mad. He'd come off the field and just be like, "Well, that was a great call." He was definitely not happy with some of the calls they got in, but it was really funny to see him just roll his eyes at plays that would come in. He would also even signal plays to me on the sidelines sometimes that he wanted to get in. I'd relay it up to DeBord (offensive coordinator), and he'd go, "Oh, okay." He'd often put it in, but sometimes not. If he didn't, Tom was upset. He felt that as the quarterback out there, you could sometimes get a real good feel for what's gonna work. So Tom got frustrated when that wasn't listened to, to a degree.

I think Tom always gave his talks, not necessarily after games, in practice or after practice. It's a long season, and there are days where you just go out there and guys don't want to practice, and you have bad practices. During those kinds of practices, normally Coach Carr has to get on the team and give it to them. I think more often, it would be Tom. If we didn't practice well, Tom was the one who was more hurt and aggravated by that, and he made a very strong point of saying, "Tomorrow, this is not going to be the way it works. We're going to come out there and practice." So he'd get on the team to a degree. What gave him the license to do that is because he didn't take days off. He worked hard. He worked the hardest of anyone. He took the captainship very serious.

I think with Tom it's kind of like a switch that goes on in these games where he just knew—me knowing Tom and being on the team—you just knew that in these games there was no way we're gonna lose. I think that's why the team had that confidence. I really do believe this because they knew they had Tom out there. Tom seemed to have a switch that would absolutely turn on in those stretches. The higher those stakes got, the better Tom got. In these last second types of games, all the play calling would be passes for the most part. You're going down. You're really putting the game in your

> Richard Nixon gave the eulogy at Woody Hayes' funeral.
> Joe Namath was the only athlete on President Nixon's
> famous "enemies" list.

quarterback's hands. At that point, it was like a switch when Tom knew they were going to put the game in his hands. There's just this look on the guy's face that you just knew this was getting done and you were gonna win. There's no way you're not going to. That's why I can say probably, geez it would be interesting to see, that in those situations I'll bet we won ninety percent of our games when Tom was playing. You take those situations and compare with other quarterbacks that we've had over twenty years or something like that, and I'd be just surprised if Tom was not at the top and then probably Griese number two.

He was telling me about the time he got locked in Notre Dame Stadium. He said he was freaked out. I think he tore his pants. He had to jump and climb out of the stadium. If I recall it right, I think he had the security guard chasing him around in the stadium. There was a gate that was unlocked and he just went through it. He was trying to get back out, and then the lock was on. It was like, "How am I going to get out of this place?" It was night. That's the kind of thing he did. He went down there and just sat and wanted to see that field and probably picture winning that game there, which unfortunately we didn't. That's the kind of intensity he had and, I think, the dreams that he had for that team.

The quarterback situation back then was definitely tough on Tom. We had many talks like that where Tom just had to say, "What more does a guy have to do to prove himself?" I had no idea. It's one of those things where you look at life and you kind of understand that it's not always fair. That's the point that we got to in saying, "Well, life's not always fair, but you've got to keep going. You've got to keep working hard." I think that's what Tom really did. It was not to say it was easy at all for him. It was very hard. This is the kind of stress that you didn't need to have or want to have at that point—and that he didn't deserve to have, but I think that really strengthened him and it has really prepared him for what he is doing now

In our last three games of his senior season, all were come-from-behind games, there was that switch I was talking about that just came on. I don't remember specific details of it, but I just remember that Tom grew into this unbelievable leader during those times—just unbelievable. I know he's been compared to every great quarterback—the Montanas of the world—that's ever been out there, but there's a reason for that. It's just because of

> Johnny Lattner, the 1953 Heisman Trophy
> winner from Notre Dame, didn't even lead the
> Irish in rushing or receiving that season.

this type of switch that he can turn on during that time. I think the thing that separates him is that he never would ever consider the game that we could lose. That thought just would never go through his head. I remember that the touchdown to Marquise Walker—I think it was a backside post route—Tom just read the defense and made a great play. I think a lot of that comes from the preparation. He knew what they were going to do. He knew he had a backside read and took it. A lot of times what we're coached to do Tom would not do. He would take some gambles on a bigger throw, but they're calculated in the sense of that's what the defense was giving him but maybe sometimes that's not what the coaches wanted to see out of it—they didn't call the play to have what Tom was throwing. There's a lot of risk there. Not only is there a risk of having an incomplete pass or having something bad happen on the play, but there's also the risk that if it doesn't work out the way you wanted, now all of a sudden you've got the coaches to answer to, too. So there's kind of a double risk there when you start doing some things in that play that the coaches don't want you to do.

> **In our last three games of his senior season, all were come-from-behind games, there was that switch I was talking about that just came on.**

I do remember that in the '99 Penn State game, Tom went off the field with a limp. He had practiced that all week and would just come off the field laughing. There were actual 'acting classes' on the practice field for that particular play. When he was walking off the field, even during the Penn State game, I couldn't stop laughing. It was so funny.

I think in our last game against Ohio State, Tom was the one who just took over as far as play calling. He was just telling me every play he wanted during that game. He was demanding it. You could see him on the field, and he was getting that—his face was like, "You'd better get this play in." I think DeBord probably sensed that too at halftime when they talked. That game was one where Tom not only took over physically being the quarterback but even was demanding plays that he wanted to be called.

That Orange Bowl game against a very good Alabama team was amazing. I've never seen anyone 'on' like that. That was pretty impressive. For Michigan to come back from two fourteen-point deficits in one game is unheard of. Michigan has never been seen as the total come-back team. Michigan usually gets ahead and lets their defense win games, but Tom just found a way to reverse that.

I think what I remember from that game is the night before. Before games, Tom and I would always sit and relax and talk. We always had these pretty serious discussions. This was the last game of both of our careers. We were sitting there reflecting on it and it was just a real emotional time for both of us. This was more at a level of just being human—not football players, but just being humans. We talked about that the night before—just moving on and what we were gonna do and the experiences that we have had. The emotions came out after the game was over. It was such an amazing game. After the end of the game, Tom came over to me and grabbed me, and we gave each other a hug. He just said to me, "I've loved the time I've spent here with you." He thanked me. We just had a lot of respect for each other. That

> **He just said to me, "I've loved the time I've spent here with you." He thanked me.**

kind of peaked at that moment. Knowing that was the way we ended our time as Michigan football players—just the fact that you can do it in that type of fashion is unbelievable.

That Orange Bowl game would definitely be the one memory I'll always have. It was such a special time for us, such a special moment for me as well. That overtime portion of it with just the feeling like 'you're not really living this, it's so unbelievable, almost surreal,' and experiencing that was what will really stick out in my mind.

What will always be a special off-the-field memory would have to just be our friendship. Just spending summers with him. At the golf course. Going to work at Merrill Lynch. Working out. Hanging out at night. Just being best of friends in a lot of ways. I know Tom, to me, he made my Michigan experience, my college experience, that much better. Just because we had such a good friendship. Most of all that I remember from Tom is not really the football, it's more the kind of guy I think he is, and friend that he is. Even to this day. He hasn't changed at all even with the success he's had, and I think that's really rare. That's what I'll remember the most about Tom.

Tom was a great student. We had the same major and took a lot of the same classes. Tom was a very good student, very diligent. Academics definitely mattered to him. I think he graduated with a grade point of 3.3 or 3.2. It was important to him to take good courses, not just get by, but take some business courses. He really loved business. We had our internships at Merrill Lynch, and we really loved talking about all that stuff. He was a very

The NFL half-time is eight minutes shorter than in college football.

serious student. It was important for him to get his work done, get his papers done. He worked hard at that.

We were very competitive. He was competitive about his grades, too. He would write a paper, and if he got a bad grade, or a teacher kinda ripped on it, or made some comments he didn't like, it would really irritate him. I can even remember him getting a little upset about some grades he got if it wasn't what he wanted.

I saw Tom last summer in Portland at Lefty's wedding. We just had a great time. That was the last time I saw him, but we talked every couple of months or so. The thing that impressed me was I talked to him a couple of weeks ago, and it was the first time since the Super Bowl. I was talking to him about, "What have you been doing?" It was great to hear that it was still the same Tom. He said, "There's some great things about this, but there's also some crappy things about having success." He said everybody was treating him differently, and the fact that he can't go out anymore. He was like, "Kap, it's just me. I'm the same guy. Cool things have happened to me, but I'm still the same guy. I just wish it didn't have to be like this all the time." He called me, and with his busy schedule and everything like that, it was cool to see that he still remembers us little people.

I absolutely knew Tom could achieve great things. His whole life story is just—give him a chance. I think sometimes coaching staffs have made mistakes and haven't given him a chance early enough. But you give him a chance, he'll succeed. I don't really care what it is—just give him a chance, he'll succeed. I think that's a very good way to describe how he operates.

This year he got a chance, and he succeeded. I think that's why he won't be a 'one-hit wonder'.

Later when he's done with football, I would love to start some kind of business with him, such as owning our own golf course so we could play. That would be really fun. That's my dream.

It was extremely ironic to see those two former Michigan teammates, Charles Woodson of Oakland, and Tom Brady come to that situation where two Michigan guys are deciding who's gonna go to the Super Bowl. It

> Academic All-American teams have been picked every year since 1952. Nebraska leads all colleges by a wide margin in number of players selected. Maybe the *N* on Nebraska's helmets stands for *Knowledge*.

doesn't surprise me at all. It's almost like in a lot of ways, God has designed that he is the 'Comeback Kid.' Even when calls go in his favor that probably shouldn't go that way, it's pretty incredible. It's pretty ironic that the end of Charles' season kept Tom going.

I was sitting watching the Super Bowl with my friends. Everyone was like, "Why doesn't he just take a knee and end regulation." I said, "Watch this. I will bet anyone in this room that they will win this game here. I will bet any one of you that he will drive them down and if not win it, give them a chance on a field goal to win this thing." Everyone was like, "Oh, give me a break. Come on." And he did it. It did not surprise me at all. I'll lay that bet down every time for the rest of his career when he's in that situation. I think I'll win ninety percent of those.

One or two words that I would use to describe Tom Brady would be 'class' and 'love for people.' Tom is a genuinely great guy. There are people you meet who are more of a fake thing, but Tom is just extremely classy, extremely genuine, and just has a great love for people.

> In most states, sports betting pools are legal as long as "the house"—or person running the pool—doesn't benefit.

> In the early part of the twentieth century, a college football game was seventy minutes long and five yards got you a first down.

> The NFL since 1968 has given every player the Wonderlic test (a human resources test measuring the ability to acquire and use job knowledge). In a recent year, 118,549 non-NFL people took the test and only four had a perfect score of 50. In 30-plus years, the only NFL player with a perfect score was Pat McInally of Harvard in 1968. McInally starred with the Cincinnati Bengals as tight end and punter.

THE POISE THAT REFRESHES
MIKE DEBORD

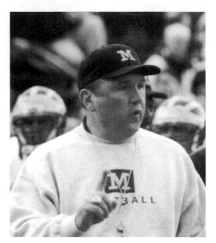

When Tom Brady appeared on the Michigan campus in the Fall of 1995, he met Mike DeBord who became a vital factor in his collegiate career. DeBord was the Offensive Line and Tight Ends Coach before being promoted to Offensive Coordinator in 1997, the season the Wolverines won the National Title. He is now the Head Coach at Central Michigan University.

W hen I first saw Tom Brady back in the Fall of '95, he had California attire on, he had a California haircut. I don't know what you'd call the haircut, but it was definitely from the West Coast, it wasn't from the midwest. You could tell he was a kid from California that was coming into the midwest.

I don't know if a lot of people know this, but before the 1997 season, it was as close of a run at quarterback between Brian Griese and him that I think you could ever expect. Probably in some ways we could have even gone with Tom Brady for that season, but what we relied on more than anything was Griese's experience—he had more game experience and he was older—so we kind of went with that. At that training camp and that spring before we really saw a guy that we all felt was going to be a great quarterback.

After the 1996 season Lloyd Carr talked to him because he was actually considering transferring. After the 1997 season he knew he was going to be the quarterback. I think it was like after the 1996 season when he didn't know if there was any light at the end of the tunnel for him. One thing I really feel good about was Tom and my relationship. It started building when Tom first came and then when I was a position coach, I think we started having a great relationship. And then when I became coordinator, I became a lot closer with the quarterbacks and he befriended me in a lot of things. I feel great about that.

There's no doubt, it started with Griese when he was a quarterback and then when Tom was a quarterback, those guys had great knowledge of football. I mean, great knowledge. Tom would spend as much time studying film as any student athlete could ever do and he did it early. He would come in and he would say, "Hey, Debo, what do you think about these couple of passes." or whatever. And if I felt like they were things that we could really get taught in such a short time and if I felt like they were things that we could put into the game plan, then we put them in, because of his knowledge and what he saw.

The thing that I valued more than anything with Tom was at the end of the week when we would sit down on a Thursday or a Friday after we'd practiced and after the game plan was in and we would sit down and I would say as we went through every

Tom Brady was a 365-day quarterback.

situation, "OK, what's your favorite passes?" I would always call his best passes early in the game, just because he knew what was good against what coverages and he also knew what he liked to throw the best. So, I just really trusted Tom Brady a lot.

Tom was outstanding in terms of practice. Tom Brady was a 365-day quarterback. He wasn't an in-season quarterback or he didn't pretend to be a quarterback. He was a quarterback and he had a mentality that every single second that he had available he was going to study quarterback play. I think he really set a standard around there for a guy like John Navarre now and other quarterbacks that were underneath him of how you study the game and how you really put that to work. When he went out to the practice field, he was relentless. He was a guy that was practicing at a fast tempo and he wanted to get a lot of throws in and he wanted to get good looks from the defense so that it would give him a game look.

The game preparation helped at the end of those games and he was just as calm as a cucumber. All the games that Michigan won while Tom Brady was quarterback, and many were won in the fourth quarter. Number one, let's start with Tom Brady's character. He has as great a character as any person I've ever been around. He is the best. I think that he's got the character to fight through tough times. And when you have that, then you can finish. If you don't have any character when you're fighting through the tough times, you're not going to be worth a crap in the fourth quarter, no matter how well prepared you are or whatever. Probably the greatest example that I'll always remember was the Penn State game his senior year. Penn State ran a defense that you never knew what look they were going to be in, you never knew what coverage they were going to be in, and you never knew what blitz they were going to be in. And I mean they blitzed all the time and they kept coming at us and coming at us. Well, early in the game we got after them and we got up. Then we hit a period in the middle of the game where they were blitzing us and changing up coverage and it seemed like they had our number. We won that game in the fourth quarter on a lot of drives that we put together that Tom just went out and executed. It goes back again to me to his character. If a guy didn't have great character, he's going to get rattled. He's going to get frustrated, he's going to have that attitude of "Hey, are we going to do this," instead of "We are going to do this." It goes to his knowledge, his preparation and all that now comes into effect.

In the Penn State game we made him practice limping off the field for the injury just once. I think we all were laughing as Tom made his way off the field. In fact, I'll be honest, I don't think we told Tom to do that. I think that was a little bit of Tom's intelligence kicking in there. I don't think we were smart enough to think about that and he was.

> **I think there was a great amount of trust by all the players and coaches with him.**

Every one of his teammates truly trusted Tom Brady and again, it goes back to the character issue. They trusted him a lot. So I think that's where it started, was the trust. And then Tom Brady was an outstanding leader. I'll give you an example. In fact, it was in the Penn State week. Penn State had again so many blitzes and coverages and all those things that it was a tough week of preparation. Practice, at one point, on like a Wednesday, wasn't going very good. I didn't think the tempo was going good, I didn't think that certain things were up to the speed that you need for a Wednesday. And Tom was just coming back from a play and I was passing him, and I said, "Brady, you couldn't lead nothing. You are the worst." And he looked at me like he wanted to fight and what he did then was he pulled that team together and he got that team to practice at an up tempo. He got them to practice with a purpose. And I really believe that that game was won on that Wednesday, just by what Tom Brady did as far as leadership on the practice field. And then when they were in drives and things, they knew Tom Brady was going to pull them through the game because of what he displayed in practice all the time and what kind of a person he was. I think there was a great amount of trust by all the players and coaches with him.

We both had the same last game at Michigan—the Orange Bowl game—my last game as a coordinator. I went on to become a head coach and Tom sets all the records. As you recall, in the first half offensively, we didn't do a lot. We tried to go in with our basic philosophy of running the ball and throwing it and controlling the ball and Alabama had a front where they had their linebackers about a yard off the ball, and they were going to make it tough on us running the football. And they really basically said, "Hey, we're going to make you beat us by throwing the ball." And we went in at half-time, we talked, Lloyd and myself, and we talked about "Hey, we're going to have to really come out and we're going to have to throw the football the second half to win this game," a lot more than what we thought game plan-wise because of what Alabama was doing. So, we got with Tom and we went over what throws he liked and what throws we liked and we put them all together and then we just went out and I told Tom that we're going to have to really open it up throw-wise. He obviously smiled and said let's go. And then he took the game over. A lot of people don't know but in some of the passes, it was an either/or type of thing where he could throw one side or he could throw backside to David Terrell when he was one on one. Just Tom Brady's knowledge of "there it is. It's one on one coverage. Let's go ahead and hit the backside guy." And he did that a lot, even in that drive and he showed to me what he's all about as a quarterback. He would dink the ball off when really we could dink the ball off and he put the ball down the field when we had to put the ball down the field. When you go back to watching him in the Super Bowl, go watch the last drive. He did the exact same thing again. He dinked the ball off when he had to dink the ball off and he threw the ball down the field when he had to throw the ball down the field. Tom Brady, to me, is a guy that's bought into the team philosophy. Let's just do what we have to do. I don't have to throw the ball down the field every time to show I'm a great quarterback. If I just do what the defense will allow me to do, we'll win. And Tom's always had that philosophy. He's always taken care of the ball, and he's always played within a team philosophy.

> **He's always taken care of the ball, and he's always played within a team philosophy.**

There was a story in *Sports Illustrated* about getting stuck in Notre Dame Stadium. I didn't get to read that story. The season before that 1998 year when he was going to be the starter, he actually went to Notre Dame Stadium and ended up getting locked in and a security guard chased him out and he had to jump over a fence and ripped his pants.

I can't recall any funny stories or anything like that. I just remember he was always very mature and very poised, and really into football. I mean, really into football. Those are the things I remember. I think there's a side of Tom Brady that people that don't know him don't know and that's the side that he really cares about people, he cares about your family, he cares about everything about you. An example of that: I don't know if it was the 1998 year or the 1999 year but I was on summer vacation and I stopped in at the Dairy Queen in Saline and there was Tom in there getting something, and we started talking. He asked me how my kids were doing, my wife was doing, things like that, and I said "Well, one of my sons is working right over at the hardware store right now, in fact." It was right across the street. And so he said, "Well, Coach, enjoy your vacation and I'll see you in about a week or two." I said, "All right." So we got in our cars and took off. Then the next day I found out that Tom went across the street, went in to the hardware store and then spent some time just talking to my son. That's Tom Brady. I mean Tom Brady is as down to earth as you'd ever want. People worry about all this recognition he's getting with Sports Illustrated and what was he, a judge on the Miss USA contest. I think they worry about "will this change Tom Brady?" I'm going to be very, very surprised if it ever does, because of his character. I don't see that every changing him.

People ask me my best Tom Brady memory. I don't know if it will be a memory, but all of the games that he won as a quarterback in the fourth quarter. All the comebacks and just having a feeling when you called a play that it was going to work because of Tom Brady. I think that would be one of the biggest memories. And I think then the last memory was that I told Tom before the Orange Bowl…I said, "Hey Tom, this is your last hurrah at Michigan and mine too. If I was going to go out with a quarterback, you're the quarterback I'd want to go out with." And I meant that. And that's nothing against the guys that were at Michigan before him that I was associated with. That's nothing against them at all. Those are great guys. But, there's something very very special about Tom and I told him that he was the guy that I would want to go out with. And then he exchanged some words back to me that meant a lot to me. It's just a relationship that you have with him, just the friendship.

The one word I would use to describe Tom is character.

EXPERIENCE IS WHAT YOU GET WHEN YOU DON'T GET WHAT YOU WANT

LLOYD CARR

When Jack Harbaugh left Bo Schembechler's staff at Michigan in 1979, his coaching spot was filled with a young Lloyd Carr. Carr unexpectedly was named Wolverine Head Coach in 1995 succeeding Gary Moeller. Waiting on his doorstep was a 17-year-old quarterback from Northern California who didn't know a single person in the state of Michigan.

W hen I first saw him on campus Tom Brady made a tremendous impression. Here was a handsome, long-haired, sun-tanned California kid…I saw him after the Super Bowl and I was telling Tom that the most prominent thing that I remember about his early career here in Michigan was in the Spring of his Freshman year. We had a scrimmage outside. It was a full scrimmage and our defense blitzed him about six times in ten plays. They had a guy come unblocked and Tom was oblivious to the rush. He just stood in there, threw the ball, got hit right at the moment he released the ball, and never flinched. And every time he got back up and went back in the huddle. My first impression was that, at least on that spring Saturday, this kid had real toughness, real competitive spirit. Then, of course, the next fall he played and his first pass was intercepted for a touchdown. You can imagine that's a quarterback's worst nightmare. Here is his first time as a Michigan quarterback, in front of 110,000 people, and he throws a ball right to the linebacker, right to the guy. Of course, he took a lot of ribbing about that play. And that same fall, at some point, or the next fall, after going through the spring and really getting to show some promise, he came in and sat in my office and said, "Coach, I'm thinking about transferring." He said, "I think I'm the best quarterback here, but I just don't see down the road the opportunity that I want and so I think I'm going to transfer." And I said, "Well, Tom, what I would advise you to do is finish this season and really come back through spring practice and at the end of spring practice,

"I think I'm the best quarterback here, but I just don't see down the road the opportunity that I want and so I think I'm going to transfer."

you'll have a much better idea of where you are." Because at the time, Dreisbach and Griese were here and Griese was playing well. So I said, "There's no reason at this point for you to quit right in the middle of a season. But you talk to your Dad and I'll support you in whatever decision you make."

Well, I'll never forget, he came back the next day and I thought for sure it was to say good-bye. He sat down right in front of my desk and he said, "Coach, I've decided I'm going to stay at Michigan. I'm going to prove to you what kind of quarterback I am and I'm going to lead this state to a championship." From that day forward, there was never any doubt that Tom Brady was going to be the quarterback here because he was possessed, he had an ability to do away with all of the distractions and he stopped worrying about the other guys and devoted himself to doing the things he had to do to get better as a quarterback. Two years later, he became the starting quarterback, he started twenty-five games here and won twenty. I don't think anyone's had a higher winning percentage than Tom Brady did. I don't think anybody here has ever led their team to more comeback victories. What I remember the most about him is the first game of his fifth year, we played Notre Dame at home. We were down late in the game and on a fake play he hit David Terrell down to the two-yard line and we went in and won the game. Then, that same season, we were down ten at Penn State and after he had thrown a pass that was returned for a touchdown with six minutes to go and he made every single play. He led us to two touchdowns, ran one in for a touchdown, threw for another one. The next week we were down against Ohio State and he engineered another great drive to score the winning points on a touchdown pass to Marquise Walker. Then we went into the Orange Bowl game. Twice we were down fourteen against Alabama, who were the SEC Champions, and twice he led us back to take the lead. His legacy here is secured. He was a Captain and a guy that every single player and coach respected because of his leadership, and his will to win. Tom Brady always thought about winning. He never worried about losing. Brady is gonna find a way to beat you. I've never coached a tougher guy, mentally or physically. That's what I remember about Brady.

I'm sure it was very difficult that the guy that recruited him, the head coach, the football team and the baseball coach were all gone. By the time he arrived here in his Freshman year, the people that he knew on the campus were gone. It was difficult because when you go that far away from home (he's 2,000 miles from home) and when you walk in and find that everything has changed, you're not only dealing with being away from home, but you're dealing with a drastic change in the people who recruited you. I can remember I tried to make him feel comfortable and we certainly tried to make sure that his coaches supported him, but I can't imagine how difficult that was. Brady is one of those kids who has a resilience and he's not going to let anything keep him down for long. So whatever emotions he had, I don't remember that ever being an issue that came up in any conversations, which speaks a lot about him. This never was a problem.

Many players say it's harder to play quarterback at Michigan than it is in pro football. I think obviously that during some careers the competition is greater than it is in others. Sometimes the competition is clear-cut and then sometimes it isn't. Tom happened to be here during a time where there was tremendous competition, starting with Scott Dreisbach and Brian Griese and

> **I think playing quarterback at Michigan prepares you for pro football...**

Drew Henson. So, I think competition makes you stronger, it makes you better, and it tests you in a way that you aren't tested when you don't have to compete on your own team. I think the expectation here at Michigan is different because you don't play as many games and your expectation every single year is that you're going to win every game and you're going to win the championship. The truth is in pro football you can lose four, five, six times in a year and make the play-offs. If you had that kind of record here, you're not going to win anything. I think playing quarterback at Michigan prepares you for pro football in a way that high school football can almost never prepare you for college football. You're at an age, you're 18, 19, 20 years old, playing in front of 110,000 people, in a place where you're high-profile and your fans expect you to perform in a way that's going to help your team win. So it's much different because you're at a younger age and you haven't matured either physically or mentally, and so there's no question that it's a great proving ground.

As a quarterback, I firmly believe that you have to begin with toughness. If you don't have a guy that's mentally and physically tough, you're not going to have success at the quarterback position. Right along with toughness I think intelligence is a critical issue. Tom Brady is an exceptionally bright guy. He was a great student here. So when you have a guy like that, who

> Tom Brady majored in Organizational Studies
> and graduated with a 3.3 GPA.

Tom Brady is an exceptionally bright guy. He was a great student here.

studies the game, it gives you the added benefit of being able to have the confidence, first of all, to make a suggestion. The coach/player relationship is forever changing and evolving and because of his work habits and because of the things that he learned and the things that he gained in studying the opponents and knowing football, then he was able to make suggestions. And there's no question that he did and he wasn't afraid to make them. I think any time you have a situation where your quarterback can tell you what he thinks and you have confidence that what he thinks is important, then I think you help yourself. Certainly Tom helped us.

As a practice quarterback he was extremely competitive. We try to practice in a competitive environment. We spend a lot of our practice time with our offense against our defense and we try to put our quarterbacks under as much pressure as we can, under as many game-type situations as we can. It brings out the competitiveness in you. So he was a great practice player. He wanted to win every drill. When we went against our first defense, third down situations, he wanted to complete every pass, and he wanted to convert every first down. When we scrimmaged, he wanted to get the ball in the end zone. I always tried to tell him that the most important thing a quarterback can do is get his team in the end zone. Brady was always competing to win and that's why his teammates had such great respect for him, because there weren't any situations in which he wasn't trying to find a way to lead you.

We installed a play for a Penn State game where he had to fake an injury. I coached him regarding the limp off the field at Penn State. We spent some practice time with that particular play and honestly he wasn't a very good actor. As good-looking as he is, and he may end up in Hollywood, I'm sure he learned from that experience because he understood that it was a key part of being able to execute a play and he's done a wonderful job with it.

He wanted the ball in his hands with the game on the line and was cool under pressure. I think the truly great quarterbacks are all that way and that is something that is in their heart and in their soul. We've analyzed great quarterbacks here and Griese was that way and there's no question that Tom was that way. I think it goes back to growing up, always seeing yourself finding a way to win regardless of the circumstances. Tom did that more than anybody I can remember. But I think all the great ones were that way and we've had the great fortune here to have a lot of great quarterbacks who wanted to be down late in the game. Because the greatest victories are always those victories where the odds were against you or where the pressure was the greatest and great players have a way of responding in those moments.

I think Tom's greatest performance was in the Orange Bowl against Alabama because we had gone into the game feeling that we had to be able to run the football and after a quarter and a half, it was very obvious that we weren't going to be able to run the football. We were down fourteen and if they hit another one we're going to have a hard time. We opened the offense up and threw the football to four wide receivers and he made play after play and did the same thing the second half. So I think his greatest performance was in the Orange Bowl against Alabama, where he engineered thirty-five points and a great win.

The thing that always impressed me was that Tom was such a unselfish guy. When we opened his fifth year with the plan that he would start the games and Drew Henson would play the second quarter, I knew how difficult that decision was for him personally. I knew he didn't like it. I knew he hated it. Yet he accepedd it with a maturity that I certainly couldn't have handled and I don't know of anybody else that could have. He handled it in such a way that he gained tremendous stature in the eyes of his teammates and his coaches and everyone who knew anything about Michigan football because it was as tough as it gets. He handled it like a champion and in the end, he fought his competition off and proved that he's one of the great quarterbacks that ever played at Michigan.

> **...he's one of the great quarterbacks that ever played at Michigan.**

I can't describe Tom in one or two words but I think he's extremely bright, he's extremely loyal, he's extremely tough and he's a lot of fun to be around. He's a guy who can talk about a lot of things and yet he's one of the guys. A guy that everybody loves. I don't know of anybody that is not happy with what he was able to achieve here and of course in Boston. I don't know of anybody who doesn't like Tom Brady.

I wish all my players were Tom Bradys.

> There are only five Division One schools without University in their names: Boston College, Georgia Tech, and the service academies.

Chapter 3

When Good Shots Happen to Bad Golfers

Rob Cunningham

Gary Williams

Doug Dollenberg

W hen Tom Brady left home for a university thousands of miles away, he and his dad made a pact that every year they would spend one full week together with golf probably playing an important role in their bonding.

In the Spring following Tom's rookie season in the NFL, their plan was to play some of the finest golf courses in the eastern U.S. Tom Sr. arranged for playing privileges at Winged Foot (NY), Pine Valley (NJ), and Augusta National (GA), among others. At the last second, they decided to go to Ireland for an annual father-son golf tournament put on by Jerry Quinlan's Golf Tours of Cape May, NJ.

This chapter consists of stories from their fellow golfers on that memorable trip. The Bradys finished seventh in the tournament.

GOING TO IRELAND WAS LIKE PLAYING HOOKY FROM LIFE
ROB CUNNINGHAM

Rob Cunningham was a basketball stalwart at the University of Texas. His father Bob, of Hilton Head Island, was a star on the 1957 NCAA basketball champs, the University of North Carolina. One of a handful of champions to go undefeated, both of their Final Four games went three overtimes. The latter was against Wilt Chamberlain's Kansas team where Tarheel coach Frank McGuire had 5'8" guard Tommy Kearns jump center against Chamberlain.

Rob is a barrister and a talented writer in the Washington, DC area.

I didn't have a clue who Tom Brady was. I only followed Texas football, so I didn't know who he was. We show up at the Agadhoe Hotel in Killarney. That's where all the father-son teams congregate. They're assigned to different tour buses. They have small tour buses to take us to various locations. One thing that was pretty neat about the father-son tournament is that there was actually one father-daughter team there. They got quite a bit of attention. It was pretty neat.

There were seventy-two teams. We were shuttled around the countryside to the various courses—Waterville, Ballybunion, and Old Head. So I first met Tom Brady when we were getting onto our tour bus. He was this tall kid who looked pretty athletic. I was actually talking more to his father because I figured he was a 'wet behind the ears' college kid. That's what he looked like, not realizing he was a Patriot quarterback. I was talking to his dad, and he said, "This is my son Tom. He played basketball. He plays golf." Tom seemed to be this nice young man just like my son, very polite, very personable. I said, "What's a guy your height doing playing golf?" We're both tall, I'm 6'8" tall, and he turned to me with a big smile and said, "Well, what's a guy your height playing golf?"

Buck Williams, one of the fathers, has been to Ireland several times and was familiar with the local territory. Twenty minutes from our hotel, unbeknownst to everybody there is probably the best restaurant in Ireland, a place called Nicks. Nicks is almost world-renowned, and is in this little town called Killorglin, County Kerry. It's a very old restaurant in this small town and has a piano player every night. So on two evenings during our trip, we took a group of guys over to Nicks and had dinner and stayed around and chewed the fat and just listened to stories from everybody. It was great. Tommy didn't tell any stories—he listened. He was just enraptured. He was enthralled with stories my father was telling. The Buckleys were telling about old Carolina stories. Tom was soaking it up and enjoying the storytelling aspect as opposed to telling stories about his life and his career. He was very deferential to the legacies that we were talking about. It was clear to me he appreciated the histories that all of these men brought to the table.

When we got back to the states, I got on the web. I followed him the remainder of the summer. I followed him in through the season. I exchanged a couple of emails with Tom just wishing him luck. We became Virginia fans of the Patriots. Even my wife became involved even though she's never met him.

During the Super Bowl, I was on cloud nine. When Bledsoe got injured and the decision was made later in the week, my first reaction was "Great for Tom." My second reaction was, "The coach could not have made any other decision." That's the only decision he could have made.

For someone of Tom Brady's stature, I've never seen an athlete so unassuming. I've played college basketball, obviously. I used to work and play with

> The greens were so slick during the 1974
> U.S. Open at Winged Foot that Gary Player
> stroked a putt that ended up in a sand trap.

professionals. I used to work at Auerbach's camp. I used to work at Cowens' camp. I played with Larry Bird. Each and every successful athlete that I have dealt with, met, or played with, carry with them a degree of 'arrogance,' for lack of a better term. I think it comes with the territory.

And I didn't understand—here's a kid who is as successful as he has been, but he carried none of that. I saw no evidence of arrogance. I saw no evidence of cockiness or over-confidence.

After playing at Waterville, we had a two and a half hour drive back to the hotel, on a very narrow road, on the cliffs of the Dingle Bay. About half the way through, the bus, as a matter of course, pulls over to the side of the road for gentlemen to relieve themselves. All of a sudden, there's also a little test of manhood. You stood on the precipice and whoever could reach the water by throwing a rock was considered a true Irishman. I dragged Brady out and said, "All right, hot shot quarterback, reach the water." Try as he might, he couldn't reach the water. I gave him such grief about that. He was kind of embarrassed. He got back on the bus, and I said, "All right the big hot shot NFL quarterback couldn't reach the water." He was very demure. With his weight training, he could probably reach it now. He's apparently gotten a lot stronger.

The one thing that I vividly recall was the second night we were at Nicks, probably at least thirty other men were there, and the pianist who plays every night played a very tearful song about a son who had lost his father called *Old Man*. I can't remember who the artist is, but he had the place just enraptured, and Tom and his father were sitting there almost teary-eyed. It was pretty neat. It was a very heart-wrenching song.

DAD TALKED ABOUT THE 'OLD COUNTRY,' BUT I COULD NEVER FIND IT ON A MAP

GARY WILLIAMS

Gary Williams is a successful radio sports talk host at WFNZ-ESPN Radio in Charlotte, North Carolina. WFNZ is a CBS-Infinity-owned station and an ESPN radio affiliate. The New Jersey native and his dad were playing partners with Tom Brady, Sr. and Tom, Jr. in Ireland.

My dad and I had been to Ireland several times but this was the first time we'd gone over and played in a Jerry Quinlan's Father-Son tournament. There's upwards of eighty fathers and sons that play in this three-day event.

Tom and his dad were one of the teams there. I do a sports talk radio program, and I've known of Tom since he was in college and have known a little bit about his career. It just so happens, the final day of the event, we were paired with Tom and his dad. But we went out to dinner the night before, as a large group, and so I got to know him a little bit that evening.

At dinner that night, he had one Guinness. We all had another round, another round—not Tommy. He had his one Guinness, and he enjoyed it, but that was it for him. He didn't need to drink five or six, or twelve beers to have a good time. He had his one beer and that was it. He is exactly who he is.

This was a restaurant, Nicks, I think in a town called Killorglin. I think if you ask the Bradys, they would rank this meal as one of the great meals ever. Tommy actually made us late for our reservations because he insisted on working out after the round of golf, which was the second round of the tournament. They had this very small, antiquated workout area in the hotel in Ireland, and he HAD to work out. Everybody else is in the pub drinking Guinness, and here's Tommy down there on the treadmill trying to get in a workout before we go to dinner. So he's running late. We're all sitting in the parking lot in this van. We had about a half hour ride. Here he comes running up the stairs, wearing shorts and a t-shirt. Obviously he's been sweating. It's one thing to be in an exercise room in a nice hotel in the States. This is a nice hotel in Ireland where they're not exactly known for working out. I think they might have had a medicine ball and a broken down old exercise bike, but I'll be darned if he wasn't gonna get a workout in.

We played at Ballybunion the last day of the event. Ballybunion, if people don't know, is one of the great golf courses in the world. It was a very, very brisk, blustery day. Tom is obviously an outstanding athlete. You can see that he could be a really good golfer, but he and his dad, like most of these fathers and sons who are over there, have very good relationships. Playing golf with your father in Ireland is about as good as it gets. So we had a wonderful day. I was so interested in talking to him throughout the round just because I'm a sports nut. He kept telling me repeatedly—I kept inquiring about his future with the Patriots. I knew something about the fact that they had four quarterbacks on the roster. He kept impressing upon me that he really thought the organization liked him. I was very, very impressed by him. I thought he was extremely unassuming. He is a professional athlete even though at the time he was a guy who was just simply competing for a roster spot. This was really his last little break before going back and getting immersed in training camp and minicamps and getting back to work. I thought he and his dad—I was so impressed by what a comfortable special relationship they had. We had a great day of golf. We really enjoyed spending the time that we had there with them. I felt like I got to know him a little bit that week. He loves the game of golf. You can tell that he wants to be really, really good at golf. There were a few moments on the golf course where he would hit great, great shots, and then follow it up with a very poor shot. But I thought he had great demeanor on the golf course.

He's a good golfer. I would say his handicap is between six and eight. I know that he has not had a lot of formal instruction. The fourteenth hole at Ballybunion is a par five—probably five hundred and sixty yards. He probably hit a three hundred and fifty yard drive, and had nothing more than just a short iron into a par five and proceeded to make a seven. He was livid, but he controlled his emotions very well. You know when a guy is angry on a golf course. You also know when he's ready to blow a gasket. He handled himself really well. He composed himself to turn around on the sixteenth hole, which is another par five, and make an eagle. He chipped in from off the green and, he went crazy. He did a victory lap around the sixteenth green at Ballybunion after making eagle. And then his dad proceeded to make about a forty-foot eagle putt right on top of him. They did a high five,

> While playing golf in 1567, Mary Queen of Scots
> was informed that her husband, Lord Darnley,
> had been murdered. She finished the round.

hugged, and they were howling laughing. That was definitely the highlight of the round for them. They both made eagle on that hole. I don't know what they shot as a team that day, but it was a real pleasure. They were a treat. And his dad's a good player. His dad's very solid, probably about a nine-handicap. I know they play together as often as they can but often only means—they may play six to eight rounds together a year, and you could just tell that they thoroughly enjoyed every moment they have with each other. When they hit good shots, they always say the same thing back to each other, "Good shot, babe. Way to go, babe." They always say 'babe' when they refer to each other whether it's father or son. I thought that was really neat.

The day before we played Ballybunion we played at Waterville, and there was a Damon Huard autographed football helmet behind the bar at Waterville, a Miami Dolphin helmet. I said to Tom, "Damon Huard's got a helmet here." Huard had just signed as a free agent to back up Bledsoe with the Patriots, so he was going to be big competition for Brady. Later on we found out that Wayne Huizenga, the Dolphins' owner at the end of the previous season, flew over all the quarterbacks for the Dolphins on a trip to Ireland. So for whatever reason they had a helmet there, and, lo and behold, Damon Huard is the guy he beat out to be the backup to start the year. It was amazing.

I have a very good understanding of players in the National Football League. Tom Brady went through that week without anybody batting an eye as to who he is, other than maybe people saying, "Hey, did you know that he plays for the Patriots." People would come up to me because they knew I am in sports, and they would say, "Do you know him?" I'd say, "Yeah, he was a good player at Michigan. He was caught in a funny situation between Brian Griese and then Drew Henson came in." I try to jog people's memories, and they go, "Yeah, I think I kinda remember who he is." But generally speaking, here's a guy who, less than a year ago, was in Ireland, and just went for a week, and nobody really thought about it. I remember e-mailing him and saying, "There's no way you could ever go back to Ireland now and get through a week without people just wanting to talk with you for the entire day. Whereas, he went there and just went about his business, played his rounds with his dad, went to dinner with some people, and people just went, "Yeah, that guy's a professional athlete." It's just really amazing.

> The Dolphins' Ricky Williams is the cousin
> of baseball slugger Cecil Fielder.

I left Ireland knowing that I was gonna take special interest in following him throughout training camp. He's an Irish guy, and I have Irish ancestors so I could tell just from being over there that we all had a very, very special time.

You hear professional athletes talk about how 'the team likes me,' 'we're gonna be a good team.' Tom kept saying that to me when we were playing golf that day. I'm like, "Tom, you guys were five and eleven last year." I was joking around with him. He was like, "I know. I'm being serious, though. I really think that we can be a really good team." Then when they came down for the preseason game, he said, "You know what. They want to start me tonight." Like, "What? They want to start you?" He said, "Yeah, but Bledsoe went to the coaches and said, 'I don't think that makes a good impression. I should play the first series and then bring Tom in.'" That's exactly what they did. The game he played here in the preseason was the best preseason game he played. Then he was elevated above Damon Huard.

> **"I really think that we can be a really good team."**

It was amazing when he started playing. I didn't profess to be his best friend, but when the Pats came for a preseason game, I had him on my radio show right after that. People kinda understood that we had gotten to know each other a little bit. Then as the season progressed, our listeners to our show started saying, "Yeah, your boy, Gary, he's coming along." Then we had him on right before the Denver game when he had absolute kind of exploded upon the scene, and had all those games back-to-back, hadn't thrown any interceptions. Then he comes on our show, and we were the 'kiss of death.' He threw those four interceptions in the game at Denver. That was the other thing about him that I couldn't believe and appreciate more that as things were getting really, really hectic for him, I would leave him a message. I left him a message the night after the game at Indianapolis where he'd had another great game. The next morning, he called in to the show. I had just said to him, "If you have a few minutes, I'd love to get you on this week." Lo and behold, he called in unannounced the next morning.

> Golfer Greg Norman's Turf Farm
> provided the sod for Super Bowl XXXIII.

> More NFL games have been played at Wrigley Field than at any other stadium in the country. Mile High Stadium in Denver was in second place until demolished in 2001.

I'm not just saying this because I like him. There are no professional athletes that I've been around that are more unassuming than he is. I don't see that changing. As a matter of fact, when he got done with all the Super Bowl stuff, he e-mailed me and said, "Gary, I am so sorry that I didn't get back to you as often as I wanted to during the year with all your e-mails. Thanks for all the support." His dad told my folks the night they came down for that last regular-season game that his life changed so much that he couldn't even go to the market without people just bombarding him. Being around him and his dad—you can tell they're incredibly close and very genuine people.

I watched the Super Bowl from my house. My wife went to the University of Arizona and is friends with Tedy ("That's how I spell my first name") Bruschi. So she had a friend on the Patriots already. Then here comes Tom. I couldn't have been more thrilled. I rooted for him like I was rooting for a brother, and my folks as well. My dad was really very impressed with him, and really liked Tom, Sr. I rooted for him and will never forget the night sitting in my house watching the Raider game with my wife. When that game ended, I turned to her and said, "They're a game away from the Super Bowl." For this guy to go from being what he was when I met him to being the Super Bowl MVP in the course of an eight-month period is mind-numbing. I try to impress that upon people. I think they understand. But when he was in Ireland, he was a guy who went about his business. We were on this trip with, obviously a lot of young guys, generally between the ages of twenty-five and thirty-five and their fathers— passionate sports fans.

I rooted like a fan, like I was a kid again. I rooted for him like I've never rooted for anybody in my life. He really is refreshing. The expression that he had after the Super Bowl, when they told him that he had won that car. That's exactly the way I would have expected him to react, like a guy who was completely—like a kid, "Are you kidding me? That's my car?"

I always go back to that round of golf. Think about it. You've gone to Ireland to play in a golf tournament with your dad. Some people though take this thing too seriously—there were some people in that event who were flat-out cutthroat. We didn't play with any of these groups, but there were a few groups over there where the dads were barking at the son if they would miss putts. But Tom and Tommy, we spent the entire day rooting for each other.

I would have never took it upon myself to try to keep in touch with somebody that I would have been anything more than lukewarm about. I have no

The undersection of the University of Arizona football stadium doubles as a student dormitory.

reason to try to ingratiate myself to somebody who is a professional athlete, but I liked him—I liked him a lot. My dad who is a phenomenal judge of character was so taken by both of them that we made the effort to stay in touch. They've been exactly who we thought they were—incredibly down-to-earth people, and have gone out

> **I have no reason to try to ingratiate myself to somebody who is a professional athlete, but I liked him...**

of their way to remain in touch with us. I'm incredibly appreciative of that.

I don't want to say that he is difficult to interview, but he is so unassuming that he always defers to other people. I think that comes from always being a good team guy. I remember having him on after the game at Indianapolis when he again had a very good statistical game, and he kept talking about his receivers. You want to talk about him, but he won't allow for it. I've got a few buddies who cover the Patriots in Boston. They knew that I had gotten to know him a little bit, from a personal level, and they said, "Gary, this guy is too good to be true. He can't be like this." I said, "No, I honestly think he is." He's very easy to interview, but he's also very hard to get to talk about himself. Like, "Tom, that throw you made?" He'll talk about the left side of his line. He can't make that throw unless he gets max protection. Or, "Tom, how'd you do this?" "Well, really the back did a wonderful job picking up the linebacker,"—he always wants to talk about other people. So if you want him to talk about himself, that's hard. I don't know if he honestly can believe all this stuff. I know that he is a big sports fan. I said to him, "Tom, the only way you're going to be able to put what you did in perspective is to remove from yourself and try to sit back and think about if you, growing up us say a 49er fan, sat in the stands at Candlestick and some guy who barely made the roster a year ago became the Super Bowl MVP. Think about that." He'll say, "Yeah, I guess." That's what his response would be. He's very engaging to talk to. He's very easy to interview. But he's not easy to get him to heap praise upon himself. That is the last thing he does. I don't think that is going to change. You watch him when Vinatieri made the field goal, and they cut to him, and he's pounding Bledsoe on the shoulder pads like a fifteen year old. He provided them exactly what they needed. The karma they had going on this year, I give him as much credit as anybody, and I give Bledsoe credit obviously for deferring and handling himself and being professional. But Tom provided them with something that not many teams get and that's genuine youthful enthusiasm from a guy who is not thrilled to be there, he is elated to be there.

My competitors give me a lot of good-natured kidding. They always refer to him as 'my boy.' He's not my boy, but I try to be as objective as I can be on the air. I was critical of him when he didn't play well, but I am unabashed in my support of him. When you feel like somebody is deserving of having these things happen to him, I'm not going to apologize for wanting a guy to succeed. I was openly rooting for him and rooting for their team. I'm a Giant fan. I grew up a Giant football fan, and that's my team, but I will root for the Patriots and root for him as hard as I rooted for the Giants when they were winning Super Bowls. He is the genuine article, and that will not change. I have no fear or no concern that wealth and fame are gonna change him. He will be unassuming. He will probably blush when people want to throw him a parade or honor him in any way. He will continue to be exactly who he is, and I go back to his dad and his mom. I've never met his sisters, but I'm sure they're exactly the way he is. The local media in Boston were trying to get information on his sisters, and I'd never met them and didn't know them, but I found that funny. Of course, Tom would continually insist that his sisters were the best athletes in the family. It was like, 'Tom, at some point, take a little credit for yourself.' You want to talk about your sisters now being the best athletes in the family, and they very well might be, but my gosh. He was even doing that during Super Bowl week.

You listen to coaches and they would say to him as he came off the field, "Tommy, what did you see?" He would go through every retrogression, and they would go, "Oh my gosh. He's like 'Rain Man.'" He could see. I think the other thing about him, and again, I thought Charlie Weis did a really good job with making sure that what he did and the way they set up their game plan was to take advantage of the things he was comfortable with and he did really well. The other thing is that they didn't go deep a lot. They signed Donald Hayes, who was a Panther. I emailed Tom and said, "Tom I think you're going to like this guy. I think he was under-utilized here." Now they've got a big target. Troy Brown and David Patten were small receivers. I think he will get better. I think he will get stronger. I think he's got a really good arm. The strength of somebody's arm is not in them throwing it fifty yards; it's in throwing twenty-yard outs. He's got a gun. I don't think it's gonna be, "Well, he's some kind of fluke, and the defenses will figure him out." No. They tried everything. What he saw just in the playoffs in terms of the different defenses that he faced, he couldn't have faced three more different defenses in the Raiders, the Steelers and then the Rams. I thought the guy made very, very few mistakes. It was remarkable.

> William (Refrigerator) Perry, "the Galloping Roast," had a grand total of three touchdowns in his career.

A friend of mine, Dave Jageler works on the Sean McDonough show for Sporting News Radio in Boston, and they would do 'Patriot Monday' so they would always be in Foxboro on Monday. They always had Belichick and Tommy every Monday on the show, not to mention covering him. There was actually a receptionist who worked for their station who was a very attractive young girl, who desperately wanted to get a date with Tommy. Dave kept saying, "Tom, I've got this girl for you." He kept saying, "Hey, what are you doing to me? I can't have the distractions. Why do you always bring this girl up?"

We kept in touch. I sent him those pictures from the trip. I sent him a t-shirt from the station. He said, "Thanks a lot. I'll be able to wash the car with that thing." When he came down here, I left him a message at the hotel. I had not had contact with him for five or six weeks. I

> **...a very attractive young girl, who desperately wanted to get a date with Tommy.**

knew he had gotten into town, and I know he's busy, and so I'd left him a message at his hotel in Charlotte, "Tom look, I know your time is short, but if you've got a few minutes, I'd love to come by tomorrow and see you before the game." He calls me back that night about ten thirty and says, "Gosh, I hope it's not too late, but I wanted to get back to you. I'm so thrilled you called. Would you like to have lunch tomorrow? My folks are in town, and my dad would love to see you." I said, "Great, my parents are here, too." So we went to lunch. We pull up to the lobby of the hotel, and I go to shake his hands, and he goes, "Come here, man." And he gives me a big hug. I'm like, "This guy is not real. Come on." That, to me, will not change.

Until the year 2005, each NFL team will get $75 million a year in television money.

A first-year official in the NFL earns almost twenty-nine thousand dollars per year...An NBA rookie ref makes ninety-three thousand...Major league baseball one hundred and six thousand...National Hockey League one hundred and fifteen thousand.

Fantasy leagues are often called rotisserie leagues. Rotisserie was the name of the restaurant in New York City where Daniel Okrent and friends dreamed up the concept during a luncheon meeting in the '70s.

YO, TOMMY...THROW ME MY BALL RETRIEVER...I JUST HAD IT REGRIPPED

DOUG DOLLENBERG, JR.

Doug Dollenberg, Jr. is a Management Consultant with McKinsey in Washington, D.C. A scratch golfer, he and his father were paired with the Bradys in Jerry Quinlan's Father-Son Tournament in Ireland.

My dad and I got paired on the same bus with Tom, Jr. and Tom, Sr. We were on the same bus for the whole seven days. Right in the beginning, we did not meet each other. Two or three days into it, we played together. The four of us just sort of really hit it off. We had a great time that round. We had dinner a couple of times and were always hanging out on the bus and we would go back and forth. We've been keeping in touch ever since.

Tom is a very good golfer. I can't remember his handicap, but he's probably a five or eight handicap. I would definitely put him on my team, giving that guy eight strokes. There's no doubt. He's so athletic. He's the type of guy, who, if he actually got a chance to play, he could definitely get down to low single digits or scratch. He was a lot of fun to play with. I was sort of immediately drawn to him as just sort of a 'good guy.' He was one of those guys who you had a blast playing with him, very social, very personable, neat guy to just talk with. One of those guys that you could see going out and grabbing a couple of beers with and just having a great time for the night, or playing golf with, or whatever. Very neat guy.

Before we went over there, I had not heard of Tom Brady. Since I've come back here and talked with a bunch of my friends, most of my friends knew who he was from his Michigan days. I do not follow football all that close so I didn't know who he was. Because of that, he and I had some interesting conversations 'cause I'm not a football guru. I remember one of the interesting things I asked him, very blunt, when he told me he was third or fourth-string. So I said, "Tom, what does it take for you to become a starting quarterback?" He said, "Well, what I need to do is play real hard in summer camp this coming summer, and I basically need to get myself to the number two position." 'Cause he was sort of hovering around three or four last May when I played with him, almost a year ago. He said, "I need to do really well in the camps this summer, get up to the second spot. I just need to instill total confidence in the coaches and be ready in case something happens." That's basically what happened. I give the guy huge credit for preparing himself and sort of studying the goal and knowing what he wanted.

He wasn't the one who bragged about who he was. The conversation was much more about golf and what's going on, and just sort of talking about things. He was interested in what my career was and what I was doing. I asked him some questions about him, but he was not the type of guy who sits there and says, "Hey, let me tell you about this great game I played. Or, let me tell you about my Michigan days." He just wasn't that kind of guy. I don't think there was any sort of great stories that he told me. Since I didn't follow Michigan football, I wasn't able to ask him, "Hey Tom, tell me about the game when you guys played so and so." Because I just wasn't up on that.

After we got home, I started following his career. I became a Patriots fan. That's now my team—the Patriots, I would say. I became a Patriots fan and definitely followed him every week. I was e-mailing him. I got really psyched when he did get in that third game of the season. He

> **I became a Patriots fan. That's now my team—the Patriots, I would say.**

started playing well. In his e-mails, he was just as psyched as could be. He said he was having a great time and really enjoying it. Very modest guy, just like on TV, when he gives credit to the team and other players in every interview I've ever seen. That is who he is. Every interview that I hear him in makes perfect sense from the guy I met back eleven months ago.

I know very few guys who are as humble as Tom Brady is, especially guys that are that successful. I can't think of too many guys that I have met over the course of a couple of days and really wanted to stay in touch with, to be honest. It doesn't happen all that often. But when I met him, I felt he was a really cool guy. We exchanged e-mails and hopefully we'd stay in touch. And we have, not because he's Super Bowl MVP, but because he's a great guy. I'm hoping that sometime I'll get up to Boston or he'll come down here and we'll be able to play golf and go out and have a good time. Hopefully he and his dad are going to be coming down to Baltimore to play golf with me and my dad at some point this summer.

How we met? We get to the first tee, we introduce ourselves to them, and that was the first time we had actually met them—on that first tee. We hadn't met them on the bus that first day or two. We teed up, and I hit my first one, dead right, out of bounds. I'm kind of ticked off. First hole 'cause it was a pretty wide-open hole actually. I tee up another one—hit that out of bounds. The starter was sort of pushing me, "Okay, you guys just get off the tee." He didn't want me to hit another one 'cause we were gonna hold things up. I said, "Darn it, I am going to hit another one 'cause I don't play this bad." I hit another one, and I'm thinking an eight on that hole, and I guess I was a little embarrassed to be firing two straight out of bounds. The rest of my shots were pretty good.

Tom has never joked with me about those two bad holes. When we do e-mail we always sneak golf in there. He'd e-mail me in the middle of the season and say, "Now, imagine you're starting to take the head covers off your Callaway and getting out there." I would tell him, "Yeah, I've been playing some and hopefully we can catch up and play this summer." I wasn't sure if he would be able to e-mail me during the season, but he did, and I thought that was pretty cool. Then I e-mailed him a few times right around Super Bowl time congratulating him as he was going through the playoffs and the Super Bowl. Obviously he did not e-mail me back then. He was so busy those couple of weeks there. He did send me one a week or two after he had gotten home from all his travels. He told me, "Hey Doug, so sorry I wasn't able to get back to you sooner, but as you can imagine, I've had a ton going on here. I apologize." You wouldn't expect someone to be like that. He kind of felt bad that he hadn't e-mailed me back yet. I was psyched to get an e-mail from him a couple of weeks after the Super Bowl. We exchanged a few back and forth, and I was congratulating him at that time. Then he said he was heading out to California to spend a few weeks with his family.

I would think a lot of people would be saying, "Oh, that's just a fake front. He's trying to act humble." But I met him and from the four days I hung out with the guy, that's who he is. He's extremely humble.

We were driving into this town of Ballybunion, a quaint small town in Ireland. The entire town is probably ten streets wide at most. As we pull into town, right in the center square is this nine-foot tall statue of a person. As we pull up, we realize it's Bill Clinton. When we first saw it, we were just shocked. You can't figure out how the heck a nine-foot tall statue of Bill

John Daly has never flown on a plane in the United States.

Clinton ends up in this small seaside town in Ireland. But it sure did, and it was quite a laugh literally. It was goofy. Then someone mentioned that when Lou Holtz was Head Football Coach at Arkansas, Bill Clinton was his personal attorney.

Tom Brady signs his e-mails Tommy, not Tom.

This was a guys' trip over to Ireland, so I didn't meet his sisters. Some of my friends hear that I get an e-mail from Tom Brady, and they just think that's as wild as can be. Some of them didn't even believe me. I really had to convince them that it was true. A lot of people didn't believe that I knew him.

LPGA golver Se Ri Pak believes in reincarnation and her goal is to come back as a man so she can become the #1 player of both genders.

Tom and his dad, Tom Sr., on golfing trip in Ireland.

Chapter 4

The Fourth Estate
Doesn't Take the Fifth

Glen Farley

Tom Curran

Skip Bayless

Mike Silver

THE SPORTS SECTION IS THE NEWSPAPER'S TOY DEPARTMENT

GLEN FARLEY

Glen Farley of the Brockton Enterprise was one of the two "pool" reporters for the Patriots during their Super Bowl season. The astute Farley has "seen it all" during his many years of sitting in the first row of the Patriots press box.

We hadn't heard a lot of Tom Brady until the Patriots drafted him in the sixth round in 2000. He came here as a guy who—we wondered at the time they selected him, of course, they had Drew Bledsoe, they had John Friesz as a veteran backup quarterback to Drew. Drew was obviously the established franchise quarterback here. They had a guy named Michael Bishop who was kind of evolving into somewhat of a cult hero around here. He came here in the '99 draft, the seventh round pick, a very athletic guy who'd been a candidate for the Heisman Trophy, kind of a raw kid, a quarterback who used to run around à la Doug Flutie, a very popular guy here. But he was a guy whose talent as a quarterback needed to be refined. Having said that, Bishop had played well in the '99 preseason and developed a strong following just because he was such a long shot. People were looking at this guy to maybe make the team. He was almost looked at as kinda the 'anti-Drew'—almost. Drew, for all his pluses, had developed some critics around here because he was just the classic drop-back quarterback in the pocket and didn't move around a lot. Michael Bishop was a guy who people looked at and thought he had a lot of Flutie in him and he was a very creative guy. So that being said, when Brady was drafted in the sixth round, a lot of people kind of raised their eyebrows as to why the Patriots, not that a sixth-round pick is a high pick by any means, but why the Patriots were even bothering with this kid when they had three quarterbacks who seemed somewhat established around here.

Brady came in the year 2000, and Belichick drafted him and kinda weaned him along. He played a little bit here and there in the pre-season, didn't do anything spectacular, but just kinda looked like he might be a heady quarterback, which was the reputation he came in here with from the University of Michigan. Not a spectacular guy, but a heads-up quarterback who knew the game. That's what we saw pretty much in training camp 2000. Belichick kept this guy around and explained they thought enough of him that if they waived him, they were afraid they would lose him. They didn't think they could tuck him away on the practice squad for fear that they would lose him. He was a very quiet kid. First year he just seemed to be sitting over in his corner of the locker room— seldom talked to him. There was no reason to talk to him. The team was going through a five and eleven season, and he was the fourth quarterback on the team. He wasn't gonna play. He played very little. He threw three passes that year—Thanksgiving Day, I believe in Detroit, completed one. He dressed next to Drew Bledsoe because of their numbers—eleven and twelve. That was just a coincidence. It wasn't like they were weaning him along to be Bledsoe's replacement by any means. At that point, he just seemed to be soaking everything in. He was kind of a tall, skinny kid, as I recall. He wasn't a kid that anybody had a whole lot to do with that rookie year. He came back here for the off-season, and you could see in the off-season mini camps and passing camps that he had bulked up a little bit. Sure enough Belichick, early in training camp in 2001, said this was the guy who had probably improved possibly more than anyone on the team, that he had bulked up and really paid attention in the off-season camps and was kind of developing into a leader amongst the younger players on the team. Sure enough, as things unfolded, history speaks for itself. He moved up the charts very quickly.

> ## He dressed next to Drew Bledsoe because of their numbers—eleven and twelve.

In the 2001 training camp, the Patriots had let go of John Friesz in a salary-cap move. John would have made well over two million dollars to backup Bledsoe in 2001, a lot of money to pay for a veteran backup who probably wasn't going to get on the field really unless there was an emergency. As things unfolded, that's exactly what happened, but Friesz was long gone by then.

> Drew Bledsoe makes just under six hundred and fifty thousand dollars <u>per game</u> as part of his hundred and three million dollar contract that he signed before the Super Bowl season. Brady, in the Super Bowl season, made two hundred and ninety eight thousand dollars.

They brought in Damon Huard, a veteran backup who was thought to be the heir apparent to Dan Marino in Miami, but was beaten out by Jay Fiedler. He came in here to be the veteran backup quarterback, the number two guy. Brady and Bishop were gonna basically battle it out for number three. Sure enough, Brady moved past Bishop very quickly. I think the coaches didn't like the fact that for the reason a lot of fans liked Bishop, the coaches disliked him. He was a guy that while he could be creative, didn't stick to the game plan. A lot of times if things started to break down, he'd start doing unorthodox things. Brady was more of a 'stick to the game plan' type of quarterback. It really started to happen his rookie year. In retrospect, Belichick, in Detroit, on Thanksgiving Day, dressed him as the third quarterback. So it was starting to unfold somewhat Brady's rookie year, but even more so during the off-season leading into year two. As training camp unfolded, it was clear that Brady was really putting the heat on to at least be the number three guy. Then in August they released Bishop, so Brady was clearly the number three guy there. As more training camp went on, more pre-season games were played, Brady seemed to be getting more and more snaps, Huard less and less. Brady moved up the charts to the point where when the season started, he was the number two guy.

It surprised a lot of us because, like I said, he was a sixth-round pick. A plus obviously was that he had come from a big-time program like Michigan. Of course in a program like that, you're playing under the bright lights, a hundred and ten thousand people in that stadium. The pressure is on to produce. Really even as a rookie, you could see that this was a guy that really didn't look like things were gonna faze him. Even what little we saw of him as a rookie, he seemed like a poised kid. In the locker room, he seemed to handle himself very well, very maturely. That played up to be one of his strengths. It definitely surprised us that here's a guy that was a sixth-round pick in 2000, fourth quarterback on the roster, which you know, no doubt, is almost unheard of in the NFL. Generally teams keep three. But they thought enough of this guy to keep him around as a fourth quarterback and to use a roster spot on him. It definitely was a very long shot that this kid at the start of the 2001 season would be the number two quarterback to the franchise guy. That's the way Bledsoe was still looked at was that he was

> The only current Jewish quarterback is Jay Fiedler of the Miami Dolphins. The greatest Jewish quarterback ever was Sid Luckman who starred in a critical Ivy League game for Columbia the same hour his dad went to the electric chair at Sing Sing. The father of the 1943 NFL MVP of the Bears was a leader of Murder, Incorporated.

the franchise guy. I'm a Bledsoe guy, I've always been a Bledsoe guy, but I think it was clear his play had regressed over the years. He had taken a lot of hits—didn't seem so sure of himself in the pocket anymore. Things would break down and it seemed as though he might get a little jittery. He was prone to making bad decisions. Lo and behold, two weeks into the season, he's basically got a tube in his chest, and the kid that was the two hundredth pick or whatever it was in the 2000 draft was taking over an 0-2 team. But at that point, it looked like the season was gonna be a throw-away. The franchise quarterback was down and the Indianapolis Colts were coming into town, the team that a lot of people thought would be representing the AFC in Super Bowl XXXVI. So the season was really going out the window quick…down the drain real quick. It looked like it was going to be a throw-away season with a young quarterback at the helm.

> **It looked like it was going to be a throw-away season with a young quarterback at the helm.**

I can distinctly recall Belichick standing in front of us at a press conference. He had named Brady quarterback the Wednesday before the Colts game. He came out and said that Tom Brady would be our starting quarterback against the Colts and for the foreseeable future. Basically he said something to the effect, "Look, I don't expect to be standing in front of you every week trying to explain what Tom Brady did wrong and what broke down. I think this kid is gonna step in and be okay." The coach wasn't guaranteeing any Super Bowl championships at that point, but he flat out said, "I don't expect that I'm gonna have to stand in front of you guys every week and try to rationalize what broke down and why Tom did this or did that, in a negative way." He was solidly in his corner. From what he had seen in practice over the course of two summers in pre-season and what little he had seen of him over the course of the rookie season and the 2001 regular season, he felt this was a kid that wasn't going to take the season down—the season wasn't gonna unravel because of Tom Brady. As absurd as it may sound, I think Belichick felt he had even more stressful problems at that point than Tom Brady taking over as quarterback.

I think there was a group of us, based on what they had seen in the pre-season—for what you can put into the pre-season—that felt this kid would be okay, that he'd be poised enough to be able to handle some things, but I think for the most part there was a lot of doubt. There were questions still about a running game. Since Curtis Martin left and the one year with Robert Edwards, we really hadn't had any kind of running game. There were serious questions about receivers—Troy Brown had a solid year in 2000 but certainly hadn't had a season to the point that he was gonna have in 2001. Terry Glenn was suspended at that time, still the most talented wide receiver in that corps—talk about raw talent. I'm throwing attitude and behavioral problems out the window, but raw talent—the best wide receiver on the team was suspended. He'd end up contributing, I think it was, fourteen catches this year. The other wide receiver was David Patten. They really had little to show at tight end. The offensive line was a work in progress at that point. They had brought in guys like Mike Compton from Detroit as a free agent. Damien Woody was pretty solid at center. Robinson Randall, a young guy, basically a rookie, hadn't played much at all last year, was starting. Joe Andruzzi who they had picked up off the waiver wire from Green Bay. And Matt Light, a rookie offensive tackle who was a second-round pick, but a rookie they were asking to play left tackle, a real key position protecting the quarterback's blind side. Bruce Armstrong had played here forever, and as it turned out, the Colts game was where they were gonna pay tribute to him because they had cut him during the off-season. His play had waned over the years. He was a guy who, since '87, had pretty much filled that left side of the offensive line at tackle. He started off playing some right tackle, but it didn't take long for him to take over that left-tackle position. For more than a decade, it was his. So there were so many questions.

There were eyebrows raised, but not just because Brady was taking over the team, but because the team seemed to be going downhill fast—if you can call 'downhill fast' from a five and eleven season. The team had continued to regress since the 1996 Super Bowl season year by year under Pete Carroll. They had won one game fewer each year. Then of course Belichick took over and they went five and eleven in 2000. At that point there was no reason to think this was gonna turn around the way it did.

> **Rehbein really sold him on Brady as being that player.**

Belichick had said that at the end of the '99 season, they had made a plan that they wanted to draft a young quarterback, a latter-round pick. He empowered Dick Rehbein to go out and find him the guy. Rehbein really sold him on Brady as being that player. It was the late Dick Rehbein that looked at films and was convinced that this guy could be the guy Belichick was looking for. Again, I'm not saying Rehbein said 'draft this guy, and he'll lead you to the Super Bowl.' But Belichick has told the story that at the end of the '99 season, they knew they were gonna cut ties with Friesz at that point because his contract was just gonna be too big for them to handle for a back-up quarterback. They were gonna bring in another veteran backup. They did want to bring in another young guy to compete along with Bishop for the number three spot. Rehbein was the guy that convinced Belichick that this would be the way to go, with a late-round pick. The guy that might be there late, that would be worth drafting with as a sixth-round pick. It was Dick Rehbein that was really instrumental in the Patriots' drafting Brady, according to Belichick. Rehbein passed away in early August, and I remember Bledsoe coming in for kind of a quick press conference that night just to talk about what Rehbein meant and, of course, obviously we wanted Bledsoe for his comments more than Tom Brady at that time because Bledsoe was the guy still. I know Brady has spoken about the time Rehbein put in with him, but I distinctly remember Bledsoe talking about how Rehbein was so good to work with and made it fun to come to work every day. I think that went all the way down the quarterbacks. Damon Huard even spoke about it in the aftermath of Dick's death. I know Brady has talked about Rehbein as a guy who has put in a lot of time with him his rookie year and during that off-season leading into the big second year.

They handed out a short statement saying that Dick had died.

Word of Dick's death broke early in the afternoon after Belichick had his mid-day press conference. He'd had a history of heart problems and a couple of days before his death he wasn't feeling well and checked himself into Mass General Hospital in Boston and died there. Word broke at training camp that day after Belichick's press conference. They handed out a short statement saying that Dick had died. There were player interviews at that point, but the PR staff brought in Bledsoe that night, and you could see Bledsoe was visibly shaken. He might have answered three or four questions. You could see it was really wearing on Drew to talk about it, and it was tough to answer questions at that point, but he spoke very highly of Dick. From what we've talked to Brady during the course of the season, I know Tom thinks very highly of Dick as well.

Brady takes over against the Colts, and he had a decent day. It was kind of a sign of things to come in that basically he was part of a cast. It wasn't like he was Kurt Warner and throwing the ball forty, forty-five times, and throwing for three or four hundred yards a week. It was a controlled passing game. I think the thing Belichick likes in him most is in the fact that as it played out, he's a guy that makes very few mistakes, he's a very heady quarterback. If there were knocks against Bledsoe, it was that he could throw for three or four hundred yards in any given week but he could also throw three picks and make some stupid decisions that are gonna cost you. Brady was a guy that was gonna come in here and probably throw for about a hundred and seventy five yards a week. Brady's interceptions were very seldom.

Right from the start, I think he set the record for one hundred and sixty-- three passes without an interception at the start of his career. There were a couple of drops that could have been picks, but there weren't a whole lot of bad decisions. It wasn't like he had six or seven or eight picks that were dropped. He didn't put the ball in jeopardy a whole lot. It was very much a controlled passing game. The words that's used around here are that 'he managed the team well.' You hear that over and over to this day, and that's really what he did. He ran a controlled passing game. The running game, all of a sudden, picked up. Antowain Smith became the savior. The offensive line improved. Every-thing jelled together. He benefited from that but he was also a big part of it because he didn't make many mistakes at all until the Denver game where he kind of unraveled in the fourth quarter. But he bounced back from that, as well.

The first game really he was part of a cast that just put a real whoopin' on the Colts. It was 44 to 13 or something like that. It was incredible. It was just one of those days where everything went right. Smith had a good game running the ball. Brady threw the ball when he had to. The crowd was fran-tic. It was an 0 and 2 team going into that. The season was already on the brink. They managed to win that game. They didn't get on a roll because the next week they went to Miami, and they got their butts kicked. They lost 30 to 10. I remember there were some breakdowns. I believe there was a shotgun snap that looked like Brady wasn't expecting that led to a fumble that produced a Miami touchdown. Brady threw for eighty-six, or some-thing really miniscule, yards in that game. It looked like we were gonna have to put up with going through the trials and tribulations of a young quarterback who had maybe been pressed into duty ahead of his time, and it continued to look that way the next week against San Diego. The Pats were one and three. In the fourth quarter, they were down by ten points, I think, with about eight minutes left, 26-16 was the score. It looked like they were about to become one and four and if they lost that game, the feeling was that the season would be over. It looked like Flutie was gonna come home and beat them and then all of a sudden Brady really out-Flutied Flutie. He led

> The Chargers were originally the Los Angeles Chargers
> in 1960, the first year of the AFL. They were owned
> by Barron Hilton of the Hilton Hotel chain.
> Hilton owned the Carte Blanche credit card
> company and named the team to promote the card.

them to a field goal that made it 26 to 19, with three or four minutes left. Even then the feeling was 'big deal—they're still gonna lose.' It was a point where I recall vividly the Chargers had to get one first down, and they would be able to run out the clock. I think on the first down, they handed the ball to Tomlinson. He got seven or eight yards, and it was a second and two situation. It was almost academic that they were gonna pound it out and get the first down. But lo and behold, on the next two carries, they held Tomlinson to one yard, and they had to punt. Sure enough, Brady marches them down the field and throws a touchdown pass to tight end, Jermaine Wiggins, to tie the game 26-26. We win it in overtime on an Adam Vinatieri field goal. You look back and it was kinda ominous that they would win that game on a field goal in overtime, 'cause if they lose that, they're one and four and they're done. They went to Indy the next week and they won which made them three and three. If they're one and four, and going into Indy, who knows that they win that game. The Chargers win was the key game.

I saw the Bobby Knight movie being publicized, *A Season on the Brink*— that was a 'season on the brink' right there because if they lost that, they're one and four going into Indy, and coming off a five and eleven season, the whole thing with the quarterback. They go out to Denver, and Brady has the meltdown, and they're three and four. Then all the questions are about 'How is this young kid gonna bounce back after throwing four interceptions in one quarter?' It was incredible. It was so bad. Belichick tried to absolve him of some of the blame, saying, "Wrong patterns had been run. It wasn't entirely Brady's fault." Belichick was trying to come to the side of his young quarterback lest Brady's confidence starts to waiver.

They go into Atlanta the next week and they won that game 24 to 10. One of the key plays in that game was a big break where Brady threw it—almost like a "Hail Mary"—it should have been intercepted. It bounced off a defensive back or receiver into Troy Brown's arms, and he took it in for a touchdown. They win that game to get back to five hundred.

Then they've got Buffalo coming here. They win that game, then they lose to the Rams, to go to five hundred again. Then they win out.

> In a 1975 game against the Minnesota Vikings, Cowboys quarterback Roger Staubach threw a fifty-yard pass to Drew Pearson. Staubach said, "I just closed my eyes, and said a 'Hail Mary.'" That's the start of the 'Hail Mary' pass.

He had a big game against New Orleans that started that run. He threw for four touchdowns. In the Jets game the next week he had a big second half, bounced back from a thirteen to nothing deficit where he and the offense was totally out of sync. Again, another key game. We got on a roll from there.

Brady's play didn't necessarily get better in the second half of the season and the playoffs, and the plays weren't spectacular by any means, but he didn't turn the ball over or make a lot of mistakes.

There weren't a whole lot of expectations for the team, even with Bledsoe at quarterback. Brady goes out the first game and does okay. He was kind of a role player in that he did a real nice job, no interceptions, made key passes when he had to. Again, it wasn't 'Air Brady' and it never was during the season except for that San Diego game, really. The control-passing game. He made many key third-down conversions when he had to, but basically six and eight-yard routes, quick passes, timing things, so it wasn't like he lit it up. Then he goes to Miami, and he and the rest of the team were just terrible and just get totally outplayed so there weren't any expectations, but even coming into the San Diego game, it looks like they're gonna lose that game and be one and four. But then he just turned that game around, and all of a sudden, even throughout that game, it's easy to look back on now I guess, and it kinda sounds corny to say, but he never lost his poise.

I tend to tape games and go back over them after they're over, during the week. I recall watching that game over and just seeing there was never a sense of panic in him. He was always that way throughout his dealings with the press, press conferences, and everything, very calm, cool, poised, laid back, California kid. Troy Brown termed him 'California Cool.' That's really the way he is, very poised. I think the San Diego game is when people started thinking, 'Whoa. Maybe they've got something here.' Then they go to the Colts game, and that was the game where David Patten threw for a touchdown, ran for a touchdown, caught a touchdown pass. He did something that hadn't been done in, I think, twenty years. I think it was twenty-two years to the day. Walter Payton had done it before him. They're three and three, but then they go to Denver. They unravel. After that Denver game, the feeling was that this is what we're gonna go through with a rookie quarterback. It was his second year, but he was really a rookie because he

In the last 30 years, the record for the most touchdown passes thrown by a non-quarterback is held by Walter Payton, with eight. In football pileups, Walter Payton used to lie at the bottom and untie his opponents' shoelaces. That's why a lot of defenders put tape over their laces.

hadn't done much other than carry a clipboard around and chart plays his first year and wig-wag plays in—and stand off in street clothes on game day. He really was a rookie. There was just the feeling that this is what we're gonna have to go through with him.

> **I think even Bledsoe supporters were in agreement with the decision.**

As time went on, he started to raise eyebrows. Obviously when they strung a couple of wins together, people started writing, "What do you do when Bledsoe comes back, if this team is winning football games? How can you sit this guy?" It got to the point where the consensus of opinion was that you couldn't sit him. There was certainly a feeling of empathy for Bledsoe in that when he went down, it seemed as though he was led to believe that when he did feel healthy enough to come back that he would be allowed to compete for the job. That was what we certainly were led to believe in the press. Then he came back, and he started practicing. It wasn't long after he was practicing that Belichick came out and said, "Look, I can't go on with the air of uncertainty with my quarterbacks, basically having two guys getting equal amount of snaps at practice. It's not gonna work that way." He felt as though he was compelled to name a number one, and at that point, he named Brady. And it was with good reason because he was winning. It wasn't all laid on his shoulders again to win games himself but he was winning. I think even Bledsoe supporters were in agreement with the decision.

I think there was some empathy for Drew, and even Tom expressed that, that Drew's a competitor. He's been the number one quarterback here since he was drafted in '93. He stepped right in and was the number one guy from day one of the '93 regular season. It never changed except when he had been out injured, which was rare. Here he was healthy enough to play again, but he wasn't gonna get his job back. So I think there was some empathy that he really didn't get a shot to compete with Brady once he felt healthy enough. There's still a school of thought that wonders how Bledsoe might function in this offense that Brady has functioned in so well. They have changed their offense where it is more of a controlled passing game that now has a running game. Clearly, even Bledsoe supporters, most of them at least, had to admit that Brady was the guy that deserved to continue to start because he was winning.

They played 'bend but don't break' defense. They might let you get to the twenty, but once you got to the twenty, they were either gonna force you to cough the ball up or to settle for a field goal attempt. At the other end of the field, they weren't gonna turn the ball over so they were gonna make the most of their offensive chances and defensively they made you earn everything you got. They didn't shut you down completely, but they made you earn every point you got.

Tom Brady can be fiery out there. There's no doubt about it. That's another thing that has irked some people about Bledsoe over the years is that they view him as kind of emotionless on the field. They would prefer to see a guy with some more fire in his belly. But a guy is what he is. Bledsoe's never gonna be mistaken for Dan Marino out there getting in guy's faces, but I've seen him do it before. I think people view Brady as definitely more of a natural-born leader than Bledsoe.

The precedent that was set, and that was while Bledsoe was here, is that you get the quarterback on the podium after the game on Sunday, both home games and road, into an interview room. At the old Foxboro Stadium, the interview room is the weight room. So you get him after the game that way. And you get him once during the week on Wednesdays for probably about a five-minute interview period. They bring him upstairs to the room next to the press room where we work and you talk to him there. That's the way it went most of the year. Towards the end of the year, it was more of a case of they weren't doing the Wednesday thing so much, and you had to get him when you could in the locker room. To be honest with you, Brady became more difficult to get as the team won more. I'm sure a lot of that had to do with demands for his time. The ESPNs were calling at that time, and I'm sure the PR staff could tell you better than me, but obviously he became more of a national figure and everybody was doing stories and live shots and interview sessions with him. He became more difficult to get. At the beginning, I think he enjoyed it. Like with most people, it began to wear on him a bit as the season went on and there were more and more demands for his time.

Also, as the season went on, it pretty much became clear that the Patriots had been passing the torch, and this guy was this team's quarterback. I think really most people regarded the passing of the torch even before Belichick's public pronouncement of that. This guy was establishing himself as 'the guy' around here. Even before Belichick's announcement it was pretty obvious that this was a guy that Belichick really had a lot of faith in. It just seemed a matter of time before he was going to make that public

ESPN debuted September 7, 1979. ESPN2 debuted October 1, 1993. *ESPN Magazine* made its first appearance on March 11, 1998.

pronouncement that this was the guy, at least for the end of the year. They kept winning. There was absolutely no reason to change course.

All week long in New Orleans, you go out to clubs or you go out to a restaurant, and I just wondered "When are the Patriots' fans going to get here?". You felt like you were surrounded by Rams' fans. I said that, and a couple of people argued with me, but most people agreed that it was basically a Rams' town that week. Then you get to game day, and I don't know if everybody that was kinda neutral figured 'Let's go and root for the underdog.' Hopefully they can make a game out of it. The noise from the start seemed to be a Patriots' crowd. Did they all fly in here Saturday night or Sunday afternoon? Where did all these people come from? All week long, you'd look around, and there'd be Kurt Warner jerseys, Marshall Faulk jerseys, people in Ram paraphernalia and you just wondered when the New England crowd was gonna get there. It was just like they threw open the gates and they all walked in Sunday afternoon or early Sunday evening into the Superdome.

> **It's gonna hurt. This was Drew's town. This was his team.**

They're not gonna be all positive feelings. It's gonna hurt. This was Drew's town. This was his team. I'm not gonna say he was always 'King of the Hill' around here, but it was clearly his team. He took his share of knocks, but he wasn't ripped apart or anything. Then all of a sudden, not to over dramatize it, but what we came to find out was a life-threatening injury and loses his job and all of a sudden this kid can do no wrong. I think Bledsoe's gonna have some negative feelings. I think it's just human nature. Publicly Drew did handle it well.

Drew Bledsoe is a great guy and excellent player. I hope he does great with the Buffalo Bills except when they play the Patriots.

> If the Tampa Bay Bucs win ten games a year for the next quarter century, they still won't be a .500 team.

THE WRITE STUFF
TOM CURRAN

Tom Curran didn't jump on the Tom Brady band-wagon, he built it. Now with the Providence Journal, he covered the Patriots for the METRO-WEST Daily News in Framingham (MA) when he first noticed that Brady was not your standard fourth-string quarterback.

An amiable, young graduate of St. Anselm's (NH), Curran offers an insightful take on sports for the Journal.

A year and a half ago, I kind of started looking at Bledsoe and saying, "I don't think he's that good a quarterback." I think he's overrated. I don't think he's a bad quarterback, but I think he makes too many big mistakes. I felt at some point, Belichick, knowing how he hates mistakes and how Bledsoe's plays work, the higher the stakes, I thought there was a pretty good chance that they would not re-sign him. I got a story on very, very, very good authority that they came close to not re-signing him. I don't know if you remember or not, but it was kind of protracted, very drawn out. They finally re-signed him in March. I wrote last August a year after watching Brady play in the preseason of 2000, where he had a 'come from behind' win at Detroit in which he hooked up with Sean Morey. I don't know if the ball hit the ground that night with Brady playing quarterback. He was just so efficient. I remember going and watching him throw at training camp. Bledsoe has an arm that he can throw—it just comes out on a different projectory with a different motion and it's just really—he's got a gorgeous arm. But the ball never hits the ground when Brady throws. The guys are never diving, jumping, leaping, or stretching. So I said, "The quarterback of the future here may very well be Tom Brady." I wrote that in an article in 2000. It was a throwaway line in just going through the team's personnel. I said, "Obviously everything's going to rest on the play of Bledsoe. If he's not re-signed, the quarterback of the future here might be Brady." So last year, we

> "The quarterback of the future here may very well be Tom Brady." I wrote that in an article in 2000.

went along, and I started to say, "It looks to me like Bledsoe's part of the problem. He's getting a free ride here. He makes a lot of mistakes." Then after he signed the contract, I said, "It'll be interesting to see how he comes out now that he's the highest paid, on-paper quarterback in the NFL." He played so poorly in training camp that they had to play him in the fourth exhibition game much longer than any starting quarterback in the league had played just to get him untracked. Meanwhile Brady's tearing up training camp, really played well. First game of the season, I wrote, "It seems to me that guys with big contracts have a tendency to sit back and not play up to their pay checks after they sign." Some people pooh-poohed that and said, "Bledsoe's always been very well compensated." I said, "I don't know." Then I saw him not being sharp in training camp and said he should be more sharp. The second game of the regular season against the Jets might have been his worst game ever. It was just fortunate in a way that he got hurt at the end of possibly his worst game. On the broadcast it was moved up from the Public Relations desk to the broadcast booth that Bledsoe was not injured, and that he was out because of performance. That's why Brady was in for the final two drives. That was said over national television. It came out later that that was incorrect, that was not the case. But initially, that's what was broadcast that Bledsoe came out, 'cause after he got hit and hurt, he played one more series, and then Brady came in. So I think that logically people said, "He's not hurt because he played another series, so he must have come out because he just sucks today."

I was very excited that next week. The week Bledsoe got hurt, I wrote on that Tuesday, "Now we'll find out for sure whether Bledsoe's part of the problem or if he's just an innocent bystander." I went on and wrote a pretty rough column. I said, "Now we'll find out for sure, and if it is, as I think it is, we're heading straight for one of the all-time great quarterback controversies because this kid's gonna outperform him." It was a long column. Later that week I did a long story. I talked to Brian Griese, Lloyd Carr, Brady's head coach at Michigan, Tom MacKenzie, his high school coach, and Kevin Donahue, the athletic director at his California High School—person after person after person, all telling me that this kid's gonna be good. I told everybody that week, "You are gonna be surprised." I was on the radio on Wednesday, WEEI, and said, "How many wins does Belichick need to save his job this year? I hope it doesn't come to that but I think people are gonna be surprised. The kid's gonna play better than Bledsoe did." And it

NFL footballs are made in Ada, Ohio.
Each team uses one thousand per year.

just went on from there. He played very well that week. People attributed it to him just managing the game. But I had the stats from that game, and I think he had thirteen completions, seven came on third down and six or more yards to go. Brady is one of the best third-down quarterbacks I've ever seen.

It wasn't really that I said, "Wow, he's got the tools and the mechanics and the arm." It was just that I thought that every time I saw him play, he managed the team beautifully. The ball never hit the darn ground. Never hit the ground. He was the life and the spark of the team. I know it was preseason. I know it didn't matter. But it matters to those guys who are on the field, and they really played well around him. He played well in the pre-season. I wrote a long column and said, "The last thing Belichick needs at this point is to decide between an eighty percent Brady and a hundred percent Bledsoe because that's a coin flip." That's saying something to say

> **The ball never hit the darn ground. Never hit the ground. He was the life and the spark of the team.**

that a second-year player who has only played one game at that point might be, at eighty percent, better than the hundred million dollar quarterback. That's stunning, but true. You got ample proof of why Drew Bledsoe has been watching for the last four months. Brady's major shortcoming, and there were a couple, was ball handling and ball control this year. It's interesting because he had a fumble at the end of the Buffalo game at Foxboro, kind of a strip sack that turned into a touchdown almost immediately. Then he had several fumbles.

One really cool anecdote. Brady had questionable ball security throughout the season. Yet in the Super Bowl, in that first play from scrimmage on the final drive, Leonard Little, one of the strongest players in the league slapped the ball with two hands and Brady should have fumbled and didn't because he had two hands on the ball. He made a slight feint to his left and coolly completed the pass to Redmond.

Brady set the tone on the first drive of the game. The Pats started off backed up deep in their own territory. He threw a slant to Brown on one of the first few plays. They picked up twenty-five yards right off the bat. You knew 'Okay, he's the same kid.' It's an incredible fallacy because if people are

> Most NFL coaches believe that an interception is twice as valuable as recovering a fumble.

down on the way Brady throws it long, I can appreciate that 'cause he didn't have a lot of long completions this year. But even if you want to say, "Okay, Brady's about a 'five' throwing long, Bledsoe in actuality is about a 'three' because he has no control over it when he throws it deep. His arm is strong but he never puts enough loft under it. He can throw it on a line fifty yards. So if you ever watch him playing with Terry Glenn, why did Terry Glenn have so few touchdowns in his career? The guy couldn't lead him. He threw the ball out of bounds. You watch—several of the longest throws in Bledsoe's career are not touchdowns. He has passes of over seventy yards that are not touchdowns. The reason for that is he completes it, but he doesn't lead guys down the middle of the field, he leads them out on the sidelines. It's amazing.

> **Brady has the personality that transcends cliques, color and possible dissension.**

Brady has the personality that transcends cliques, color and possible dissension. He has no pretense. He is very natural. His enthusiasm and self-confidence make it so that he's not self-conscious about what his role is or what someone else's perception of him might be. He doesn't hesitate to say, "Oh, I don't want to look like a fool in front of a brother." 'Cause he just acts like Tom Brady, and has that refusal to be self conscious, and refusal to draw attention to himself—being egoless. I think one of the most interesting things is that he hasn't gone for a commercial yet. He's not doing ads—he's just Tom Brady, doesn't put the spotlight on himself. He corrects what his shortcomings are.

I talked to Bill Walsh about this. I asked him, "I hope you don't think this is sacrilege, but can you compare him in any way with Joe Montana?" This was after the Oakland game, right before the Pittsburgh game. He said, "I think he compares very favorably with Joe Montana. He makes very few mistakes, the more the pressure, the better he played." I talked to Walsh again after the Super Bowl, and he said the same stuff. He said what he did that day compared with anything anyone ever did.

Brady differs from the other young quarterbacks. He is not intrigued with finding out the level of his incompetence. He doesn't want to find out how far he can push it. He doesn't care to find that out. He already knows what

> Joe Montana did not start until the fourth game of his junior year at Notre Dame. Montana was awestruck by Huey Lewis and once sang backup with his band.

the goal is—to complete passes, exactly what he said the week before the Super Bowl: "I just complete passes and move the chains and try to win." That's all he does. He doesn't try and do it with flair or style or anything else. The great, most talented quarterbacks think that they are super men. Very reasonably. They've never found anything they can't do. In the NFL they continue to try and do things they could get away with earlier in their careers in college. They find the level of their incompetence—where their incompetence is greater than their experience. They try to do things, which maybe later in their careers, they'll be able to do. But they're not experienced to know that they can't do it. Take Bledsoe for instance, he's the fallback I have, not because I think he's a bad guy or bad quarterback, it's just the instance I have. He came into the league at twenty. He didn't know what the level of his incompetence was so he tried to find it, which meant to throw into triple coverage, to throw long, to throw rashly – so he made some silly decisions. Brady is not intrigued with finding out what'll get him into trouble, how far he can push it. Bledsoe plays that way. But I'll tell you guys that don't play that way—Phil Sims, Griese, Joe Montana—those are the kinds of guys that I compare Brady to. That is his ilk.

Michael Bishop watched Bledsoe play and didn't see a heck of a lot going on up there. Even though he couldn't probably trump it, because he was not technique-wise as able to do it, he knew he was as good as the guy making seven million a year. He knew even though the guy was making all that money, he wasn't that great. But he really thought a lot of Brady. The last thing Michael Bishop said as he left the Patriots club, "You guys are going to find out pretty soon that Tom Brady is the best quarterback here!"

> **The last thing Michael Bishop said as he left the Patriots club, "You guys are going to find out pretty soon that Tom Brady is the best quarterback here!"**

Down at the Super Bowl I get a call from Don Yee, Brady's agent along with Steve Dubin, who I haven't spoken to since November. I thought, "Oh my God, they've resigned Brady, and I'm gonna get this scoop." And I'm going crazy trying to get him. Finally I get him and say, "Is there something I need to know?" He goes, "Yeah, yeah, I just wanted to let you know I'm reading your stuff. I didn't read your stuff regularly throughout the year, but I started going onto your web site the other day and I couldn't stop because I started reading your stuff and I can't believe the stuff you were writing so early. I just wanted to say you've got a lot of guts to write that stuff out there on the line the way you did from the beginning. At first the reaction to my columns was shrugs. I think it was kind of regarded as a swipe at Bledsoe as opposed to a lauding of Brady. It was both, is what it was. It was a vote of 'no confidence' in Bledsoe, and it was a vote of 'confidence' in the way I thought this kid presented himself every other time I'd seen him play.

> **You don't normally get excited as a sports writer covering a team, but I was just so excited to see Brady play.**

The Wednesday before Brady's first start against the Colts, there was a lot of talk in town about 'Why would you go with Tom Brady if you have a quarterback in Damon Huard who actually has started games in the NFL and has played pretty well?" I was just so excited that whole week. You don't normally get excited as a sports writer covering a team, but I was just so excited to see Brady play. Belichick said, "Look I don't think I'm gonna be standing here every Monday explaining talking about all the problems that we're having with Tom Brady at quarterback." That's all Belichick said. That's how he is. That speaks volumes. Him saying that is another coach saying that 'this is exactly what we wanted to have happen.'

Brady should be made in black and white because he is that kind of a fifties-type. He's 'aw shucks.' Yet, he really takes charge in the huddle. The players have told me that. Brady was all about everybody but Brady.

> Troy Aikman wrote a book that had nothing to do with football. It was a kids book called *Things Change*, and it sold an astonishing 200,000 copies.

> Barry Sanders was tackled for losses 14 percent of the time. On approximately 400 carries, he lost more than 1000 yards.

DO YOU KNOW THE WAY TO SAN JOSE? YEAH…HANG A LEFT AT THE MASS TURNPIKE AND KEEP GOIN'!

SKIP BAYLESS

The San Jose Mercury-News recently lured award-winning columnist, Skip Bayless, from the Chicago Tribune. Skip is an Oklahoma City native and a Vanderbilt graduate. He is the author of several best-selling books including God's Coach (Tom Landry) and The Boys, which chronicles Jimmy Johnson and Jerry Jones' wild ride with the Dallas Cowboys.

T om Brady actually lives right across the freeway from me right here in San Mateo. I think both of his sisters live within three or four blocks of me, but I don't know who they are. But, I'm just amazed at the right guy finding the right place at the right time and doing something that has never been done before in the National Football League, because it broke all the rules of how you win a Super Bowl. I guess you could say that Trent Dilfer had broken them somewhat last year, but I had always been taught that you have to have a pedigree quarterback to win a Super Bowl. If you look at the history of it, it holds true all the way through, even in the Super Bowl itself, the pedigree quarterback always beat the guy from nowhere.

You can say Kurt Warner broke the mold to a certain extent, but he was on a team that was incredibly talented, and Trent Dilfer was a high draft pick. Dilfer just wound up with the perfect team and one of the great defenses in the whole history of the league. But in this case, with Brady and the Patriots, they're not an overly talented bunch. He, obviously being a sixth round draft choice, a first year starter who had gone from fourth string

> Coach Jimmy Johnson and Janis Joplin were high
> school classmates at Thomas Jefferson High School in
> Port Arthur, Texas. Jimmy Johnson didn't know she
> sang. They hated each other. She called him
> "Scarhead" and he called her "Beat Weeds."

when camp opened this past July, playing on a team that got off to a bad start, just defies all logic that I had been taught. You can't do that. I figured, frankly, that by the time he got to the Super Bowl, the stage would be just way to big for him. But what he had all year was, maybe not first round draft choice talent, but first round intangibles.

I've never seen a more poised kid who was smarter for his age than this kid was. It's like he was born wise and born poised, because nothing seemed to fluster him. He mostly made the right choices. He never made a bad choice at the worst time, and those are amazing attributes. I've seen too many kids, like Cade McNown, go up in smoke. Kids who had some talent and couldn't stand the pressure of it. So, I've never seen anything like it in sports before.

> **...he handled it with incredible humility and grace toward Bledsoe and really defused it.**

Tuesday of Super Bowl week is the biggest stage in sports these days. It's that Media Day stage, and there was a controversy about whether Brady or Bledsoe would play. I wrote a column saying that Brady set some sort of Super Bowl record for first time poise because he handled it with incredible humility and grace toward Bledsoe and really defused it. Because if he had said the wrong thing or said it awkwardly, it could have gone out of control because we were all sort of "frothing" for a big story, and he basically punctured it with his humility and his maturity. He just was real smooth with it, and I was amazed. That's when I said, "Hey, he may not win the Super Bowl, but he won media day."

> After the 1987 Super Bowl, quarterback Phil Simms was the first to say, "I'm going to Disneyland."

> To host the Pro Bowl starting in 1994, the state of Hawaii had to donate the use of the stadium rent-free and guarantee the NFL one million dollars income each year.

MEN LOVE *SPORTS ILLUSTRATED*... THEY PROVE IT EVERY FEBRUARY WITH THAT ONE ISSUE!

MIKE SILVER

Michael Silver is a Senior Writer for Sports Illustrated, who covered Brady and the Patriots during the AFC Championship game and the Super Bowl. He talks here about his interview with Tom Brady in a feature cover story for Sports Illustrated, a Sports Illustrated where Brady posed on a controversial cover sans shirt.

B rady's been in a lot of unusual situations since the Super Bowl. He played golf with John Elway in Hawaii. He spent time with Barry Bonds and Willie Mays at spring training in Scottsdale, Arizona. He was at a party in Phoenix with Muhammad Ali. He was in Indiana judging the Miss USA Pageant. Also, during the team's visit to the White House, his teammates gave him a hard time, saying that he wants to live there some day. Brady has aspirations for a future career in politics. We've all heard some athletes talk about that in the past, and it sets them up for a fall. Steve Garvey comes to mind. But I will give Brady credit. I describe him as a guy who started out on the right hash mark and is steadily rolling left, getting closer to the middle of the field. Brady says the country needs good people to lead it, and that's something to think about down the road.

I really didn't know him until recently. I think we've all sort of grown up with the mythology that if you have three older sisters, they're always bringing their friends around and you're sort of a younger brother in that scenario. Ultimately you'll be the beneficiary of that environment and the accompanying confidence with the women. It seems like Tom is the living embodiment of that American belief. He seems to be a guy who women really like, and he's very comfortable around them and knows how to treat

> *Sports Illustrated* began in 1954 and its
> first swimsuit issue was in 1964.
> The *Sports Illustrated* Swimsuit Issue has
> 52 million readers, 16 million of them are females...
> 12 million more than normal.

them. I don't know that he's acting on it as much as some people would, but he certainly seems to be enjoying that popularity.

Sports Illustrated has a new managing editor, and he was extremely excited about putting Tom on the cover. It was a huge priority early in his regime. I really felt like with a new boss that it was a story I had to get done. So even though the initial prognosis was not good, I felt like I had to keep pushing to try to make it happen.

My golf game is about as advanced as Yassar Arafat's peacemaking skills...

Tom and I went to breakfast in San Mateo. Then we went out to Wente Brothers, which is a winery in Livermore, but also has a real nice golf course. So he and his dad and Pat Kratus, a real good friend of his who played with him at Michigan and lives in the area, golfed. My golf game is about as advanced as Yassar Arafat's peacemaking skills so I sat it out. And I don't think I helped Tom's game much either because he wasn't playing that great and so I started interviewing him, thinking it might change his game, but I don't think he had his better day out there.

I think most quarterbacks are good golfers. If you look at NFL players and off-season golfers and who's good, the quarterbacks invariably tend to be the best guys. Elway's great and Marino's pretty good, Trent Dilfer is outstanding and so is John Brody. I don't know why—it may have something to do with the arm motion. I think hockey players tend to be pretty good, too. Maybe there's something in a slap shot or a downfield throw that you can equate. I just don't know enough about golf to know why that is.

Tom Brady has exceptional self-confidence. Whereas everybody else might be just blown away by the 'out of nowhere' element of the story, he might not have planned it this way, but you don't get the feeling that he's blown away either. In that regard, I liken him to Kurt Warner a little bit. His attitude, when people come up to him and say, "Oh my God, can you believe this happened to you?" deep inside is, "Yeah, I can believe it 'cause I've always thought I was good, and I always thought that if I got my chance, I'd do something with it." So there's that, and whatever that poise thing is that great quarterbacks have it's very hard to quantify and obviously the

> Joe Namath got his "Broadway Joe" nickname
> from teammate Sherman Plunkett because of an
> SI cover with Namath posing with
> "The Great White Way" in the background.

intangibles that go along with that. But just from having watched him play, if he can continue to show the kind of poise he's exhibited thus far in pressure situations, he's obviously from the 'Joe Montana family tree' of coolness under pressure. It's tough to say that about a kid who's only played in seventeen games, but if he can continue to do that, that's really good.

The Patriots seemed like a team that was left for dead when Bledsoe got hurt. I had picked them to win the AFC East, partly because I really had a high regard for Belichick, partly because I believed that Antowain Smith was gonna be a really important free agent signing and that with the running game they had a

> **They may have been a little bit of a tired team under Bledsoe...**

chance to be a lot better. And lastly, because I just hated the other four teams in the AFC East. I had to pick somebody. When Bledsoe got hurt, and they went to 0 and 2, I thought, "Jeepers, this is gonna be pretty tough." What I realized once I saw Brady play is that there was a sort of unpretentiousness about his game which really caught on with his teammates. They may have been a little bit of a tired team under Bledsoe, as good as Drew has been and as physically gifted as he is—sometimes change is good. But, at the time, the change really helped them. I think a lot of players thought the season was over. But Brady was just so resolutely confident and unruffled and in control of the huddle that I think pretty early on players said, "Wow. Maybe we do have a chance to be okay."

The feeling in the press box at Pittsburgh, it was still early, and the Pats were up seven to three when Brady left. The seven points was a punt return so I figured people were just caught up in the great story about Bledsoe coming back in. I think a lot of us in Pittsburgh, myself included, believed that Bledsoe would end up starting the Super Bowl, and I don't think people on TV were affected in as pronounced a way as I was and some of the other people who were in that stadium. Bledsoe just looked so much more like a dominant quarterback, not to take away from Brady, but it just seemed like what had happened in that game would lead to Bledsoe playing but clearly that was a visceral reaction to what had happened in the stadium because

> Almost every good football team at any level in America is one play away (injury) from being average. Average time lost due to injury in high school football is six days. Healing time due to injury to a high school cheerleader is 29 days. Among the sixteen most popular college sports, spring football has the highest injury rate.

that's not the way it went, and most of the people I know who saw it on TV didn't agree with me.

> ## "Oh my God, they're gonna win this game. The kid's gonna do it."

Obviously, in the Super Bowl, you could tell early on that Belichick had made a great decision to play Brady. He looked fine. He had a lot of poise. He was managing the game brilliantly. His stats weren't great, but that last drive certainly will help define his career for a long time.

Apparently John Madden was saying on TV that there's no way they should go for the win. I don't know if people in the press box were unanimous in that opinion, but I think a lot of us were thinking about overtime and the Rams having momentum. All of a sudden, Brady hits that pass to Troy Brown and he's running free and people are sort of looking over at each other sort of nudging each other saying, "Oh my God, they're gonna win this game. The kid's gonna do it." It was a really inspirational moment. Unbelievable.

Going in, I was just blown away when I saw the point spread, which I think was sixteen at one point, and I actually said to some people, "Did they watch the games—the people who are betting on this or are expected to bet on this—are they watching the games?" Had the Eagles blocked a punt late in the Ram game, which they came very, very, very close to blocking, then the Rams could very well have lost that game. I certainly thought New England was better than Philly and had beaten a pretty good Pittsburgh team so I thought it would be close. The only justification I could see for expecting a blowout was that it's the Super Bowl and that just happens. Three of the last five Super Bowls have been pretty darn good. I think we sort of need to let go of that line of thinking. The Rams are good, and they might not have played their best game, but I certainly don't think they were far better than New England.

When Vinatieri hit that field goal, I think the feeling in the press box was "RUN. We've got to get to the locker room." It was exciting. I thought the Rams-Titans ending two years earlier was as good an ending as I'd ever seen in a game I've covered. A field goal doesn't quite carry the drama, but having the underdog win like that was very exciting. I had a great story ready to go about Marshall Faulk and Kurt Warner, just as I did the previous week about the Pittsburgh Steelers, but those stories never saw the light of day.

> Joe Theismann holds the NFL record for the shortest punt that wasn't blocked—one yard.

My wife's brother, Mark Goyette, is a teacher at Serra High. He'd been telling me about Tom for years. When I did meet Tom in Pittsburgh, I told him that I was Mark's brother-in-law so we sorta connected, and we definitely knew each other. Tom seems to be one of those not only polite kids, but very sincere people who genuinely remember people and pay attention to things like that. Not only did he say some real nice things to me about my brother-in-law, but he certainly remembered that connection. During the interview, we were together quite a while. Later in the golf round, he started asking me questions, technical questions about working for SI, and just sort of the way my career had gone and asking me about my wife and kids. He seemed to be genuinely interested. Some other athletes have shown an interest like that, but it's not the norm. I'd say most twenty-four year olds don't. Usually when that happens, it's a guy who's older and known for sort of being more worldly. To have a twenty-four year old guy who's living a whirlwind existence in the wake of sudden fame to seem to be interested, that was cool. Likewise, since the story came out, he made sure to let me know

> **...it's certainly not the norm and definitely not for a twenty-four year old...**

that he enjoyed it and appreciated it, told me some very complimentary things. Again, that's not unprecedented, but it's certainly not the norm and definitely not for a twenty-four year old who's probably had about seven million things written about him in the last two months.

Mark Goyette had told me, probably when Tom was a senior in high school, that I was gonna be writing about this kid. I had lunch with Tom's sister Nancy during the story. Unfortunately a lot of it got cut out of the article, but she went to Cal, like I did, and when I called her to set up the interview, the first thing I said to her is, "I've heard that you're a real good athlete—" she had gone to Cal as a softball player—"but apparently you're a terrible recruiter." She started laughing. I would hold her personally responsible for Cal's continued football futility because if she could have persuaded her younger brother to come there, I think they would have been a lot less awful than they were during those years.

Nancy talked about how it's obviously been a huge change with the sudden fame, and she told me about a couple of experiences where other people's hysteria sort of infringed upon her ability to have a normal interaction with her brother, which is obviously an adjustment for her. And she talked about how—there's this story that Tom told that I put in the story about how he went to spring training as a kid and asked for Chili Davis's autograph when he was a Giant, and he got blown off a couple of times. It's a famous story within their family because it's the ultimate spoiled, pampered athlete who blew off an adoring young fan. And yet now Tom's trying to figure out a way to set boundaries just for logistical sanity. I guess they were all in Hawaii for the Pro Bowl having dinner, and a woman came up and said, "Oh, can you sign my jersey, or whatever?" Tom looked up and politely said, "I will, but I'm eating now, and I want to finish my dinner and I'll be glad to do it when I'm leaving." She said that everyone at the table was stunned. It was like this landmark moment. They had never seen him just not be one hundred percent amenable. She said later Tom looked up and noticed that the woman was getting ready to leave. He ended up calling her over and signing it anyway while he was eating because he didn't want to make her just sit around. That, to the family, was a real landmark moment, just seeing him set any boundaries.

I think Tom is smart enough to know that the most important thing is having credibility within the structure of the team. That's what Montana always pulled off, that's what Elway always pulled off—to name a couple of people who are brilliant at that. John Elway was the biggest thing ever in Denver sports by far and one of the greatest players in NFL history. But in that locker room, he genuinely exuded the aura of someone who was one of the guys. Obviously he couldn't be one of the guys because he was John Elway, but he sincerely wanted to hang out with the offensive linemen and not be 'larger than life.' And guys felt like when they saw it day in and day out that it wasn't an act, and they played hard for him. When I covered the 49ers, they wanted Montana, since it was so tough to pin him down sometimes, to just do a one-a-week press conference for the local writers and get it over with. He always refused because he just thought it was stupid that here he was a part of the team, and one guy on the team would have to talk to the media and it wouldn't be the same for everybody else. Those are two great examples. I think Tom is shooting for that. He's smart enough to know that's the main reason why his team responded to him because they did know he was one of the guys. Now, he's going to be set apart as someone who's not one of the guys and that's part of the deal. I think his teammates will give him some slack, because they know the deal. If he does, not only succumb to the distractions in terms of having it detract from his preparation or mental

> Superstitious Denver Bronco Terrell Davis demands that the name tag above his locker always must read "Joe Abdullah," and Bronco center Tom Maler won't wash his practice gear during the year because he feels that he's giving the equipment "natural seasoning" to shield "evil spirits."

clarity, but if he does allow himself to become this sort of cheesy object of commercial profit or whatever—if he starts doing dumb commercials or just giving off the air of someone who's a little too into "it," then I think he might have some problems. But I think he's smart enough to guard against that.

The great ones do handle it. We don't know if Brady's great yet, but we do know he has poise and the ability to block out pressure and perform. He believes he's not handling it very well. He believes he's overwhelmed, that he runs the risk of both alienating his teammates and detracting from his preparation by doing any of this. Obviously, he's a work in progress. Tom has said his biggest fear is to end up a "one-hit wonder." But, he's clearly got the poise, the intangibles, leadership skills, intelligence. He's obviously not physically deficient either—he's more physically gifted than people give him credit for. If I had to guess what makes quarterbacks excel, based on what I've seen from spending a lot of time around them, I'd say he's a keeper.

Some of the many discussions we had with Tom's agents had to do with their trepidation about Tom being on the cover in any sort of provocative pose. This was coming off the Charles Barkley cover with chains. We have a new managing editor, Terry McDonell, and ultimately Don Yee, Tom's agent, said to me, "Before we

Late in the photo shoot, we look up and he's got his shirt off...

agree to this, would you give us sign-off power? Would you allow us to approve the cover shot before you use it?" I said, "Look, I can't enter into discussions like that so I'm gonna get you on the phone with Terry." So Terry and Don Yee spoke about this, and I know Terry didn't grant anything like that 'cause we never would. I think Terry told him this was a nice happy story, and we're gonna do something tasteful. So they got this guy, Brian Lanker to do the photos. From what I heard about his past work, he's done some very, very tasteful classy covers. Curt Schilling and Randy Johnson, in a black and white Sportsmen of the Year cover I think was his most recent. So I felt real comfortable with it. After golfing, we were in this restaurant part of the winery, and his dad and Pat Kratus and I were sitting over

> Curt Schilling has the most strikeouts by a
> right-hander in one season in the National League
> in the last century (319).

> The NFL chain gang gets eighty-five dollars
> per person, per game.

there drinking red wine and eating, and Tom's over there doing the photo shoot. Late in the photo shoot, we look up and he's got his shirt off, and we all sort of looked at each other, open mouthed and half laughing and half stunned. Tom looked over at us and said, "You know what. Don't worry about it. It's just a head shot." We all sort of like rolled our eyes and said, "Yeah, right." I know that Tom didn't freak out when he saw the cover. He's a smart kid. He knows what he's doing. I don't think the cover was that racy, but it is pretty funny when you think back to the initial discussions.

> **I figure if we're going to start putting Boston athletes topless on the cover, let's equalize it.**

A lot of people have commented on the cover. I'm sure his teammates will let him have it. He's the second prominent Boston area athlete that we've had shirtless on the cover. We had Nomar Garciaparra on our baseball preview last year. Now we've had Tom. My reaction to SI was that you need to let me go and do a story on Kristine Lilly, one of the best players on the Boston Breakers, the WUSA soccer team. I figure if we're going to start putting Boston athletes topless on the cover, let's equalize it.

Tom Brady and Kurt Warner are two guys that if somebody told you going into that season that they were gonna be Super Bowl Champions, let alone Super Bowl MVPs, you would have said, "What?" But if you had bothered to ask them, each would have said the same thing, "Yeah. If I get a chance, we could." I think they had very different life circumstances—Kurt wasn't much older than Tom when he won, but had been through incredible amounts of life experience and had lived a more accelerated existence.

I don't think Tom is naïve. It's just—he was in college two years ago. He spent one year as a fourth-string quarterback, and he worked his way up to backup, and Drew Bledsoe got hurt, and he hasn't lost a whole lot since.

Tom is a guy who played on a National Championship team—took Michigan to big bowl games and was still drafted and never got cut. So it's a big story, but to me it's not comparable to a guy who was stocking shelves at the Hy-Vee, and off the NFL radar screen for years. I think the prevailing wisdom in the NFL has changed from 'you've got to have your franchise quarterback' to 'you know what—you don't need your franchise quarterback.' We'd all say now that Kurt Warner is a franchise quarterback and at

> More U. S. kids today play soccer than any organized sport, including youth football. The reason so many kids play soccer is so they don't have to watch it.

one point Trent Dilfer was believed to be long before he won the Super Bowl, but I think that now, when people see the market for Drew Bledsoe be very cool compared to what it would have been a couple of years ago, people say, "Yeah, it'd be great to have a star quarterback, or a quarterback that we would consider to be a star, based on his physical characteristics and pedigree, but, you know what, if we just get a guy who runs our system and has some guts, we might be able to win with him."

Every talent evaluator should be asking himself the question: How do we miss on a Jeff Garcia, a Kurt Warner, a Tom Brady? They spend a lot of money scouring the earth to find talent everywhere. They pride themselves on it, and yet the best player in the league was an Iowa Barnstormer from Northern Iowa and the Arena Football League.

Mark Goyette, my brother-in-law who coached Tom, is pretty good about reminding me of his comments about Tom. He's probably told me a few other guys are gonna be good, too, so I don't know. He just says that Tom is one of those kids who teachers loved and adults loved, but he wasn't one of those kiss-asses or phonies. You could tell he was raised well. They had a day for Tom at Serra High School so Mark got to see him a little bit before I got together with Tom for the story. He said he saw Tom and that Tom mentioned that he'd met me and was asking Mark about his kids and things that Mark didn't expect from a guy he hadn't seen in years and who had a lot of other things going on. I do believe that that's sincere and Tom was probably genuinely interested.

Tom calls Nancy, Julie or Maureen and gets pretty good advice when it comes to buying gifts for women. He caused quite a stir among his teammates with the gifts he bought some of their wives for Christmas, even. It was like the famous "Simpsons" episode where Apu was treating his wife like a queen on Valentine's Day.

> In 1985 when the Patriots beat Cincinnati to qualify for a Wild Card Playoff Spot, the fans tore down the goal posts. Some fans carried one of the goal posts out onto Route 1. When the goal posts touched some electrical wires, five fans were severely injured.

Chapter XXXVI

Son of a Gun, We Had Big Fun on the Bayou

Hank Stram

Bobby Shea

Bob Manning

Dion Rich

FURTHERMORE, HANK FEELS THAT THE WASHINGTON GENERALS ARE DUE
HANK STRAM

The Antebellum-style home behind imposing gates sits thirty-five miles from where the crowning glory of Hank Stram's notable coaching career took place. Built during Stram's two-year stint as coach of the Saints in the middle 1970s, the mansion has been Stram's home and base through a highly successful second career as an analyst for CBS Radio's broadcast of Monday Night Football. It was in New Orleans at Tulane Stadium that Stram's Kansas City Chiefs delivered a crushing defeat to the Minnesota Vikings in Super Bowl IV, one of the most important games in the history of professional football.

The moving pocket, use of the double tight end and stacked defenses came from Stram, the only man to coach in the AFL all of its ten years. His team, Kansas City, had the AFL's best record, 92-50-5.

Fans have vivid memories of Super Bowl IV in large part because of NFL Films, which miked Stram for the occasion. It is one of the NFL Films most repeated segments, in part because of the constant and humorous chirping of Stram and in part because it was perceived as a major upset. The most asked question about that segment according to Stram is about the rolled-up paper he waved throughout. "I just tell them the truth," Stram said, "It was my grocery list from my wife, Phyllis."

In January of each year, Stram spends a lot of time working on his seventy-six-step formula that has successfully predicted the Super Bowl champion for twenty-seven consecutive seasons. He was one of the very few so-called experts to pick the Patriots to win the Super Bowl.

John Lennon's death was first reported to the nation
by Howard Cosell on Monday Night Football.
In 1999, Monday Night Football became the
longest-running prime-time entertainment series ever,
breaking a tie with Walt Disney at 29 years.

I've got a special formula that I use. I get calls from all over the country wanting this formula but I'm not giving it out. I've done it when I was coaching—same formula, and then when I got into broadcasting, I did the same thing. I've been involved with every Super Bowl. Of the thirty six Super Bowls, thirty four have been right on the button. I had a pretty strong feeling about Belichick. I've known Bill, and he's a great coach. He's got a great imagination, especially defensively.

My formula didn't vary, whether Bledsoe started or Brady started. It's a plus and minus thing for what the teams do—I've got ninety-four categories and you get a plus or a minus, and the team with the most pluses is the one that I pick. It was very obvious that the most pluses definitely went to New England. I thought that if they beat the Raiders, they would go all the way. The Raiders did a foolish thing. They called timeout in the snow with little time left in the game, and provided New England with an opportunity to sweep off all the snow where the kid was going to kick. They cleared it off as nice as could be, and the kid kicks the field goal and wins the game. I do the formula during the playoffs, during the season. I do all the games every week as to who I think is going to win, according to the formula. I just do it as a hobby on my own.

I saw Tom several times during the season, and I was just amazed at the poise, the confidence, the way he handled the team, the way he threw the ball—the whole bit. You know he's going to be a super, super star.

At the end of the regulation in the Super Bowl, I certainly would have gone for it. You're there to win the game. I got a kick out of Madden. At the telecast, he said, "if I were the coach, I'd just go for the tie and play for the overtime." Then, you know, the kid takes the ball and, 'boom, boom, boom.' Gets them in position, and the game's over.

Steve Sabol and his dad, Ed, the founder of NFL Films, were great friends. We played tennis and golf together and were friends for an extended period of time. They asked me several times during the course of the 1969 season if they could wire me for sound, just as a rehearsal because they wanted to start something different. They called me the night before the Super Bowl and said they wanted to wire me for sound in the Super Bowl game. I thought they were crazy. He said, "Well, we've got to do this. We've got to do this. There's never been a head coach wired for sound." Actually, this

> When Knute Rockne was killed in a 1931 plane crash,
> where seven other people perished, it was the largest
> disaster in U. S. aviation history up until that time.

was the biggest game that's ever been played. He says, "We are going to wire you for sound and we've got to do it. The only story of that kind that was exposed was of Knute Rockne, and it was fictitious from the real deal, and we want to wire you for sound. It will be great for the American Football League." I said, "Well, you've got to do it, huh?" I called him "Smoosh." I said, "Smoosh, you've got to do it, right?" He said, "Yep, we've got to do it." I said, "I've got a great idea. Go over and see if Bud Grant would do it." He said, "oh no, no. We think you're going to win the game, and we want you to do it." I said, "Well, okay, fine. I'll do it under these conditions. Nobody must know that I'm wired for sound—no players, not Lamar Hunt, our owner, nobody on the team—nobody. That's one requirement, and the other requirement will be that if after the game is over, and you make the film, then I have the first right of refusal. If I don't like what I see in the film, then it's kaputski, and we don't do it." He said, "That's fine. We'll do it. That's a deal." So I said, "Why don't you get somebody else to do it?" He said, "No, no, no. We've got to have you do it." He said, "We tried it with Norm Van Brocklin one time, but we couldn't use it because everything was a bad word." Anyway, that's how it all took place.

As I watched the Super Bowl at New Orleans—looking back at the very first one I coached in Los Angeles, I obviously didn't think the growth of the Super Bowl could ever happen like it did. You didn't know what to expect, and really after the game in Los Angeles, going back to Kansas City after the game, all I heard about was the parties and everything they had—the jubilation about the Super Bowl and that kind of stuff. The players didn't even talk about the game. They just talked about how much fun they had at the parties. I didn't know all those things existed at all, but each year and I haven't missed—thirty six years in a row after the conclusion of the game, I said, "I don't know how in the world the League is going to make it any better than it is this year." For those thirty six years, I've been saying the same darn thing, and it's always been better and better and better. So, you know, it's a great compliment to the League.

> **...one reason— because he's got great escape ability skills.**

If I was Belichick in the game, I would, without a doubt, have gone with Brady instead of Bledsoe—one reason—because he's got great escape ability skills. Bledsoe is a fine pocket quarterback, and he's a smart guy. He's got a good arm, but he doesn't have any escape ability. You know doggoned well that if you put him in the game, they're going to rush the devil out of him. So as a result, I didn't think it was any contest. I didn't even give that a consideration. I thought he HAD to play Brady.

After the Super Bowl, after I had predicted New England, I got a lot of calls. You know that Tuesday Media Day before the game, we have to go through that every year—who's going to win the game and all that kind of stuff. I got there at eleven in the morning and didn't get back until seven at night, and they all thought I was crazy because I predicted New England to win the game. I got all kinds of calls from all over the country wanting the formula—all that stuff. Anyway, that's how it all took place.

I don't know if I should have picked the Patriots because of what happened in Boston early in the AFL days. At that time, the Pats were playing in the college stadium right there in Boston. The first time we ever played them as a team was at Harvard. We beat them at Harvard, then after that we played all the games in Boston University Stadium, a nice stadium. It was always a competitive game, but normally we beat them. We played up there, and we had about two minutes left in the game, and they're ahead by a point, if I remember right. This was in the sixties. We signaled for a fair catch. We had good position. The first play was a reverse pass, and we got down to the one-yard line with only a few seconds left.

Now we're going to throw a slant pass, and we're going to win the game. So, Cotton Davidson, our quarterback, goes back in the pocket and the people in the stadium now have all surrounded the playing field and all over the perimeter of the end zone when we were about to throw the ball. The whole background of it was full of people. Cotton throws the ball and one of the fans runs across our defense, and watching Cotton throw the ball, he goes across the field, knocks the ball down—that's it—we lose the game. I didn't see him do it. The coaches were already down from the press box. We're on the sidelines, and we thought somebody on the defensive side knocked the

> As a result of a public contest in 1960, the team nickname of Patriots was chosen. Many years later when considering a name change, they decided on the Bay State Patriots, but changed that because they're worried about Bay State being abbreviated in headlines.

> In the history of the Patriots, they have played home games at Harvard Stadium, Boston University Field, Fenway Park, Boston College and in 1971 they made their debut at Schaefer Stadium in Foxboro. Schaefer was the one stadium to have when you're having more than one.

ball down. After the game, Cotton comes over to the sideline and says, "Hey coach, a guy in a khaki jacket knocked the ball down." I said, "Oh cripes, no wonder we didn't win the game. Our quarterback must be smokin' funny cigarettes." Cotton is going nuts, and we're ignoring him. We think he's nuts…takin' the loss too hard. So anyway, we go in the locker room and he showers and comes back out and says, "Coach, I'm telling you, a guy in a khaki jacket knocked the ball down." When we get on the plane, Cotton comes up to me—I'm in the first seat on the plane—and says, "Coach, God, all I can think about is the guy in the khaki jacket knocking the ball down." I said, "Yeah, okay, okay Cotton. When you go back there to the back of the plane, tell Wayne Rudy to come up here. I want to talk to him." He's our trainer, and I thought, "God, Cotton must have lost his marbles or something." Anyway, Wayne comes up to me and says, "You know something coach. A guy in a khaki jacket knocked the ball down." I said, "You better go back and check it with Cotton. He must have got a hit on the head or something. What's he talking about?" He said, "No, no. A guy in a khaki jacket knocked the ball down." So, we blew the game. Then we get the films, and, sure as heck, there's a guy in a khaki jacket. The funniest thing about it is Phyllis, my wife—she's got a good sense of humor—Billy Sullivan, team owner, is a good friend and a good guy so Phyllis sees him and says, "Hey Billy, how come you're not wearing a khaki jacket? What did you do with the khaki jacket? You knocked the ball down." The other funny thing was that Joe Garagiola was doing The Today Show for NBC, and he said, "Hey somebody said a guy in a khaki jacket knocked the ball down." I said, "You, that's exactly what happened." He said, "You've got to be kidding me." I said, "No." He said, "Send me the film." I said, "Fine, I'll send you the film." He's going to play it on television. Anyway, it was a big deal because he showed it on television, and it was a big joke. Everybody laughed like heck about it. They won the game. I was 'irrigated.' That's what my mother used to say, "Hey, I'm irrigated."

> **"I was 'irrigated.' That's what my mother used to say, "Hey, I'm irrigated."**

The Bengals, owned by the Paul Brown family, were named after the Massillon (Ohio) High School Tigers, whom Brown coached before he became head coach of Ohio State and the Cleveland Browns.

In 1971, the Boston Patriots were renamed the NewEngland Patriots, and the following year made financial history by paying their first cash dividend of fifteen cents a share.

WHEN THE BIG EASY CALLS, YA GOTTA ACCEPT THE CHARGES

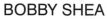

BOBBY SHEA

Bobby Shea of Belmont, Massachusetts is a policeman for the city of Concord. A Patriots fan for thirty-five years and a season ticket holder for the last ten years, he attended his second Pats Super Bowl in New Orleans.

This season wasn't looking too good when Bledsoe got hurt. Then the season started progressing a little bit. You saw a different team under Brady. You saw more of a take-charge leader, a rah-rah guy, who seemed to read defenses better. He'd throw a nice screen pass. He'd hit the wide receivers so they could catch the ball on the run. But Bledsoe would throw behind them and screw up their timing. You'd see the team pick up a little—played a lot harder when Brady was in the game. As the season progressed, you started really believing in them. The team was very well coached under Belichick now. They didn't miss too many assignments. The fans were really getting into the Patriots. Then when they finally beat Miami, they clinched a playoff spot. My good friend, Bobby Manning is a die-hard Patriot's fan. He's a big Bledsoe fan, always has been, and I was up until a few years ago. But I thought Bledsoe had lost it. I just thought he made a lot of bad reads, a lot of mistakes in crucial periods, like letting the clock run out. I decided to get tickets to the Super Bowl because I thought they were going to beat Pittsburgh. I called my travel agent in Concord, Mass. Most of the Super Bowl packages cost two thousand dollars and were geared toward Pittsburgh to tell you the truth. When I called the travel agent, she said I was the only caller that called beside her son. She had booked my package before in 1996. I went ahead and booked the tickets, because if the Pats had lost, it would have cost me a twenty-five dollar fee, and that was it. I couldn't lose, but we had to fly in and out of Baton Rouge about an hour's drive from New Orleans.

> **You saw more of a take-charge leader, a rah-rah guy, who seemed to read defenses better.**

I paid $250 for my flight, and when they beat Pittsburgh, the flight went up a thousand dollars for the same flight to go to Baton Rouge. When I tried to get my ticket, we couldn't get anything in to New Orleans, all the flights were booked. The trip didn't include a game ticket. I'm a season ticket holder, but I didn't get a Super Bowl ticket. My uncle did get them in the lottery. Bobby Manning got us a place to stay in somebody's house about ten minutes from the Superdome.

Bobby and I have been friends for years. We went together in '96. He's another die-hard Patriots' fan. We have a hard time watching the games together on TV so we talk on the phone back and forth. It seems like we booked the flight on a Wednesday, the middle of the week before they played Pittsburgh.

On our flight to Baton Rouge, there were other people going to the game, but we didn't really talk to them. On the way down, we were just concerned with how well they have to play, like mistake-free. They have to do ball control. They've got to keep the ball away from St. Louis 'cause their offense is so really tough They have to play mistake-free. They can't afford to play and have turnovers. When we played St. Louis before, we turned the ball over a couple of times, and that really hurt us. We figured the defense had to play really well, and had to come up with a touchdown, or the special teams had to play really well and come up with a touchdown. They needed to play well on all cylinders. That was what we kept talking about. We talked about Brady having to play mistake-free. Basically that's what was going back and forth all the way down. I felt like they could win.

People saw the way they won this year—they won a couple of close games. They never quit. That was the best thing about them. When they played St. Louis, I think they learned a lot. They blitzed constantly in that game, and Warner just picked them apart.

They never quit. That was the best thing about them.

In the '96 Super Bowl, we played Green Bay. The whole state of Wisconsin was there. I don't think anybody worked that weekend. But this time, I thought the Patriots had ten times more fans than the Rams. I knew a lot of people that drove down for the game, too. I didn't hear that happen in '96.

We get in Thursday night about seven o'clock their time. We picked up the rental car and drove to New Orleans. We checked into the house we were staying at, and we went to Pat O'Brien's in New Orleans. We hooked up with some of the local Boston sportscasters. We met Tom Curran who used to write for the METROWEST *Daily News* out of Framingham. Now he writes for the *Providence Journal* out of Rhode Island. We met Chris Collins from New England Cable News and Pete Sheppard, a local sportscaster on WEEI, the all-sports station in Boston. He's a big Brady guy. Tom Curran is a big Brady guy. We talked to those guys till like four o'clock in the morning. Then we were back there again Friday night and it was mobbed. They were very confident. Tommy Curran was just praising Brady and was very confident. He gave us some insight on a few things about Brady over Bledsoe—things he had heard.

We were hanging with the sports reporters and it was a great time.

Then Friday night we ran into Tom Curran again. He and Bobby went at it like you wouldn't believe, arguing over Brady versus Bledsoe. And Wendy Nix, who's a sports reporter from Fox said, "Will you two calm down and be quiet?" It was actually kind of funny. They were like Bobby Knight yelling at each other. I just stood there and laughed 'cause I'm used to it. We were hanging with the sports reporters and it was a great time.

Saturday, we went to the NFL Experience. I wasn't impressed. I thought it was better in '96, that the merchandise was better. It was bigger this time, but I just wasn't impressed with it.

Sunday we went to the game. We got there early because of the security reasons. We were just looking around to see if we saw anybody. We didn't want to run inside too early. We wanted to stay outside— just savor the moment. We ran into five or six people we knew from back home. It was a great time. We got to talk to Sports Review—see, Bobby and I love talking sports. That's why anyone would enjoy talking with Tom Curran. It was just a great time, one of the best times of my life, especially when they won.

After we went inside, Bobby made a key statement to me. He said, "I hope they come out as a team during the introductions." I said, "Yeah, I agree." I had these headsets so we could listen to the Boston sportscasters calling the game, Gino Cappelletti and Gil Santos from WBCN in Boston.

On each of the seats was a seat cushion with a pouch overhanging the front of the seats. The pouch contained neat goodies, including a little radio. The radio had the TV play-by-play, the National Radio broadcast, plus the home announcers for each of the two teams. You could get any of the analysts or could get the Rams or Patriots regular announcers.

> Bobby Knight, Dan Issel and Dave Cowens have the same birthday—except Knight was born eight years earlier.

During the game, I was just euphoric—from the opening gun when the Patriots came out. I liked the way they were playing. They were playing very physical. They were really hitting them hard. They were knocking Warner down. They were really hitting the wide receivers. Bobby and I had commented on how physical they were. I thought when Ty Law made that pick, that turned the game around right away. When the Patriots got first possession, they were pretty deep in their own territory, and they moved the ball to midfield. I thought they got a little conservative in the third and fourth quarters. I thought they were going to go for it with a minute twenty one to go.

Bobby started yelling at me later in the game when the Rams tied it up. He didn't think Brady played that great the first half. Remember when Brady threw the ball to Patten—the bomb—I think to open up the third quarter. He missed him. If he had caught it, it was a touchdown. He overthrew him. Bobby said, "If he hit that, the game's over." He likes Brady. He says, "The kid's got real guts." That winning drive, Bledsoe could have never done, I don't care what anybody says. There was one play, may have been the first play, when Brady stepped up, it was only a two-yard completion he threw to Redmond, but they had him. They

> **That winning drive, Bledsoe could have never done, I don't care what anybody says.**

were going to try to knock the ball out of his hand. He got the ball off to Redmond. Just that play, Bledsoe would have taken a sack, or he might have fumbled the ball. Brady just sees the field so well. It's like the ball he threw to Troy Brown, then he threw the ball to Wiggins, and they kicked a field goal. He stepped up, and threw a bullet to Brown. Bledsoe doesn't do those things. He used to. He just doesn't do them anymore.

I was very confident that Vinatieri would nail the field goal. We just went ballistic. Everybody was yelling, screaming, whistling. As a long-time Patriots' fan, you've seen so many bad things happen. It was good to see a good thing happen. It was just one of those magical seasons you'll never forget.

> Twenty years ago, two-thirds of all NFL field goals were made. Now, better then 80 percent are successful.

> The Rams, who began as the Cleveland Rams, were named for the Fordham University team.

As we walked out, people were offering twenty to fifty dollars for the ticket stub. I wouldn't sell mine.

After the game, we went to the Patriots' party. It was wild. There were players there. I liked the one in '96 a lot better. That year it was more exclusive and there weren't so many people there. This year, the people who bought club seats for the new Pats stadium were given a free pass so they could go this time, and it wasn't that great. There were a lot of idiots there. In '96, it was somber, but you got to talk to the players. This time it was just a bunch of idiots. You were happy because everybody won.

When we got home to Boston, people were envious, because this time we had won, and everybody wished they had gone. I just had a hunch the Pats were gonna do it.

Belichick and Rehbein saw something 'cause they elevated him to the back-up spot…They saw something, but other teams would have given up on him.

It's still all people talk about. On sports radio, they try talking about the Bruins or the Celtics, nobody really cares. Baseball has started now, and people talk about the Red Sox, but still it's the Patriots—"What are they gonna do with Bledsoe?" Stuff like that.

I think the Patriots are more popular than the Red Sox.

I think the Patriots are more popular than the Red Sox. I think baseball is changing. Young kids don't play it or follow it anymore, not like they used to. I think the Patriots have been a big draw in the past few years. One thing about the Krafts, they market very well. They do a lot of things. Their merchandising does very well. Also, I think people can relate to the Patriots. I think basketball was really big in the eighties. The Bruins haven't made the playoffs in so many years, and if they do, they're usually one and out. They're labeled a 'bad franchise' 'cause they don't spend the money, and I think people are just tired of it. The Red Sox—well people are just sick of losing. Under Dan Duquette, they were a complete disaster. They brought Pedro in but I think a lot of people lost respect for them. They just disenchanted. I believe that they are an 'old people's team.' I think baseball has changed. Young people don't relate to baseball anymore. I really don't think they do. You don't see kids playing it in the parks

> In 1971, Tony Conigliaro screen-tested for a role in *The Godfather*. Al Pacino got the part.

anymore. I see people turned off by the Red Sox. It's an older sport now. The young kids love football. You walk around now, you see everybody wearing Patriots' paraphernalia. You don't see people wearing Red Sox paraphernalia, not young kids that's for sure.

I don't think Belichick is a big fan of Bledsoe. You mention Brady playing in front of a hundred thousand, the kid wanted a challenge. I think Bledsoe has always been a super star since he was a young kid. People always worshiped the ground he was on. Now he's having a hard time accepting that the people don't want him. He doesn't like being number two. He's never been number two his whole life. I think he's having a hard time accepting that. You certainly can't blame him for feeling that way.

I think Kraft gave him a big contract 'cause they were having trouble selling seats. They had a horrible year last year going five and eleven. Bledsoe was his drawing card. But this year, I think he sold almost all the club seats. We ran into Dan Murphy, Vice President of the Patriots in charge of the new stadium. He had given us tickets to that Super Bowl party. We partied with him Friday night down at Pat O'Briens. We were with him for four hours and then we met Tom Curran again. That's the night Curran and Bobby went at it. Curran was a great guy. He was telling us a little insight about Belichick and Pete Carroll.

Brady has great moxie. That's the best thing about him. I don't think the Patriots have had that under Bledsoe. I don't think they have. The offense has just been struggling for years. They'd blame the offensive line. I used to say to Bobby, "They blame every-thing else but Bledsoe. The kid—his skills

> He said, "He's another Jim Everett." He is. He's Jim Everett.

have diminished." There was a guy back here, a sports fan, who died about a year ago. He said, "He's another Jim Everett." He is. He's Jim Everett.

At the beginning of the year, two sportscasters in Boston, Pete Sheppard, on WEEI, and Fred Smerlas, a former All-Pro football player were calling for the ouster of Bledsoe, actually the year before that. They were calling for a change. They thought his skills had diminished. They both worked a real post game show after the Patriots' broadcast. They've been saying for about a year and a half that "Bledsoe needs to be benched." "They need to change." "Something's wrong." "He's not delivering." They caused a little bit of a stir. They caught a lot of flak, but in the end, they were right.

Last year was just the best. It was an unbelievable season, and Brady was phenomenal. It was a great time. It was a blast. One of the best times of my life. I'll probably never see it again in my lifetime. You know what's so good about this team? When Baltimore won, they had a bunch of absolute jerks. This team—everybody could relate to. They were like a lunch pail group. They worked hard. But you know what? I think Belichick's one of the best coaches in the league. I don't care what anybody says. It was one of the best times in my life. It was an experience I'll never forget. You know what else was nice about it? We got to meet a lot of sportscasters. You get the inside story, too. Hanging out with Tom Curran was worth the trip alone.

You know when Brady's really gonna own the town—when Bledsoe's out of here.

On Tuesday before the Super Bowl, we went down to Foxboro to pick up tickets for the game. The line out the pro shop was about a hundred people deep. That was outside. There was probably a hundred people inside. And there was no Brady stuff. You couldn't get a Brady shirt. He came out of nowhere. He took the town. You know when Brady's really gonna own the town—when Bledsoe's out of here.

In 1986, Matt Millen, currently president of the Detroit Lions, punched Pat Sullivan, the Pats' general manager, in a tunnel at the LA Coliseum. Sullivan had yelled at Howie Long of the Raiders. Pat Sullivan said that Millen hit him with his helmet. Matt Millen said his fist got hit by Sullivan's face.

During a 1979 game against the New York Jets at Shea Stadium, a remote control model airplane crashed into the stands at half-time, hit a Patriots fan and killed him.

The Arizona Cardinals are the only NFL team to play full-time in a college stadium—Sun Devil Stadium, home of Arizona State. The Chicago Bears will play the next two seasons at the University of Illinois.

LADIES AND GENTLEMEN OF THE JURY, THE BLEDSOE DEFENSE RESTS ITS CASE
BOB MANNING

Bob Manning is a Massachusetts State Trooper and a die-hard New England Patriots fan. He is a staunch Drew Bledsoe backer and proud of it. He and his good friend, Concord (MA) policeman, Bobby Shea were two ring-tailed tooters after attending Super Bowl XXXVI.

S ports radio is big up here, and they talk about which team is most popular all the time. But the Patriots, even in preseason, have been outdrawing the Red Sox for a while now. Diehards up here—of course, I'm a little biased because I like the Patriots more than I like the Red Sox, especially with the way the last management, the way the sale of the team and everything went. It really turned a lot of people sour. I've always been one to think that when—Boy, Kraft has sold out that stadium ever since he bought it—every single game. I'm biased 'cause I like the Patriots better, but I think the tide has turned. Bobby and I lean more toward the Patriots. Bobby hates the Red Sox anyway. I think that the tide has turned. This team, the way they won anyway this year, captured the hearts of a lot of people.

By the end of the Super Bowl, our defense was sucking some serious wind 'cause they had played their hearts out. We hung on there to win. It was a great, great victory, Brady does, and Belichick deserves a lot of credit. There were sports writers up here, some major sports writers, that publicly in their columns personally insulted Belichick when he got hired—calling him "Pond Scum. He's a stiff; he's a moron; he's this; he's that," but he and Scott Pioli deserve a whole heck of a lot of credit for turning that organization around. I think it was a big win for him anyway because he comes out

> Patriots player personnel director, Scott Pioli is married to Bill Parcells' daughter, Dallas.

> The Super Bowl was not called the Super Bowl for its first three years. It was called the World Championship of Professional Football.

of Parcell's shadow. People thought Parcells was God around here. He's kinda showing his colors.

Brady shows me a lot of character. Looking back on it, that was his football dream season, but I think he was a product of the system. I think he's dealt with great coaching. Let me say something—Drew Bledsoe excelled with great coaching under Bill Parcells. The minute he had mediocre coaching, he went downhill.

Drew Bledsoe's game was very plain and simple. Drew Bledsoe was the best quarterback, with the exception of this past season with Tom Brady, and judgment is still out, that the Patriots have ever had. He came in here as a highly touted rookie. He, in my opinion, learned an extremely lot under the coaching system of Bill Parcells. He's never had the same system three years. He's passed for more yardage than, I think, the only other quarterback might be Dan Marino in his first eight years in the league. He has faults, but he is a quality, quality quarterback. He's a quality individual. The reason I stick by him is because fans around here are too easy to turn their backs on someone. He's always been very professional, never blamed anybody else on this team for anything. He's always taken the burden himself. Speaking about some of his faults, I think Drew Bledsoe, like most quarterbacks, when he was coached under, at that time what I thought was one of the best coaching groups in the league, which was Parcells, Belichick, the year the Patriots went to the Super Bowl, I thought that Drew Bledsoe played very well. So did most people around. The minute that system changed and they got mediocre coaching here, Bledsoe went downhill. I think the team went downhill fast. Bledsoe realized that, and he tried to do too much on his own. Every year around here, it's always been that Drew Bledsoe has to win the game. I don't think that a quarterback in the NFL that can fit and handle that pressure—certainly not Drew Bledsoe because he certainly isn't the most athletic guy in the league.

I remember that Mo Lewis hit on Bledsoe which I thought was one of the most vicious hits I'd ever seen. I couldn't believe one—that Bledsoe got up,

Two of the greatest quarterbacks of all time, Johnny Unitas and Dan Marino, have the same middle name, Constantine, and both are from Pittsburgh.

In 1969, the famous "Joe Namath" Super Bowl, Army assistant football coach Bill Parcells watched the game at the house of Army's head basketball coach, Bobby Knight.

Who said it was a man's world?
Galynn, Tom Brady, Julie, Maureen and Nancy

I hope the "Gong Show" never goes off the air.

Jack Arute interviews Tom Brady after a Michigan victory.

Tom Brady (12) with his Serra High School Team

Tom Brady with former Michigan teammate, Brian Griese of the Denver Broncos.

Kurt Warner and Tom Brady
prior to Super Bowl XXXVI

The "Sisters"— Maureen, Nancy and Julie

This guy Mickey sure has a lot of friends!

two—that he went back in the game. I remember saying to myself I don't care what kind of game it is or what he is, how could Belichick even put him back in the game after undergoing that hit. He was one sick guy. I think he's one of the toughest guys to ever play football. I think people forget what a quality individual he is—what a good player he is. I don't think he's the greatest quarterback ever to play the game, but people around here want him to be something that he's not. He's not John Elway—he's not Brett Favre, but neither one of those quarterbacks ever won anything until they had a complete football team around them. Drew Bledsoe, if you want to give the quarterbacks the credit, took this team to a Super Bowl along with a lot of other star players and a great coaching staff and they lost—to a better team. A game that I was

> **I think people forget what a quality individual he is—what a good player he is.**

at, and I personally believe that they had a chance to win that football game if their head coach was into that game. I believe Bill Parcells did not prepare like Belichick and his coaching staff prepared for the other Super Bowl. The Patriots were in that game. They had started to take control. The coaching staff and the players made some errors and it cost them.

Bledsoe threw four interceptions in that game, but one of those interceptions was a 'Hail Mary' at the end of the half. If I'm not mistaken, one of them was a bad interception and one was at the end of the game when they were trying to play catch-up—maybe two were—at the end of the game when it was obvious what they had to do, and the lights were out after Reggie White made that sack after the touchdown, and you could kind of see the writing on the wall.

But Drew Bledsoe is who he is. When he beat Minnesota up here in Foxboro in what some people consider his greatest game, he was a God. He was a 'Hall of Famer.' But see what happens is the press up here takes you and puts you on another pedestal. They build you up, and they build you up, and then they just love to tear you down. Drew Bledsoe is a good solid quarterback. With great players, he can be great. That '96 football team—think of who their subs were: Keith Byars, Dave Meggett, all playmakers. Those guys would come into a game as subs and make huge plays. If you remember, Bledsoe very often threw to the backs. He threw to Keith Byars. He threw to Dave Meggett. He threw to Curtis Martin. He obviously threw to Ben Coates, who was maybe the best tight end in the game during that span.

> Dean Cain, who played Superman on TV, holds the NCAA record for the most interceptions in one season.

He had a decent offensive line. He had a left tackle who some people considered one of the best in the game at the time who was playing at the top of his game. They had a solid defense, and they had a running game. They take all those weapons away, what has Brett Favre done the last couple of years other than being an individually great athlete? He's had his ups and downs. What was John Elway, other than being an individual great athlete, until they got Terrell Davis and one of the best offensive lines the game's ever had? What has Dan Marino ever won? Nothing. Because he's had to do it all by himself all the time. He's never had the complete game—never once. Drew Bledsoe isn't the greatest quarterback who ever played in the NFL. He's certainly the best quarterback the Patriots have had. Right now, to the fans, Steve Grogan is a God—because he's retired. He was one tough S.O.B. When he played, they hated him. They booed him 'cause he was always trying to throw the ball downfield and going for the touchdown. They hated him part of the time during his career and that's when he was a veteran. Then Tony Easton started to become what most people would call a baby 'cause he could only take the ball here or there and he couldn't throw the ball downfield. They wanted Grogan back. But when Grogan was the starter up here, they crucified him. Now he's a God. He's a living legend up here because his toughness grows in retirement—his image of being tough. Actually he's a better quarterback in retirement than he ever really was.

Bledsoe will land on his feet in Buffalo.

Drew Bledsoe's a good quarterback. Bill Belichick doesn't think so, and I understand why, but Drew Bledsoe's a good quarterback. A lot of teams would take Drew Bledsoe. They used to like first round draft choices, and this and that, but Bledsoe will land on his feet in Buffalo. He's a victim of the salary cap; I think if you look back, Bobby Grier turned out to be a big mistake. Pete Carroll turned out to be a big mistake. During those years, out of every offensive lineman that Drew Bledsoe played with in the three years of the Pete Carroll regime—and even the first year of the Belichick regime—there's only one that is still playing and that is Damien Woody, center. Nobody else is playing that played with Drew Bledsoe during those three years on the offensive line. No one else is even still playing in the league.

I'm not a Brady hater. I'm a Patriots' fan—number one. How do you argue with a guy who just won the Super Bowl? Every decision Belichick makes, he comes out on top. Bryan Cox took some shots at the administration and the Head Coach when he signed with New Orleans. He said, "Everybody thinks this team had a great coaching staff. We weren't the best team in the league. We won because we had the best coaching staff in the league." He goes, "But the administration around here doesn't know how to deal with players. I think he was insulted that the Patriots maybe didn't come and knock on his door. Supposedly they didn't offer him any money and New Orleans was chasing him down so he signed with him. I liked him here. I liked him under Parcells with the Jets. I thought he was a very good football player.

The media around here billed this team as "team first," "team first" and everybody was getting along. Drew Bledsoe—a lot of players have said that Bledsoe could have divided that team, and he didn't. Bledsoe believes Belichick gave him the impression that he was going to have a chance to get his job back. Bobby and I had talked about this extensively. I really believe that if Bledsoe had continued not to play well, Belichick would have benched him. I don't think Belichick liked him. I have no idea about Charlie Weis. We don't get enough about that. What I disagree with is that just because he was playing bad, you don't just throw the guy away. I think Bledsoe could have come back and done very well with that football team. That's my opinion. My buddy, Bobby Shea, disagrees with me, but I think he could have snapped out of it with the right coaching, with that coaching staff. I think you would have seen the old Drew Bledsoe.

I think Brady will do well in the future. I do respect other guys who say that he has signs of greatness. I can see that. I really do like the way he deals with this football team. He gave this football team an attitude that it did not have. He's a different kind of person than Drew Bledsoe in the respect that's he's more of a rah-rah guy. I didn't think he deserved the MVP of the Super Bowl…as great as I thought he was in that last series, and he made some great plays. One of the greatest plays I ever saw, he didn't do this all year long, that very first play, that one or two-yard dump off to Redmond. One of the Rams guys got his hands on the football, and Brady held it. That was a great play. Brady fumbled more than any quarterback in the NFL last year. Tom Brady led the league for quarterbacks—more fumbles than any other quarterback—a true fact.

A couple of years ago, the Patriots lost a play-off game to Pittsburgh, and Bledsoe got crucified around here because they were a lousy team. They had a lot of guys hurt, and they weren't playing that well. It was all on Bledsoe's shoulders. They couldn't run the ball for a down. A Steeler came around Bruce Armstrong, and he hit Bledsoe from the blind side when

> Recovering fumbles is largely a matter of luck, while intercepting passes is largely a matter of skill.

Bledsoe was trying to throw the ball. He fumbled it, and Pittsburgh recovered it and they won the playoff game. We lost by 7-6, something like that. It was a low scoring game that we lost. Everybody was all over Bledsoe. He got hit from the blind side as he was trying to make a play. Nobody was open, and he was trying to find someone open. The Oakland game, Tom Brady was trying to make a play. He was holding onto the ball until somebody got open. Woodson comes in right from the side that Brady should have seen him and he didn't see him. If the referee doesn't overturn that play, or if that's Drew Bledsoe—trust me, the fans—they would have had to get a police escort to get Bledsoe home safely that night. Was that the game? No. Brady came back in and he did the job. Drew Bledsoe used to do that. Now people say Bledsoe can't do it anymore. I say, "Show me a quarterback who can't run—can't put the ball in the end zone really on his own. But when you get inside the twenty with absolutely no running game and no target over the middle, okay—show me a quarterback in the league who can throw the ball in the end zone when all the defensive backs and teams do is put eight guys back in the end zone or seven guys and rush four. They cover every spot of the football field. Show me a football team that will be successful when that's the defensive philosophy and you can't do anything else but rely on the arm of your quarterback. You're not going to be successful in the NFL.

Drew Bledsoe should have a high and very special place in the heart of every Patriot fan.

> Bledsoe attended Washington State.
> Pullman, Washington, home of Washington State University, has a population of twenty-five thousand. Martin Stadium, the home stadium for the Washington State Cougars, holds thirty-eight thousand.

> In the late 50s, the Cougars had a home game during a blizzard. The paid attendance was 1. The Athletic Department gave that paying fan a lifetime pass to Washington State football games.

ST. PETE, I JUST WANT TO USE YOUR PHONE AND THE BATHROOM, I'LL BE RIGHT BACK

DION RICH

Dion Rich of San Diego is the most famous gatecrasher in the history of sports. His most formidable challenge was Super Bowl XXXVI in New Orleans.

I'm originally from LA, during the height of the depression. The depression hit October 29, and I popped out November 29. I remember the roof leaking. I remember going to school with holes in my shoes. I remember trading peanut butter and jelly sandwiches for minced ham sandwiches. And I remember going to school in a Model-T Ford—very humiliating. So I knew from that time on, I always wanted to have money. So I saved my money and worked hard ever since and turned my efforts toward gate crashing in my later years.

Super Bowl I goes back to the Los Angeles Coliseum in 1967. Obviously, it was the first Super Bowl I crashed. That's when the Packers beat the Chiefs 35-10. I knew a lot of the Chiefs' players so I went in with the Chiefs' bus, and I put on one of the Chiefs' jackets—one of the coach's jackets—because he was up in the booth. He didn't need the jacket. I was on the sideline the entire game. Then after the game was over, I went in to the Chiefs' locker room, but it was dead. Lockers rooms are extremely dead when the team loses. So then I proceeded to go into the Packers' locker room. That's the place to be. Lo and behold, I see Pete Roselle, Bart Starr and Vince Lombardi on the podium so I just hop up on the podium. Meantime while I'm up there, Bart Starr gets off the podium. He was 'most valuable player' that first year. I have a picture of just Roselle and Vince Lombardi and

> The first Super Bowl, in 1967 at the Los Angeles Coliseum, had 32,000 empty seats even though the most expensive ticket was $12.

myself, and there's another guy on the podium at the time. When I got back to San Diego, people say, "Oh Dion, oh boy, we saw you at the World's Championship Game."—it wasn't called the Super Bowl then. From then on, it was kind of a ritual for me. I missed Super Bowl III only because of a skiing trip that I had planned and couldn't get out of. Otherwise, in retrospect, I would have forgot the skiing trip, gone to Super Bowl III, and I would have crashed all thirty six Super Bowls.

At Super Bowl VII, the NFL finally found my true identity. The reason for that was that Super Bowl VI, I was on the field with Landry. After that I was on the podium with Duane Thomas, of the Cowboys, and Jim Brown and the CBS announcer, Tom Brookshier. I danced with Landry's daughter at his victory party after that. From then on, NFL Security saw me, and they said, "We've got to get this guy outta here." That was Super Bowl VI.

At Super Bowl VII, I crashed Pete Roselle's Friday night party on the Queen Mary. I'm standing there with the Rams' ticket manager and Chargers' ticket manager who both are very, very close friends of mine, and this big guy, man, he's about two hundred and fifty pounds and six foot, five, and he walks up and he says, "Is your name Dion Rich?" Boy, I looked up at this guy. I gulp, and say, "Yes." And he points at me and says, "If we catch your blankety blank butt on that field Sunday, we're throwing you out. Do you understand that?" I said, "Yes sir."

Two weeks later in *Newsweek* magazine, there's a beautiful shot of Don Shula and myself. That was Super Bowl VII when the Dolphins beat Washington 14 to 7. It should have been fourteen to nothing but Yapremian picked up that botched field goal and threw the thing and the next thing you know Washington scored seven points.

So it went on and on and on—one Super Bowl crash right after another. Then Super Bowl XXII, in San Diego, I was tipped off by a friend of mine on the San Diego Police Department that they were going to follow me. They trailed me the whole time. I crashed the game, but I stayed off the field and out of the press box and out of the locker room.

> When Don Shula retired, he had more
> victories than over half the NFL teams.

> The only person to score back-to-back fifty-point
> games in the history of Long Island High School
> basketball is Jim Brown, the NFL legend.

At Super Bowl XXIII they finally put a sting operation on me. At that point, someone called me at my home and they said, "Is Dion Rich there?" I said, "Speaking." They said, "This is *South Florida Trade Winds Magazine*, and we'd like to do a story on you. Where are you staying?" This was a ploy! They already knew what flight I was coming in on. I said, "I'm staying at Ft. Lauderdale on the beach, and I have the telephone number, but I don't know the exact address." I gave them the phone number so in a matter of minutes they had the address. They followed me the entire time while I was wondering when they were going to do their story. Anyway, it's time for the trophy presentation. I'm ready for the presentation when Pete Roselle hands the Vince Lombardi trophy to Ed DeBartolo, of the 49ers, and up comes the sergeant from the Miami Vice Squad. He says, "Okay, Dion, you're out of here. This is the last of you."

> **I'm able to crash all the parties I want as long as I stay off the field, out of the press box, and out of the locker room.**

Felix Eads, the secret investigator, who had trailed me the entire time, says, "Dion, you've got to stop this. You're costing the NFL thousands upon thousands of dollars to trail you and keep track of you." I said, "Okay." So they give me my territory now. I give them theirs. I'm able to crash all the parties I want as long as I stay off the field, out of the press box, and out of the locker room.

Now what you really want to know is about the Patriots' Super Bowl XXXVI. I had no idea that I would make it. Believe me, I had more than one friend of mine in the media tell me that I wasn't gonna make it. Well, the way it worked out, I crashed the press room. I crashed the working press room. I had several radio interviews because of an article that was written by Les Carpenter in the *Seattle Times*. He wrote a real nice article on me that came out Tuesday prior to the Super Bowl. It was because of that Rick Reilly, of *SI*, who is one of the most coveted sports writers, not only in the United States, but the world. He is one fantastic writer. He is great. I had no idea how great he was, but now I'm reading every back issue of *Sports Illustrated* that I can get my hands on. He interviewed me on the Friday prior to the Super Bowl in New Orleans. I had no idea how great it was gonna turn out, but I've had nothing but compliments on the article. In fact, I've had a few compliments already on the article that came out in a recent *Sports Illustrated*. I had to crash the New Orleans Hyatt where the press stayed the day of the Super Bowl. They had that all roped off. You could not enter—just people who stayed there, residents and media only. I was real lucky to be able to crash. I started to walk through, and they turned me away because I had no credentials. A woman called a name and I said, "Yes," and she put a ribbon around my head with a credential to get into a party so I just zipped right on in. I asked her how she knew who I was, and she said, "Oh, I think I recognized you." So I just used somebody else's name and walked in. That guy, he won't have any problem. He just shows his ID and they'll give him a credential to get into the party. I crashed that party.

I was waiting for Rick Reilly. How can I be the world's greatest gatecrasher without crashing security to meet him in there? I couldn't say, "Hey, I can't get in." From there on, Rick Reilly followed me in. I had no idea I'd make it. I didn't plan on making it. There's no comparison, this one was a lot tougher than the earlier Super Bowls. They scan everybody with the scanners and the metal detectors and everything. I saw a very narrow passageway that I thought I might be able to get through without being scanned. So I put my fourth finger up to my eye and then I pointed to me, and Reilly's probably about twenty feet back. I said, "Keep your eye on me." I zipped right on in. The article said I was in within six minutes. I would have been in sooner except I stopped for two pictures outside of the Superdome. I figured this might be my last chance to get a picture before being incarcerated. Who knows? But I was in, and we have a picture of Rick Reilly and myself. I'm gonna send him a glossy of that picture of the two of us inside the Superdome with the untorn ticket and with the scoreboard in the background.

Anyway, I went in an area where they were scanning everyone that went in. Even if you had credentials you had to be scanned. I circumvented that because there was another narrow passageway that I spotted. After that, I got a picture outside. As luck would have it, I went in a side door, and Rick Reilly followed me the entire time. I was so fortunate to be written up by one of the greatest writers in the world. I couldn't go in the Media entrance because I didn't have credentials, and they would have scanned me. I went through another small passageway.

Normally the fans went through a first place where they do something and then went about twenty feet further and they did something else, and then you were in. But I circumvented both those posts.

After Rick Reilly came in, he looked up a photographer to get some pictures. We got pictures with my camera and another photographer's camera. From then on, I ran into a whole bunch of people I knew, and he ran into people he knew. By this time it was half an hour or so before game time so

> Before Super Bowl XI, there was no national anthem.
> Vicki Carr sang *America The Beautiful*.

he went up into the press box with his credentials. I watched the game from a no-show seat. I could have watched it from where I had a ticket—that wasn't torn—but earlier I hurt myself when I hopped off the media van. I had hurt the bottom part of my foot and didn't want to walk any farther. There's a place in the Superdome that's blocked off and you can't walk all the way around. I got tired of walking and just sat in a no-show. That's nothing new for me.

I have pictures—one on the front page of the *New York Times* with Chuck Noll, a picture with Vince Lombardi, and with John Madden. I have a picture on the sideline with me and McCafferty, when Baltimore won. I don't have a publication of it, but it was on television. I have another picture with Flores and Vermeil after Oakland beat Philadelphia in the 1980 Super Bowl.

To be a great gatecrasher takes a little tiny bit of skill. It takes a lot of luck, a lot of timing, a lot of desire, a lot of hard work, a lot of connections, and I clean this up if I'm talking to a mixed group, and a lot of intestinal fortitude.

I'm in demand a lot to give talks. I make it clear. I answer the most prevalently asked questions. They say, "Are you ashamed of what you do?" I answer, "Absolutely not. I do more volunteer work in one month than the average person does in an entire lifetime," which I do, and I have letters to back that up. I do a lot of volunteer work in San Diego.

I'm the only guy who's gotten two letters from the Academy Awards. The first letter said, "What the heck are you doing here?" The second said, "Don't come back even if you have a ticket." My advice to a novice gate crasher is 'make sure you eat the minute you crash a party.' Because I know from past experience, it feels a lot better to get thrown out on a full stomach than it does an empty stomach.

One of my fortés is crashing the Olympics, Super Bowl, Kentucky Derby, the Americas' Cup in Australia. I've got a picture with Kentucky Derby winning jockey, Jerry Bailey, on the front page of the Louisville paper with a complete write-up. I had superimposed on that same front page a shot

> John Madden lost his long-time partner after Super Bowl XXXVI when Pat Summerall retired. Pat Summerall's real first name is George. He is called Pat because when he was a kicker with the New York Giants football team, the newspapers would print: "P.A.T.-Summerall." P.A.T. stood for "Point After Touchdown." Summerall played minor league baseball against Mickey Mantle,

with me and Steven Seagal in the front row of the Oscars with the big giant Oscar in the background. I don't limit it just to the Super Bowl. Once they put that sting operation out on me in Super Bowl XXIII, I branched out from there to the Oscars, the Americas Cup, the World Series, the All-Star Game, and the Final Four.

At the Kentucky Derby, you have to crash one of the entranceways because they have wristbands for each and every section. There's a cement fence, probably about four feet high, you have to scale. You do that when the feature race is going on. Then while everybody's looking at the race, you climb the wall, then you find the guy with the happiest smile on his face, and you run in with his entourage. I have pictures that the New York Post had on me in the Winner's Circle with his entourage, and then one with me and Jerry Bailey. I've never been kicked out of the Winner's Circle, but after the Winner's Circle I went up to the podium to make my speech on CNN, ABC, ESPN worldwide. I was up there with the owner, his daughter, the jockey, the trainer and myself, D. Wayne Lucas and Jerry Bailey at that particular Kentucky Derby. I'm ready to make my big speech—first time ever. About that time, a gal tugs on my shoulder and says, "Sir, do you have a credential?" I said, "No Maam, I don't." She says, "We saw you on television last night." I had been on the Lexington TV the night before at a big party. I said, "How did I

No respect—he should have said 'that world's greatest gate crasher.'

look?" She said, "You're out of here." One of the officials said, "Is that that gate crasher? Get him out of here." No respect—he should have said 'that world's greatest gate crasher.' So they got my attention. I was PO'd about that time. I crashed the Turf Club, got a picture with Connie Stevens and Jerry Hall who is Mick Jagger's ex-wife.

Once, after the final game of the NBA Championships, I was able to wiggle my way in to the Celtics locker room and put a Celtics jersey on. I have a picture at the All-Star game in Miami of me sitting at the press table. I sat there the whole time. One of the reasons I was able to do it—it said, 'Wall Street Journal,' and the *Wall Street Journal* guy hadn't gotten there yet so I turned it over so it didn't say anything. I made some long distance calls home to San Diego to tell people that I was sitting at the press table. Michael Jordan was right there, and I didn't get a picture with him. I've got pictures of almost three hundred celebrities, and I should have got a picture with him.

I not only amaze other people, but I amaze myself in how I'm able to do it. What people don't know, is there's so much luck involved and so much timing involved—luck and timing both.

Chapter 6

Turn Your Radio On

Sean McDonough

Dave Jageler

Pete Sheppard

SEAN McDONOUGH IS A HARD ACT TO FOLLOW ...MAINLY BECAUSE HE TAKES THE MICROPHONE WITH HIM

SEAN McDONOUGH

Sean McDonough has climbed the media ranks in quick fashion since his graduation from Syracuse University. He is a star with the Sporting News Radio Network and ABC Television.

We have a show on Mondays called Patriots' Monday. We had Tom Brady and Bill Belichick on every week, usually in person. There were a couple of times we had him on over the phone. We did it from Foxboro Stadium so most of the time he was on with us right in person.

I know a kid named Travis who played basketball at Michigan who was there the same time Tom was. Trav is a great guy, and he called me up when Tom first got drafted by the Patriots. He said, "I hope you have a chance to meet this guy Brady because he is just one of the greatest people I've ever known. You'd really like him, etc." That was always in the back of my mind. I'd never met Tom during the year he was here as a backup.

When I first met Tom, I mentioned that I knew Travis, and of course he had a lot of nice things to say about Travis. Then week to week, he was so humble, so anxious to talk about anything but himself, and just praise everybody else. If you ask Tom Brady a question he doesn't like, he doesn't bristle at it, he just kinda makes a face like, "Aw shucks. Why'd you have to ask me that?" He got very embarrassed. About two thirds of the way through the season, I was beating the drum on the radio show for Patriots' fans to log on and vote for him for the Pro Bowl because I really thought he deserved it. When I brought it up on the show one day when he was there, he looked at me like, "Can we talk about anything else but this? All I really care about is winning games." It was almost like "You've got to be kidding

> The first coaches' TV show was in 1952, hosted by Bud Wilkinson at the University of Oklahoma.

me, talking about the Pro Bowl." That's the way he is. I remember at the end of the year, I did the Citrus Bowl for ABC. I spent about an hour with Lloyd Carr, his Michigan coach, a couple of days before the game, and I was mentioning I was doing the show every week with Tom and what a great guy he was. I told him he seems too good to be true, and after a while I just realized, "No, that's the way he is."

And Lloyd said, "Sean, I felt the same way. When I first met him, I was like—'Come on. This has gotta be an act.' I just realized as time went on that Tom Brady was one of the greatest people I've ever known, never mind coached. Everybody I've ever met who knows him well, feels the same way—that he's just legitimately, sincerely a nice, decent, thoughtful, intelligent guy, who happens to be an outstanding quarterback, too."

It's ridiculous to compare anybody to Joe Montana, but I think Tom Brady is that type of quarterback. Maybe from a physical standpoint, he doesn't have the strongest arm, the quickest feet, anything, but I think he just has the right combination of football skills, the smarts, the instincts, the leadership ability. There's no doubt in my mind that he's gonna be one of the top quarterbacks in the league for a long time. Would that surprise me? No. I don't think there's anything flukey about what he did. I don't think it was that teams were caught off guard. I think if anything, he could do more. I think the Patriots just sort of asked him to do the bare minimum that he needed to do to help guide them to the Super Bowl. I think the Super Bowl game was a good indication of that. They leaned heavily on the defense, and to a lesser extent on the special teams and just asked the offense to do enough. Don't turn it over, get first downs, keep the defense off the field, and score some points when you have an opportunity. I think the real test was at the very end of the game when the situation was, 'Okay, offense, you

> **It's ridiculous to compare anybody to Joe Montana, but I think Tom Brady is that type of quarterback.**

have to do it. You have to move the ball.' That's why Tom won the MVP because of that last drive. He'd had an adequate game up until then, but I don't think he had an MVP caliber performance, in large part because they didn't ask him to. I think as the years go on and he is asked to do more, if anything, he'll just display his skills that much more. Unfortunately, the reality of his profession is that he could go out permanently the first play of the next year with injury.

I was in New Orleans from Tuesday on at the Super Bowl. Early in the week I definitely thought the Patriots had more fans there, but later in the week I started seeing more Rams fans too. People around the country, the odds makers, the experts were taking the Patriots lightly. A lot of people thought the way they won the Oakland game was a fluke, that they shouldn't have won, and that an injustice had been done to Oakland. I think those of us who had watched them play realized they were a real good solid football team. Shoot, they easily could have beat the Rams when they played them earlier in the season. If Antowain Smith hadn't fumbled on the two-yard line right before the half, they had a great chance to go in at halftime ahead ten points. The Patriots were clearly a better team in the playoffs than they were back at midseason when they had played the Rams. Even though they lost, I said to myself, "You know, this is a playoff caliber team because if they can hold their own with the team everybody thinks is the best team in the NFL, they certainly can be a playoff team." That's really when I became a believer, even though it was a loss. Most of the fans around here were convinced by what they saw during the year that there was nothing flukey about what the Patriots had done. They were legitimately a good football team, deserved to be in the Super Bowl and could play with anybody. They certainly proved that.

> **They were legitimately a good football team and deserved to be in the Super Bowl and could play with anybody, and they certainly proved that.**

New England is much more a pro football area than it used to be. That really started when Parcells came. They went from having very low season ticket sales and not selling out the stadium, but I think they have about twenty thousand people on the waiting list for season tickets. Boston is much more of a pro football town now than it ever was before. Or if they have another five and eleven or four and twelve season, we're looking at a lot of people jumping off the bandwagon. The popularity of the Patriots, Celtics and Bruins is much more contingent upon the winning and losing than is the popularity of the Red Sox. The Red Sox fans are there no matter what.

It's been a joy talking about Tom Brady. I love to talk about people I really like a lot.

The Boston Celtics eight-peated.

CINDERFELLA WAS RAMTASTIC
DAVE JAGELER

Dave Jageler joined WWZN at the same time Tom Brady became a Patrios starting quarterback. Previously he worked in the Charlotte, NC market.

From a reporter's perspective, it was just how amazing how Tom Brady handled the media despite the fact that he had never started a game in the National Football League. The Boston media, as you know, can be ruthless. He comes in and he's the fresh face and the good story. Every week these people would ask him a lot of the 'big picture' questions: "Are you surprised at how well you're doing?" "You've won four games in a row, how huge is this for you?" He was incredible at just focusing. The media couldn't break him down. "No, I'm just focused on the next opponent. I'm not worried about what I've done. I've still got to get better." It was like he had a script that he was going to stick to in these press conferences and it didn't matter what the question was. I thought that for his age and experience level that he

> **...he did a tremendous job of playing the Boston media like a fiddle.**

did a tremendous job of playing the Boston media like a fiddle. He came across as genuine. If asked about the playoffs when they were six and five, some guys might say, "Yeah, hey, if we win three of our last four games, we're gonna get to the playoffs." He was never like that. It was always, "I'm not even worried about the playoffs. I'm just worried about beating Buffalo, or beating Cleveland." He sounded like a coach. The media accepted those answers. The media respected the way he handled things. He showed that skill throughout the year. When he was the starter, everyone would ask, "How much more difficult is it now that you're the starter to get ready for the game?" He said, "Not at all. When I was the fourth-string quarterback, as a rookie, I prepared myself like I was the starting quarterback, whether it was watching film for hours on end, or studying the game plan at home or during meetings and such." Maybe that eased his transition—the professionalism he had even as a rookie when he knew there was no chance he was going to play, preparing himself like he was a starter. When he actually became a starter, it wasn't a life-changing experience. He was prepared for the opportunity.

I had seen Brady play in Charlotte in the preseason game because I worked in Charlotte at the time. When he had started, everyone's expectations were low. I was listening to the talk radio shows when I first moved to Boston in September. It was like, 'Well if Bledsoe's out five weeks, they might go one and four,'—it was gloom and doom. They were 0 and 2, and they had looked terrible against Cincinnati and against the Jets. Their franchise quarterback was out, and there was no way that this team could more than win three or four games the rest of the year. Then they go out and beat Indianapolis like a drum, and it's like, "Well, okay, that was a fluke." Then they go out to lose to Miami the next game, and Brady doesn't play well.

The game that really sold me on him was the San Diego game when he led them back from ten points down in the fourth quarter with a game-tying drive, throwing a touchdown pass in the last two minutes, and then leading them to a victory in overtime. He threw for over three hundred yards, with tremendous poise, and from that point on, I was sold on his ability to throw the football. He didn't put up the great numbers necessarily 'cause the game plan was to be mistake free. They didn't take a lot of chances. He wouldn't throw the ball fifty times unless they needed to. The only games he really did that were the San Diego regular season and the Oakland playoff games. You saw he put up good numbers when he did that. But I was sold. I told my friend back in Carolina very early on that when Brady took over the team, he just had that leadership ability and he had the respect of his teammates. I said that something special was going on very early in the season when they got on that roll and got back to five hundred. This team was playing hard for Brady. It started to become obvious that it was going to be tough for Bledsoe to get his job back when he came back, and ultimately that proved true.

> The youngest coaches in NFL history were Harlan Svare, thirty-one, 1962, Rams; David Shula, thirty-two, Bengals, 1992; John Madden, thirty-three, Raiders, 1969; Don Shula, thirty-three, Colts, 1963.

ENJOY A SHOT OF THE TRUTH.
MAKE IT A BOTTLE...I'LL BUY

PETE SHEPPARD

Rhode Island native Pete "The Voice" Sheppard teams with former NFL-er Fred Smerlas on a popular sports talk show on WEEI Radio, Boston. Sheppard and Smerlas were among the very first to sing Brady's praises and took considerable flak for doing so.

T he only time I saw Tom Brady in 2000, his rookie season, was he came in for a couple of series, one on Thanksgiving Day in Detroit, which he was nowhere near ready at the time. You could tell. He was very raw. The turnaround we saw in the 2001 preseason, particularly in the Carolina game, was unbelievable. And you could tell, and I personally think that if Belichick had his way, he would have started Brady from day one, from the first game of the season. You could tell by the way he was talking at some of the press conferences, especially when Brady vaulted— you know, Michael Bishop became an afterthought—he vaulted over Damon Huard. Most of us thought Damon Huard was going to be the second-string quarterback going into this year, but when Belichick picked Brady over him, you knew something special was happening. Then we saw him in the Carolina game, the exhibition game, and he looked fantastic.

At the time, there wasn't a bigger Drew fan in the world than myself, but you just saw some things. And, again, it started in the Cincinnati game opening day—the Pats started off okay in that game, but then you see things that don't show up in the stat book. They go four series in a row of three and out, and things like that don't show up, even though Bledsoe had a decent game. I hate to see anybody in the league get hurt and have career-ending injuries, but the Mo Lewis hit—in the Jets game was, in a lot of ways a blessing in disguise. Even in that game when Brady came in for Bledsoe, I

> There have been two players in NFL history who later owned teams. George Halas, of the Chicago Bears, and Jerry Richardson, of the Carolina Panthers.

could see his leadership qualities take over right away. There was no question in week three when they played the Colts. In that first series, there was just something special about this kid that you knew—at least I knew—and I think Freddie did, too, as well, that this was not your average back-up quarterback. There was something special going on here. It took a few games for people to cross the bridge onto our side. People tried to make it out—Bledsoe versus Brady—Bledsoe bashers versus Brady praisers.

> ...I could see leadership qualities right away take over.

We took a lot of heat for it on the air at first, but eventually you started seeing how smart this kid was, and again the leadership and the decision-making. Even if he had a bad series, he would go over to Coach Belichick and explain what had happened. Belichick would say this in the press conference. "I didn't complete this pass because the safety was coming here, the linebacker was zone-blitzing, and I didn't pick up such and such defensive end dropping back." He knew exactly what every player on the defensive side of the field was doing. Bledsoe never had those kinds of reactions—ever.

I believe Brady can throw deep. He certainly did in college. He destroyed Alabama in the Orange Bowl. This stuff about the reason for his success was that the Patriots changed their offense to suit Brady is totally untrue. Charlie Weis told us that all season long and reiterated it at the Super Bowl. It had nothing to do with changing the offense. It had to do with Brady making better decisions than Bledsoe. Plain and simple. He's not gonna try and force the ball downfield.

I personally thought this year that one of the greatest games he ever had was the game against Denver. He was phenomenal in the first three quarters and four minutes against Denver. Even though the Patriots ended up losing thirty-one to twenty, he completed his first eleven passes. He was thirteen out of sixteen at the half, and he was gunning the ball down the field. He did that several times. Certainly the San Diego game, when they were down ten points with five minutes to go and they came back to tie it up and win in overtime, was one of the key games of the whole season. That was the most yards he threw all year—356 yards. In the New Orleans game, he was phenomenal, four touchdown passes. The touch passes. He proved to me he could do it all. He did throw the ball deep in the Indianapolis game—the

> At halftime of a New Orleans Saints game in 1968, Charleston Heston drove a chariot and rode an ostrich while filming the movie *Number One*.

first one. And there were a couple of plays where he overthrew some receivers going deep, but so does every other quarterback. Look at Kurt Warner's stats of throwing the ball in the air—in the air, mind you, over thirty yards. It's nothing spectacular. But certainly Tom would be the first one to tell you that's a bit of an area he can improve on. He overthrew Patten the play in the Super Bowl that just missed him by a couple of feet. That's gonna come.

To me, this was basically his rookie year. I've never seen anything like the poise that this kid had all season long. He doesn't make many mistakes, and if he does, they're not costly mistakes. He made a mistake early in the Miami game this year, the first game where he turned the ball over on a bad snap. But he does not make turnovers or cause turnovers or throw interceptions that are run back for touchdowns. He did it once in the Cleveland game when they played Cleveland at home. His turnovers don't usually hurt you. When they come, they're not gonna kill you. He's too smart.

Bledsoe was as professional as he could be, but there's no question there was some dissension there. There's no doubt about it. As far I'm concerned, that's Drew's fault. Play better.

We do our post-game show either here at the studio or at another location right across the street from the stadium. We were not the flagship for the Patriots so there was another FM station that was their flagship that had much more access to him. However, this year, we have a thing called Patriots' Monday. We just took it from the other station and Brady and Coach Belichick and a couple of the players are gonna be on with us all the time. It's unfortunate it didn't happen a year ago. I think Brady's gonna actually be on our radio show every Monday, or Tuesday if they have a Monday night game. So I'm looking forward to that.

After the Super Bowl, I did a one-on-one interview with him. I think he's fantastic. He speaks like a seasoned veteran. He really does. He doesn't say all the cliché stuff that you would normally hear from a lot of guys in his position. He answers your questions honestly, tells you what's going on, honest— if he screwed up or if he should have done this or that. He doesn't shy away or hide from any of the questions. I thought he was very refreshing.

> Monday Night Football ratings have gone down seven years in a row. Even when *Monday Night Football* ratings hit an all-time low, it still ranks in the top five during prime time for the entire year.

Bledsoe's one drive against Pittsburgh was fine. He had an excellent touch pass after to fullback, but, while falling down, he also threw that stupid pass over his head that could easily have been disastrous. And how about the first series? The first series, he did the same exact thing he does when he went head-on against Mo Lewis. He runs to the sideline, he stands up, and he slows down and he gets belted. The same exact thing. No learning from it at all. He does the same thing

I didn't know this until last year when I really did some research on Brady about being a California kid. I know the Cal Bears wanted him really bad to stay out there. That tells you a lot about a kid who probably could have gone to Cal, a pretty good team, but nothing spectacular. He probably would have been one of the stars of that conference. Instead of being a starter right away and being a super star, he chose to go to one of the most prestigious football schools in the country where there were three guys ahead of him who would be NFL guys. He chose to work and fight and scratch and claw his way up the ranks. That says a lot to me right there. I don't know if his dad tried to talk him out of it or whatever. But that tells you a lot about somebody's character. He was willing to put instant fame on hold, go to Michigan and try to work his way through so much adversity to get to the top of the ranks there.

So people were wary after his great first game. "It's a one-game wonder. It's a one-game wonder." I kept saying, "No, it's not."

"This kid is gonna be it. You can tell by the decisions he makes."

Then of course the Patriots went to Miami the next week, and they fell flat on their faces. They lost thirty to ten. Brady had bad stats and was only seven of fourteen for eighty yards, and he did fumble once which led to a touchdown. However, when you look at their field position in that game, they were pinned inside the ten-yard line I'd say for three-quarters of that game. They were not gonna risk throwing the ball down the field with Miami's defense early in the season in Miami where the Dolphins hardly ever lose in the month of September or early October. I said, "You've got to throw that game out the window. You can't judge that game. You say he was a one-game wonder at Indianapolis. You guys can take the same approach for this game and not go nuts. This kid is gonna be it. You can tell by the decisions he makes."

And of course the next game was the San Diego game I believe which won just about everybody over. They were down ten with five minutes to go. That's when people started to really see what he could do. People called in,

"Bledsoe never would have led them back with a ten point deficit with five minutes to go." Even though Bledsoe has had his share of comebacks in the NFL, actually a lot more probably than people realize. You could just tell there was something special going on. It just catapulted from there.

My on-air partner is Fred Smerlas. He thought the same thing. We were both on the same page from the beginning on this one. Sometimes that's not the case with a lot of radio hosts for different shows, but we really were. We didn't know what was going to happen. I could just tell from the way Brady was so poised in leadership qualities, and the way he was throwing the ball, and his decision-making. It was such a vast improve-

> **Drew was always tough. No one ever questioned his heart or his toughness...**

ment over what we had seen with Bledsoe. Again, people said, "Aw, you can't go by wins and losses." They'd bring up Trent Dilfer who was like 16 and 0 last season, but Bledsoe was six and nineteen his last two and a half years. And against teams that were over five hundred, he was four and twenty-one. Four and twenty-one! Some horrible showings, particularly in the national spotlight. That has nothing to do with his toughness. Drew was always tough. No one ever questioned his heart or his toughness, but that, a lot of times, does not transcend into leadership ability. That's what I thought this team was lacking—leadership ability, big time. Particularly too many series of three and out, too many series of three and out in crucial situations, and bad decision making in a lot of games.

After the San Diego game, they went to Indianapolis the next week and absolutely destroyed them. Again, that was the David Patten game where he ran, threw and caught a touchdown pass for the first time since Walter Payton did it exactly twenty-two years ago to the day, which was phenomenal. But Brady was outstanding in that game—the whole team was.

The Atlanta game he was good. He was always consistent. There was a stretch there of three or four games where he completed almost seventy percent of his passes. Even when they didn't win, even in the loss against the Rams on that ESPN game about two-thirds through the season could have been a completely different game. They should have won that game. Smith fumbles on the one-yard line. Kevin Faulk, in the first series, has the ball go through his hands and intercepted on the Ram twenty. Otherwise

> Do you confuse Miami (Ohio) with Miami (Florida)?
> Miami of Ohio was a school before Florida was a state.

that's a totally different game. The Patriots, in my opinion, would have won. And again, Brady leading them down the field at the end just to make it close was another tell tale sign. You could just see the confidence building week in and week out. What I loved about him the most was if he had a bad series, or a bad quarter, or even a bad half, as he did in the Jet game, he didn't let it bother him. I personally think the Jet game was the biggest game of the year for this team. They were down thirteen to nothing, and Brady came back in the second half and led the team, and they ended up winning the game seventeen to sixteen. Most people around here will point to that game as something really special. He proved a lot to a lot of people who didn't believe in him in that particular game. A lot of people were screaming for Bledsoe to come in in the second half. The best part— Belichick said he never even considered it. And I believe him.

> ## "Brady has done more with less, and Bledsoe has done less with more."

It's the same system they had for Brady as they did for Bledsoe. Because they threw a couple of short wide-receiver screens, people said, "Brady throws more passes behind the line of scrimmage than Bledsoe ever did." Well why is that? Because the plays work. What's he supposed to do? Force the ball twenty-eight yards down the field if somebody's not open? He threw the ball down the field fifteen, twenty yards when he had to for the most part. And he connected. And look at who Brady had to throw to. Jermaine Wiggins, David Patten, Troy Brown, and Terry Glenn, who came in for one game against San Diego, which he was brilliant in. I've always said this, "Brady has done more with less, and Bledsoe has done less with more."

Can you imagine Brady on the Patriot team from '95 when they lost to the Packers? There's no doubt in my mind the Pats would have beaten them. Take the first play of this year's Super Bowl, that first pass—no hesitation, just a nice little square-in and boom. Brady nails it for an eighteen-yard gain. That says it all right there. Bledsoe would have got sacked.

At the Super Bowl, I was sitting in the press area next to a guy from the *St. Louis Post Dispatch*. When the Pats got introduced as a team, he taps me on the shoulder and goes, "Uh-oh." I said, "What do you mean?" He said, "We're in trouble, aren't we?" I said, "You guys got no chance of winning this game. You have no chance to win this game at all." He goes, "You know

> Rich Kotite, former head coach of the Eagles and the Jets, was once Muhammad Ali's sparring partner in Miami.

what? I'm starting to believe you." I said, "I'm telling you. You have no idea what this defense is about to do to you guys. I want you to focus on Marshall Faulk for this entire game, because he's gonna be black and blue ten times over when it's done." Sure enough, Faulk just got absolutely annihilated every time. When he was away from the ball was the best part, which I'm sure wasn't showing on television, but if anybody's got a replay of that game, and you watch Marshall Faulk, he just got abused every single play whether he had the ball or not. He was just pounded. When the Rams were about ready to go, and this is when Tebucky Jones picked up the fumble when McGinest got called for the holding call, but right before that, a guy sitting next to me goes, "Oh, the Rams got 'em here." I said, "They're not scoring." He said, "What?" I said, "They are not scoring inside the ten-yard line. You can write it down right now. Get your note pad out. They're not gonna score." Then when he fumbled and Tebucky Jones ran it back, the guys were looking at me like, "Holy cow, give me some lottery numbers." Of course, the penalty happened. He said, "You still think they're not gonna score?" I said, "No. Their emotions are gone. They're probably gonna score on the first play." Then sure enough there goes the quarterback sneak into the end zone.

> **I just dropped to my knees. I started bawling. I didn't care who saw me.**

I don't know if I should take pride in this or not. But when we were in Pat O'Brien's or some of the other local watering holes in New Orleans, every bartender and waitress said the same thing, "Man, you all can drink." The Pats fans drank that town dry. All the waitresses and bartenders said the same thing, "You guys tip way better, and you guys are a lot of fun to be around, and you people drink more than anybody we've ever seen in our life." So I'm sure it was a happy bunch. This area was so starved for a winner with the Red Sox, Bruins and Celtics, especially the way the Red Sox started off so great last year and then lost it so badly down the stretch. People were calling Boston 'Loserville'. The way this team came together, it just unified the whole area, particularly the Boston area, but New England as a whole. It really was something special. I'll never forget it. I was fifty feet from where the ball landed on the field, as I was waiting to go into the locker room, when that ball hit the ground, I just dropped to my knees. I

> Sam Malone's character in Cheers was patterned after former Red Sox pitcher, Bill Lee. Bill Lee once demanded number 337 from the Boston Red Sox because 337, upside down, spells Bill Lee's last name.

started bawling. I didn't care who saw me. I know media's not supposed to cheer and all that stuff. I was going crazy. A cameraman from a local TV station picked me up. We were just hugging and crying and I didn't care. I didn't care what anybody thought of me. You know what, the St. Louis people all came over and congratulated to us. They were all classy about it.

In late Spring the fans leanings are about seventy-thirty in favor of Brady. There are still the Bledsoe people out there that just won't let it go. They don't get it. They just can't see past Drew—Drew—Drew. More importantly, they don't want him to be traded for anything less than a number one pick. They'd say, "Well Trent Green got a number one pick." The Patriots were lucky to get a number one pick, even if it was next year's draft. But the market's changing. Especially recently when Brian Billick comes out, an offensive coach who likes to throw the ball down the field, comes out and says, "I don't want this guy on my team. He makes too many mistakes." That's gonna stand for something.' What does that tell you? I think that's the reputation he has. Good passer, not a good quarterback, good passer. He's a step above Jim Everett. That's really all he is. He may be one of the most overrated quarterbacks in the history of the game. I really believe that. And I don't think I ever would have said that five years ago, but having watched him every single game for his whole career and the improvement and where he had to improve on and what he hasn't done, it's ridiculous. They think Drew got a raw deal from Belichick that he didn't get a chance to earn his spot back—that's why some of the Bledsoe people are praying that he doesn't get traded, that he stays this year and that Belichick will give him a fair shot to win his job back.

That was one of the greatest days ever when Belichick said, "Brady's my guy." I was saying for two weeks that Belichick was gonna come out and say it, he's got to come out and say it, because otherwise he is going to go through every week with a quarterback controversy. There's no way you can do it. You can't have it this late in the season, especially after week six when they were really starting to come together. You could see that there was something special happening. And the controversy. That didn't shock me at all. I really expected that. It just goes to show you the kind of faith Belichick had in Brady. And believe me, if he thought Bledsoe was a better quarterback, he would have played him because he's that kind of a coach.

I think Brady is going to sign a long-term deal. I don't think it will happen midway through the season, but I think he's definitely here for the long haul. Belichick, that's his guy, I think he fits in well. Charlie Weis will be here for at least two more years. The only out is if he gets a job offer for a head coaching job. I think he fits in great here. And he's only gonna get better. The Patriots re-signing Antowain Smith is huge. They're adding a couple more weapons now with the receiver, Don Hayes, they just got from Carolina. Certainly that is gonna help out next year, having Don Hayes, and Cam Cleeland as a tight end. The Patriots have four or five tight ends right now. We'll see what hap-

> **People really should take a step back and see what he did this year with the weapons he had.**

pens. Certainly that was sorely lacking last year. Jermaine Wiggins and Rod Rutledge did not get the job done in the regular season. Certainly Wiggie was great in the playoffs, particularly the Oakland game. He had four catches all year and had ten in that game. They can get production out of the tight end, and they added Hayes, and that's just more weapons for Brady. People really should take a step back and see what he did this year with the weapons he had. It's just unbelievable. Troy Brown obviously is one of the most underrated players in the NFL, but even on most other teams, he's only your second or third guy, as good as he is.

> Calling Bill Belichick "Billy" is like calling Attila the Hun "Tilly."

> Roger Maris was Roger Maras until 1955. He didn't like for fans to call him "Mar-ass." Maris still holds the national high school record for most kickoff returns for a touchdown in one game with five.

> Mean Joe Greene's name is not Joe. It is Charles Edward.

Chapter 7

Super Bowl, Super Pats, Super Guy

Steve Sabol

David Nugent

Paul Johnson

John Friesz

Ken Flanders

Debbie Rogers

Mary Hilliard McMillan

IF YOU RUN NFL FILMS BACKWARDS, IT LOOKS LIKE THE PLAYERS ARE HELPING EACH OTHER UP AND SHOWING THEM ON THEIR WAY
STEVE SABOL

NFL Films was established in 1964, when Ed Sabol, Steve's father, convinced then-NFL commissioner Pete Rozelle that the league needed a motion picture company to record its history. NFL Films has mushroomed well beyond the role of mere historian. The entity has won 73 Emmys for outstanding cinematography and sound, and it represents the quintessential standard for sports filmmaking. From theme programs, such as NFL Films Presents, to team highlight films to emotional behind-the-scenes detailing the nuts and the bolts of HBO's Inside the NFL, NFL films, as an independently operated arm of the league, captures the essence of football like no other visual entity. No story of Steve Sabol could be complete without a story or two of NFL Films dealings with George Halas or Sabol's exploits on the college gridiron four decades ago.

George Halas, who died back in 1993, had a love-hate relationship with NFL Films. Halas used to sell seats on the visitors' bench at Wrigley Field. After Minnesota Vikings Coach Norm Van-Brocklin complained to the League office, then NFL Commissioner Rozelle asked me to shoot footage of the bench as he proceeded to investigate. But I told Rozelle, "I've already got that." So I sent Rozelle the footage and sure enough there were those guys on the bench. Rozelle confronted Halas and found out that Halas actually sold seats on the bench. They fined Halas and when Halas found out the footage came from us, he tried to have us banned from the sidelines. He also detested the close-ups we took of people like Dick Butkus and Gale Sayers. He said, "I don't want any face shots cause

> *Inside The NFL* on HBO is the longest running
> series of any kind of cable television.

the players will see that and want more money." It helped when we made an extra effort to include clean-cut Bear fans in the highlight films. Because back in 1967, Halas became enraged when one of our films showed a fan lunging for a ball in the stands with a pistol tucked in his belt. Halas kept saying, "Those are not Bear fans. We don't have people like that come to our games. We have good fans." But Bears' fans in the 60's made the Indy 500 infield look like a parliament. They were wild. Halas didn't want that. So the next year I went to Washington and got a close up of Redskins' fans with their camel hair coats, pretty sweaters and scarves. Every year I'd splice those shots into the Bears films, so until the day he died, he'd say, "See those are Bears' fans." He never knew. That was one of our running jokes at NFL films. We always had an assignment for a guy to go to Washington to shoot "Bears fans."

With Brady, it's a great story, just like the Warner story—like the John Unitas story updated. It's one of those fairy tale kind of things that happens once in a generation. The only thing is—with Warner, it happened two years ago, and now we've got another story that's just as incredible.

Our video on the Patriot season is the biggest selling sports video of all time. Part of that has a lot to do with the story of Tom Brady. He's an integral part of that tape. He has outsold every other sports video that's ever been made—five hundred and fifty thousand copies, probably more—by Father's Day, it'll be even more. It does shock me, but the thing is, it's the story. We figure that this story and this season was so unique, it touched a lot of people and they want to relive it through our video.

We always debut our videos in the victors' hometown. The one in Boston was great. That's just something we've always done. Whatever team wins the Super Bowl, two weeks later we have a big premiere in that home city.

Running NFL films is like the supreme job. Every day is like winning the Super Bowl. Well, maybe not, but I sure am lucky…and Tom Brady's performance made our job easier.

Let me tell you the story of the "Fearless Tot from Possum Trot." What happened was I was raised in a suburb of Philadelphia called Villanova, Pennsylvania. I had great grades in prep school but I had a lousy SAT so I ended up going to school in Colorado Springs at a college called Colorado

> The Chicago Bears wear blue and orange because those are the colors that team founder George Halas wore when he played for the University of Illinois.

College. I wanted to play football out there so one of the first things I did was change my hometown from Villanova to Coaltown Township, Pennsylvania. It was a non-existent town but had the ring of solid football to it. Everybody knows that western Pennsylvania is where the football studs come from. I'd never seen a coal mine but if coaches thought I was been rubbing shoulders with guys like Mike Ditka and Leon Hart, they'd have to start thinking. I carried it off all freshman year and nobody caught on. Guys would come up and ask me why I hadn't gotten a big scholarship from Notre Dame or Ohio State or someplace, and I'd just say, "Aw, I was just third string."

But I didn't play much in my freshman year so I knew I'd have to do something to impress the coaches. So when I came back for sophomore year, I told everyone that I was from Possum Trot, Mississippi cause you can't ignore anyone from a place called Possum Trot. Then I knew I had to change my name. I had an honorable name but it didn't have the ring of greatness. I wanted something real lethal like "Sudden Death." That fit my initials, too—Steven Douglas Sabol became Steve "Sudden Death" Sabol. Then in the program for the very first game, we had "Sudden Death" Sabol listed by that name. Also I bought an ad in the program that said, "Coach Jerry Carle wishes "Sudden Death" Sabol a successful season." Everybody thought the coach put the ad in there but I paid for the ad myself. Coach Carle was a regular Bear Bryant; he never smiled. The last thing he'd do would be wish me a successful season, but a lot of people took it seriously. I thought it was all pretty funny. But the coach didn't have any scholarships to give so he couldn't run off any players like me.

> **It was a non-existent town but had the ring of solid football to it.**

Unfortunately I only weighed one hundred and seventy pounds so the nickname "Sudden Death" just didn't seem to go with my build. Nevertheless in the final program of the season, I ran an ad that said "Coach Jerry Carle congratulates "Sudden Death" Sabol on a fantastic season."

So before junior year, I added forty pounds—I really bulked up. Then I started sending out press agent stuff to both the local and the Denver papers. One ad told everyone "The Possum Trot Chamber of Commerce extends its wishes for a successful season to its favorite son, "Sudden Death" Sabol. Another advertisement included a picture of me in a football uniform at about the age of ten when I played on a Midget League team. Then came a hundred tee shirts made up with the drawing of a possum and the inscription "I'm a Little Possum Trotter." I gave half of them away and sold the rest for one dollar.

So with my own money, I'd paid for newspaper advertisements, colored postcards, brochures, tee shirts, lapel buttons and pencils on which were written such legends as "The Prince of Pigskin Pageantry now at the Pinnacle of his Power." And "One of the Most Mysterious, Awesome Living Beings of All Times." I sent out news releases reporting incredible accomplishments of "Sudden Death" Sabol on thc football field with sidebars describing his colorful campus life. And as testament to my ability, the sports editors swallowed all this stuff hook, line and sinker.

> **...the sports editors swallowed all this stuff hook, line and sinker.**

Now football practice itself was tedious. It was a period of intense boredom punctuated by moments of acute fear. So I began writing the game program itself. And I did a column for the school newspaper entitled, "Here's a Lot from Possum Trot." I also was the team cheerleader, and I began plastering the walls of the locker room with posters and slogans and slipping fight songs onto the record player. Then I shipped off a press release to our rival, Concordia College team's hometown paper. They were unbeaten at the time. The quote says, "Sudden Death says Colorado College will Crush Concordia College." Their game plan was simple. They wanted to break my neck. But I loved it. It makes the game more personal. This one big end was particularly anxious to break something. He seemed very capable of it, too. So at halftime I go up to the referee. I'm putting on my "choir boy look" and say, "Mr. Referee, Sir, that end—well I hate to say it, but he's playing sorta dirty and I wish you'd watch him."

So on the first play, I asked the quarterback to call my number on an end sweep. Sure enough this big oaf really clobbers me. I whisper in his ear, "You're nothing but chicken ____." Naturally he takes a swing and there's the referee standing right there, throwing down his flag, and yelling, "You're out of the game." We beat Concordia thirteen to nothing.

I had a good year. I was good enough for first team All-Conference and we won four games, which is about twice what we normally won. The news was going all over the country about Steve "Sudden Death" Sabol. It was carried on the AP wires, and I got a letter from a disk jockey from, of all places, Possum Trot. There really is such a place, but it's in Tennessee, not Mississippi. That was fine by me because I always had a sneaking hunch I wanted to come from Tennessee anyway.

So I go back for my senior year but I fought hepatitis all summer so I had to drop out and go back to Philadelphia. I started lifting weights to get back in shape. Back in those days, most athletes didn't lift weights. Darned if I didn't work so hard at it, I was actually named Mr. Philadelphia. Well I couldn't let that honor pass me by, so I had 8 x 10 photographs made showing me all aripple and holding a spear. Underneath the picture was my name and these modest words. "Acclaimed as the Greatest New Adventure Hero of the Year." That was an inspiration I got from my huge comic book collection where I have all-time favorites such

> **...these modest words. "Acclaimed as the Greatest New Adventure Hero of the Year."**

as Captain America and Batman. The pictures were immediately dispatched to editors, press agents and fans. I had the mailing addresses of influential people well catalogued from my Dad's business.

That was a good start on the year but I was worried the people back in Colorado had forgotten all about me. So I went to a printer, and I had stationery made with "Universal International" and wrote all these letters. "You have been placed on Steve Sabol's mailing list and thus will be able to follow his movie career." Then came the information that Steve Sabol had been cast as a supporting actor in Universal's forthcoming film "Black Horse Troop." Which is a name I got from a march by John Philip Sousa. The movie would star William Holden, Steve McQueen, Eva Marie Saint and Steve Sabol. The letter was stamped "Approved for immediate release by order of Central Casting." I'd had a stamp made up with that title on it. But I didn't send the letter to the newsmen back in Colorado Springs. They were starting to get a little suspicious. So instead I sent them to friends in the Colorado Springs area who were most likely to leak the news in the right places. It worked. Local columnists fell all over themselves informing the readers that "Sudden Death" Sabol was Hollywood's newest star. I must have had a hundred calls from people wanting to know if it's true that Steve McQueen is really a jerk. But I told them, "No, he's really a great guy."

So the next summer before returning for my final year of Colorado College, I did a grand tour of Europe and in Madrid I got inspired again. El Cordobes, was the biggest bullfighter in the world at that time. There were picture postcards of him all over Spain. I said, "Now that's class." So when I

> Former Colorado Rockies Manager Jim Leyland was once a second-string catcher for Perrysburg, Ohio High School. The starting catcher was Jerry Glanville.

got back home I shelled out some more money, actually my Dad's money. I got a couple of crates of colored postcards of myself in a football uniform. At the back of the postcard, is "Steve 'Sudden Death' Sabol, all-time All Rocky Mountain Football Great." At the bottom it says "The Prince of Pigskin Pageantry." So in the fall, I go back to Colorado College. I had a new maroon convertible; I had a five-bedroom apartment even though I lived alone but I could think better when I'm alone. I had a picture of me signing with the Cleveland Browns for $375,000. But the topper was when Coach Carle got upset because outside Washburn Stadium I put a sign that said, "Washburn Stadium, Altitude 7,989 feet," which was exactly 2,089 feet higher than it actually was but I wanted to psyche out opposing players when they came there. So I had a plaque remade for the visiting team's dressing room that read "This Field is named in Honor of Morris Washburn who perished when his lungs exploded from a lack of oxygen during a soccer match with the University of Denver in 1901."

> ### I got a couple of crates of colored postcards of myself in a football uniform.

The Fearless Tot from Possum Trot might be the only football player in history with a better "rags to riches" story than Tom Brady.

> Mountain climbers "pass gas" violently at high altitudes.
> At 11,000 feet, the stomach's resistance to the expansion
> of gas is greatly reduced. Always try to be the lead
> climber. That's a free tip from your Uncle Rich.

Tom Brady Jr., John Gould,
Bob Cunningham and Gary Williams
at the 19th hole in Ireland.....or
maybe it was the 20th hole.

©Jim. Mahoney

Tom Brady Sr., Julie, Mo, Galynn and Nancy

Hey, it was tucked!

Hey! You're in my seat—I was the Employee of the Month!

©Jim Mahoney

I'm going
in tomorrow for
an estimate on
a haircut......

Tom Brady on
the sidelines
with injured
quarterback
Drew Bledsoe

THE BEST DEFENSE IS THE ONE STANDING ON THE SIDELINE
DAVID NUGENT

David Nugent, a defensive end from Purdue, was the 201st overall pick in the 2000 NFL Draft, just the second spot after Tom Brady was picked at 199th. They ended up being roommates and close friends.

T om Brady and I both came here in sixth round, both from the Big Ten, we had big rivalries so coming in, we kind of knew each other that way. Over the course of training camp, we were all trying to feel each other out, trying to see whose personalities fit well together as far as roommates. Tom approached me one day and asked me if I would like to live with him. It's been a great relationship since then.

What sticks out about him is just his toughness. I remember one time in one of our college games, I hit Brady so hard. I had no idea how he got the pass off, but he completed the pass probably forty yards down the field. I got up and said, "You gotta be kidding me." That's just the thing that sticks out about him. He's tough. He took some hits this year that I don't know how he got up after. He just popped right up and got back in the huddle. He's a tremendous passer and a tremendous competitor.

During our rookie year, we were ending our stay over at the End Zone motel in Foxboro. I still hadn't found a place to live yet, and was getting kinda panicky about it. When we were in the hotel, we all just left our doors open and everybody walked in each other's room and looked around. He just walked in my room one night and sat on the bed and we talked. I think he was probably still making up his mind as we talked whether or not he wanted me to live with him. He just said to me, "I'm getting a place. Do you want to live with me?" He explained all about the place and it was Ty Law's old place. The more he talked about it the more impressed I was—it sounded really

> The football helmet was invented by Dr. James Naismith, the same man who invented basketball.

cool. I said, "Yes. I haven't seen the place yet, but I'll take your word for it that it's a good place." We've been living together two years now.

I felt that it would be good for us to live together because he's a lot like me. We're both not wild guys. He seemed like he would be an ideal roommate. He seemed respectful. He had a lot of the qualities that I would want in a roommate, and I'm guessing maybe he saw the same thing in me.

> **...they had some kind of sports psychologist at Michigan and he learned a lot of interesting things from that guy...**

We used to come home from practice just dead tired, and sit on the couch and talk about practice. Both of us were frustrated with our playing time. With Tom, he's such a competitor, and even though he was drafted sixth round and was fourth-string and all that, he saw no reason why he shouldn't be playing. Even with Drew out there, it was killing him every day. But it was interesting because I guess they had some kind of sports psychologist at Michigan and he learned a lot of interesting things from that guy that he passed on to me. "All you can worry about is yourself and what you do. It's not the coach's fault. It's not your teammates' fault. It's just you. And once you learn that, it's such a 'freeing' deal because you don't have to worry about anybody but yourself. You just focus on getting yourself better." That's one thing that he taught me a lot last year.

I know that he knew he was just a rookie, and it's hard for the coaching staff to trust a rookie so he knew eventually his time would come. It made it that much more frustrating when Drew signed the big contract, and they brought in Damon Huard. But even when that happened, he wasn't going to throw in the towel. I remember him saying, "You know what? So what. I've still got to take care of myself and do what I've got to take care of."

He had the confidence that he was going to play. I don't remember him outright saying, "I'm going to be the starter here." He just knew that his time would come. He was quiet, but you could tell that's how he acted.

Going back to our being frustrated, I remember him talking about what he went through at Michigan and that compared to what he went through here this year.

I think Tom was obviously disappointed because he had expected to go higher than sixth round in the draft, too, probably just like me. With each round that goes down, you're just like, "You've gotta be kidding me." But he's made the most of it obviously.

The one thing that sticks out, and I don't know what part of the year it was he got up in front of the team to give a speech. I was thinking, "Tom not this." But just the way he spoke to the guys on the team—with such passion. You knew that he didn't want to waste any time waiting his turn for the appropriate time. He knew his time was now. He knew the team's time was now. He knew that. And then we all figured it out, too.

Tom definitely felt that the intensity level of our practices were not what they needed to be and Tom went to Lawyer Milloy to talk about what was needed in practice to get better results. I remember watching that interview on TV after that game. And you could just tell that he could not wait to get back out on the practice field. He knew that we had some flaws in the way we were practicing. For a guy in his second year to be able to command that kind of attention on the team and say, "Hey guys, we're not practicing right." I think that might even have been when he gave the speech. He said, "Let's really focus. Let's turn things around here 'cause we have good guys on the team. We can do this." And that made everybody on the team want to do their best to win.

One day we were all in the team meeting room and the coaches had left. Tom got up and what he said was cool. He was saying that if everybody could just miss one less ball at practice or make one more tackle in practice, if everybody, with that combined effort, could do something like that it's just going to make the team so much better. And he just told the guys, "You know what? I'm going to do my part. I'm going to try to be error-free on my part. If everybody can do the same thing, we're going to come out of this on top."

It was a crazy situation. The team's veterans were there, and you've got Drew sitting up there on the front row and even I was uncomfortable for him. But as Tom got going, just like I said, the passion that was coming out of this kid—you could just feel it in the room. Everybody was like, "Yeah, yeah, I feel what you're talking about. Let's do this. We're going to go out and practice today and we're going to turn things around." It's this quality—this charisma that he's got that just makes everybody want to follow him.

I think it really did make a difference. When he said to go out and everybody just give a little bit more effort, then that combined effort is just going to make great things happen—even on an individual basis. I went out there that day, and I remember just hitting the sled harder, hitting the offensive tackle harder—everybody does that and it will make a better team.

> The best run defense is a poor pass defense.

Last season's off-season was huge for him. Not once did I ever hear him talk about how Drew's not there or Mike Bishop's not working out hard, he totally focused on himself. In the off-season, he got bigger. He got stronger. Even on our off-days, he would try and find a receiver to go out to the field and throw routes to him. If he couldn't find a receiver, then guess who he went out there with? But I'm so slow that he would just have me stand there where the ball would be thrown and then he would just turn around and act like I just ran the route. He was going to get work done regardless. He rubbed off on me, too, and made me focus on myself.

After that you could see a lot more participation in our program—a lot more people were willing to stay afterwards to run routes with him, to do the extra things because he's willing to do it.

During training camp Tom was moved ahead of Damon on the depth chart, but you know what, he never even talked about it. I don't know if it was just something he expected to happen but he never once bragged about it, never talked about it. He and Damon and Drew were good friends so he'd never say anything about it.

> **...a lot more people were willing to stay afterwards to run routes with him...**

Obviously, it was unfortunate what happened to Drew, but I remember the series when Tom went in. I just knew things were going to change. I was like, "This is huge. Something is going to change here." Then after we lost that game, and during that week of practice, he came home and we're talking and he was saying, "Things are gonna change around here. We're going to start getting things done. You're going to see this offense get fired up." He was like, "It's not going to be dull anymore. Practices are going to be fired up. We're going to get stuff done."

I remember in the Miami game, Brady's second start, a lot had gone wrong in that game. When we came home, it was all about what he did wrong. He didn't say anything about offensive line, about the running backs, about how the receivers ran their routes, it was about his timing and what he did wrong. He did say, "This is what I'm going to work on this week." I think the next game was against the Chargers, and he had a great game that day. It was tremendous.

I don't think anybody's going to believe this, but right as we broke five hundred we were talking about the season and about how practice was going and he just interrupted and said, "We're going to the Super Bowl." I mean the way he said it and how he looked, I knew he wasn't just saying it. He was totally serious and confident. To me it seemed that he was going to just do everything in his power to get there. That made me want to do everything I could do and that's exactly what happened to our team this year. Everyone captured his enthusiasm and his desire to be the best that we could be. That's what ultimately happened.

I remember he made that remark real early in the season—too early for anyone to ever even think anything like that.

The way Tom said it, and the relationship I have with him, I know that he's not going to BS me. I believe him! He's our quarterback so obviously that's a key position if you're going to go to the Super Bowl. I knew that if he was going to do everything he could do, and if I could do everything I could do, and if everybody would do that—we had a chance.

Critics have said Tom has gotten too much credit for this year, but they don't know all he does. It's not just on the field. There's so much stuff that Tom offers off the field—his leadership. What he brought to this team was a young fiery competitor who just put a spark in everyone's butt this year. He just woke everyone up. "You've got a lot of great talent on this team." He just came in and said, "Listen, I'm not going to back down. I don't care how young I am, whatever. I'm going to go in there and give it my best and everybody else should too." You just can't argue with that. And for the critics who say that his role on the field was minimized—that's my answer to that.

Tom has always said he wanted to be a football player and not a celebrity. Obviously that's hard to avoid with all that's going on—winning the Super Bowl, being named the MVP. It's hard because he doesn't want to disappoint people. There's a lot of offers that are coming his way right now, and he doesn't want to turn people down, but you only have so many hours in the day. We try and get out once a week—go have dinner or go see a movie or something. But it's comical. You go out to dinner, and on your way out, you get a standing ovation from the whole restaurant. You go to a movie, we're walking out, and there's a whole line of people asking how he enjoyed the movie. That's all fun stuff to be a part of.

It's funny because when we went out, before he started playing, nobody knew who he was. Now I'm looking outside a door right now. We've got ten footballs setting outside our door, banners up on the walls. It's incredible.

> Jim Thorpe was the first president of the NFL.

They're just from people who drive over here and drop stuff off. They just leave it to get signed—like it's an autograph shop.

After we came back from the Super Bowl, and he'd just left for Hawaii for the Pro Bowl and it was absolutely nuts over here. I had to call a patrol car because people were just coming over and staring in the windows and dropping off posters on the front door, balls, girls calling every five seconds screaming into the phone—just nuts. He enjoys it. He definitely wants some 'Tom' time so it's hard to turn people down. I'm sure he got advice from Drew on how to handle it since Drew had been through it for so many years.

One time at an Outback Steakhouse restaurant, we had a waitress come over and sit down at the table and declare why she was best suited to be his girlfriend. That was pretty funny. Then she wanted to take a picture, prom style, with her hand on his chest or whatever. He was like, "Absolutely not."

He's gotten to do some pretty neat stuff—meeting Muhammad Ali. He gets to meet all kinds of people right now. I get in on some of the things. I know we are going to the Kentucky Derby together. I get invited to some of the parties. One of the nights of Super Bowl week, he had interviews with Martina McBride at some concert. Two friends and I got to sit in the VIP section while he was up there. I got to meet so many people, that was great for me, like Tom Arnold, N'Sync was there—that's for my girlfriend, she loves them—John Elway, Steve Young, Joe Montana, L. L. Cool J, all those people. There was just an endless amount of celebrities there. That's cool for me because I don't get to do that every day.

My life has definitely changed some because of the Super Bowl. It's fun because I'm getting to do some things that I'd never dreamed about doing. It's kind of funny. I'm like the secretary at home and get to answer all the phone calls. Some interesting people call over at the house. It's a neat ride for me, too.

We don't talk about football all the time. We talk about going out. We're young guys so obviously we talk about girls—just typical stuff.

One of the funny things that happened during rookie year was that John Friesz and Drew put glitter in all the air conditioning vents in his car and turned them all on to high. He had a date that night and when he started the car—they were hiding around the corner—all this glitter just shot out everywhere— all over his face—everywhere. All over his face, all throughout

In 1979 Ali beat Lyle Alzado in 8 rounds.

the car. You know he couldn't get that out in time for his date that night. She was probably wondering what this freak's doing with glitter all over his car.

We had a third roommate, Chris Eitzmann, here last year. We used to mess with each other all the time. Tom would be sleeping in his room and Chris and I would dress up like goofballs and just go running into his room. We knew he was sleeping and we'd just start spanking him and hitting him and jumping up and down on his bed screaming just waking him up, banging pots and pans—whatever. We'd get these boxing gloves and just go in there and start pounding on him.

Then one time I was sleeping and both of them came in, and I had another friend in town, and they held me down while they took a permanent marker and drew all over me. I didn't know what they were doing. It didn't feel like they were drawing on me, so I was just like, 'whatever, get out of here.' A couple of hours later I get up and go downstairs and they're just dying laughing. I'm like, "What?" I go over and look in the mirror and I've got magic marker all over my face, all over my legs and arms. I had to go to church that night looking like that. It was funny.. but not at the time.

Our friendship has evolved over these last two years. We knew each other before all this so he knows that I'm one guy he can absolutely trust. So many people are starting to come his way, wanting his friendship. He knows I've been there the whole time. We've had our talks at night about what's going on. It's like a team—I'll be there for him, as he will be for me.

He's got to be aware of people coming his way now. Neighbors that used to maybe not like us now bring over balls, whatever. It's funny. He has been a great roomie and has added a lot to my life.

> Lee Corso and Burt Reynolds were roommates
> at Florida State in 1957.

> Quarterback Brad Johnson, who started more games at
> Florida State in basketball than he did in football,
> is the only NFL quarterback in history to
> complete a touchdown pass to himself.

BUT MR. BRADY, THE MOSQUITO IS THE STATE BIRD OF MINNESOTA
PAUL JOHNSON

Paul Johnson is Tom Brady's first cousin. He lives in Tom's mother's small hometown of Browerville, Minnesota. He runs a very successful Internet business at www.pickleboy.com. Tom Brady and his sisters would vacation in Minnesota every summer.

He was a chubby little kid. I remember us just wanting to beat the crap out of him 'cause he was a very, very aggressive kid.

My grandpa, Gordon Johnson, had a dairy farm when Tom and his sisters were growing up. They would come up for a few weeks every summer and stay with Grandpa Gordon. We were always excited to have our cousins from California come to visit. My brother and I spent a lot of time taking those kids out to these big gravel pits we have on our motorcycle and spending hours in the gravel pits. We would go to lakes and Grandpa would actually take all four of the kids fishing in a boat. It was quite a fiasco there—tangled lines most of the time. When the girls got in to fifth and sixth grades, the boys here would be excited to know that our 'pretty cousins' from California were coming back. My friends definitely took notice of those girls. Tom was still a chubby little kid at that time, but he was very athletic. He was throwing stuff steady. The whole family— Galynn's an avid tennis player. Tom, Sr. was a very good athlete. Tommy's uncle, who is my uncle, too, is in Browerville's Hall of Fame here for basketball. He played when they said 'if there had been three pointers at that time, he would have just blown out the record books for points.' The girls were fabulous in fast-pitch softball.

I know Tom, Sr. still likes coming up. He says with the mosquitoes and the cold weather he could never live here—he likes California.

When Tom was at Michigan, we always watched as many games as we could get. When someone comes up and says, "My cousin's got potential to become an NFL football player," realistically if you play the percentages, your changes of winning Power Ball are better than having a first cousin do what Tom Brady did. If Tom can somehow keep his head on straight and not let all the fame and fortune wreck him, if he can keep that work ethic, nothing can stop him. I know that he has said his biggest fear is to be a one-hit wonder. He may not even realize how driven he is. If he doesn't get hurt, I think he can really break some records.

My brother has one of Tommy's footballs that he has signed. They were just out to California and were with Tom and Galynn about three weeks ago. Tommy sent one to give to a charity or something, and my brother is going to find a charity and donate it to that so they can sell it. They sent my dad and me and my Grandpa an NFL jacket, the DVD of the Super Bowl, sweatbands, nice NFL shirts and a nice real heavy-duty travel bag with a Super Bowl logo on it. It was really nice that they still remember us 'cause they could go the other way, too, and be in that ritzy class and forget about those 'hillbilly' relatives in Minnesota.

When they used to come and spend time here in the summer, Tommy played a lot of sports. He actually busted a few of Grandpa's windows playing baseball.

I still talk to his sisters quite a bit. Of course, to talk to Tommy anymore is just about impossible. I had his e-mail address and once in a while I would get an e-mail from him, but I'm sure he's had to change his e-mail address 'cause he was getting thousands of e-mails.

When my grandma died a few years back, Tom was playing for Michigan. He had to take a separate flight back and get back to the workouts. He was a super busy guy then, but I did take him out fishing to my dad's cabin. We discussed things, and he's a normal kid. We sat there and laughed and had a good time. He thoroughly enjoyed something as simple as that, and I think he still would. He's just that kind of guy. Even if they ask him to highlight his favorite things, with all this stuff that he's been exposed to now, it would still be to spend time with his family.

We got to watch every game because they got my grandpa that package on satellite. We watched these guys creep up every week— just 'not supposed to win, not supposed to win,' and they just kept winning. Every weekend, we would all get together at Grandpa's and say, "Hey, these guys are great. That defense is rated little or nothing in the NFL—close to last, and we were shocked. "Boy, somebody hasn't figured out yet that these guys are for real."

> The Minnesota Vikings have not been in the
> Super Bowl since the Lou and Bud Grant era.

We thought about going down for the Super Bowl, but it sounded like it would be very difficult to get tickets. That's such a big-money thing.

Belichick's daughter, who's seventeen, has got the hots for Tommy. It was something to read all that in the *Sports Illustrated* about all the women in the pageant, the mothers of the contestants in the Miss USA Pageant, how they were begging him to date their daughters. I'll give him a hard time about that and about how he was chumming with that chick, Nikki Ziering, from *The Price is Right*, and about how they were partying on Donald Trump's plane when they were flying out there. He's a normal twenty-four year old. I know he broke up with his girlfriend. He's got too many women after him now.

Former Vikings kicker, Fred Cox, invented the Nerf ball.

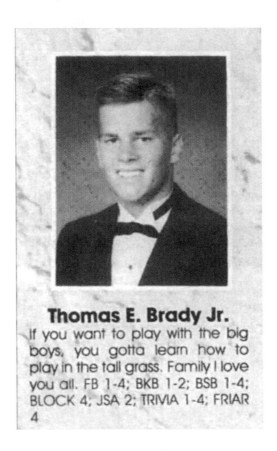

Thomas E. Brady Jr.
If you want to play with the big boys, you gotta learn how to play in the tall grass. Family I love you all. FB 1-4; BKB 1-2; BSB 1-4; BLOCK 4; JSA 2; TRIVIA 1-4; FRIAR 4

HE WAS IN THE LAST QUARTER OF HIS CAREER AND PRAYIN' FOR OVERTIME

JOHN FRIESZ

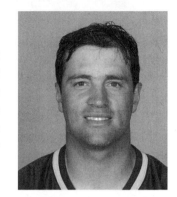

John Friesz' goal when he was a high school quarterback was to get a college football scholarship. His dream came true when he became a star at the University of Idaho. He considers his eleven years in the NFL as a wonderful bonus. His last two NFL seasons were with the New England Patriots.

The first time I ever heard of Tom Brady was when he was drafted. I was playing for the Patriots at the time. I honestly didn't follow much of college football, really sort of even lost a little bit of what was going on with my alma mater. Draft day I checked out the Patriots web site to see who we drafted and was a little bit surprised that we even drafted a quarterback but that was really the first time that I'd heard his name.

The first time I saw him was actually in our first quarterback meeting. He was sitting down. We called it 'quarterback school.' It was six hours a day, I think, maybe even eight. It was three or four hours, lunch break, and then another three or four hours—very intense, different than anything I've ever been involved with. It was our first indoctrination of the offense. We'd take a little bit of a break and people would talk. I was getting to know Charlie Weis, the offensive coordinator, for the first time. I was getting to know Dick Rehbein, the quarterback coach, for the first time. I had known Michael Bishop who was one of the four quarterbacks and I had obviously known Drew. Brady talked a little bit just sort of giving us a little bit of background—kind of letting us all know a little bit about himself. But for the most part, it was strictly a business-type setting and didn't really get to know him on a personal level until we started practicing.

One of the first things I noticed about Brady was in the classroom, and I've told a lot of people this. He's one of the few quarterbacks that I've been around as a little bit of an older player where I started to know the correct questions to ask. He was maybe already understanding what the NFL is about. So many times a rookie quarterback will come in and not ask the correct questions. What I mean by that is they open their mouth and they really sort of let everybody know that they really don't know much at all. You can learn a lot from a person from what they ask. If they ask very basic questions, then the coach and everybody else knows where they're at. They're at a very low understanding of the game or what we're trying to do. Brady always asked very legitimate questions—questions that showed that he understood the things that were underneath that question. He already knew his ABCs and it was a little bit surprising that he knew those ABCs because the game is different from college to pro. I was very much impressed with him mentally.

> **He already knew his ABCs and it was a little bit surprising that he knew those ABCs because the game is different from college to pro.**

His retention for what the coaches gave us seemed very high compared to almost every rookie quarterback that I'd ever seen. Physically, nothing stood out. He threw a pretty ball. It generally spiraled. It was generally pretty accurate. Drew and I would talk a lot about him, and we both felt that he had enough physical ability. He wasn't a person who blew you away physically. That's not meant to be a slam on his part at all. It's just there were other things that were more obvious that he was head and shoulders above his peers, and again that was the understanding of the game and those issues.

The fans in New England, maybe even more than management, loved Michael Bishop. They thought that Bishop should be starting over Bledsoe. It really sort of got going in the preseason the year before Brady's rookie year. Pete Carroll was head coach—and I don't want to get into slamming Bishop because I liked him. The coaches would give him three plays to get ready for in a preseason game and they would just flip-flop the plays depending on which hash mark we were on. It was strictly a one-two-three reading, and the coaches would go over it with him and he'd get in those games and he'd drop back looking the other way, throw it into a crowd, and the guy would make a catch. The fans just loved it. He was exciting. He didn't know where to go with the ball, so he'd drop back, stand around and take off and run and use his physical abilities, which he had a ton of, as far as being able to run or throw hard, but to know where and when to throw it with accuracy wasn't going to happen.

That first year, it was an interesting thing because Brady did have a good preseason. They had invested a draft pick in him. It was obvious to us, the players, that he was definitely a guy who deserved to be on the roster. Teams don't usually keep four quarterbacks, but Seattle did several years ago. I remember hearing about that, but it's a very rare situation where four quarterbacks will be kept on a fifty-three man roster—extremely rare. And it's pretty much stupid to do it. If anything I thought that I may be the odd man out, not because my salary was too high, but I just didn't fit in with Belichick and his people. Bledsoe had proven to be so durable over the years that I thought that they felt like maybe they could roll the dice and go with two young guys. But the reality and reason I think that Belichick stayed

> **...it's a very rare situation where four quarterbacks will be kept on a fifty-three men roster— extremely rare.**

away from that was because the year before he was in New York with Vinny Testaverde going down. They saw what happened when they didn't have a veteran backup that had played and how that cost that team. It was an interesting situation. I never thought that they'd keep all four. What made sense was to keep Bledsoe, myself and Brady. But again, the media and the fans were all swept up in this Bishop thing. At that time, if you would ask anybody outside of a very close circle of fans that really knew the game out there, if you said, "Name the four quarterbacks on the roster," I don't know that they could have named anybody past Bledsoe and Bishop. It was really unbelievable.

When Belichick was with the Jets, they had Ray Lucas there. As a back-up quarterback he was a guy that would come in on occasion and spell Testaverde and they would do some different things with him—running the ball, running options, getting him out of the pocket—doing things Testaverde couldn't do. I think Belichick, being a defensive coach, under stands how difficult it is to put a game plan together in a given week. Now you throw on top of that, the fact that you've got a pocket passer—in that case it was Testaverde—and a mobile guy that could come in and do a number of different things that you could never really prepare totally for in Lucas. He was able to say, "Well, we've got that same thing here. We've got a pocket passer in Bledsoe. And we can activate or de-activate Bishop on any given week. We don't need to do that till Friday so other teams are going to have to prepare for a number of trick plays and that's exactly what they did. There were times when Bishop was actually the number two and I was de-activated to the number three spot with the understanding that if Bledsoe went down, I'm in. That was a gamble on the coach's part because once the third guy goes in, if it's in the first three quarters of the game, neither of the other two can return no matter what. Then there were other times, I'd say probably two-thirds of the season, I was the number two guy, but teams didn't know that. That's one of the reasons why they felt like they would try that with Bishop that first year.

Brady did get in one game on Thanksgiving Day in Detroit. I had played the week or two weeks before that and had sprained my knee. I was hobbling around, but they were starting to, and this is my opinion, write the year off. I was bothered pretty good by the injury, and Belichick called me in and said, "I appreciate how you're trying to fight through this, but it's clear that you're not a hundred percent." His reason to sit me down that week was that we had a bye week after that and then we had a Monday night game after that so it was going to be a long time until we'd be back on the field. This would give me an opportunity to heal. It was all a nice gesture on his part, and I didn't argue with it. I couldn't argue with it because I was hobbled, but at the same time I'm pretty sure they were thinking that this would give them an opportunity to get Brady in there a little bit and maybe not get in a game but at least he'll be a little bit more bumped on the chart and see how he responds to it.

> **...he's the hardest working quarterback that I've ever played with.**

He seemed pretty calm when he went in the game. He seemed really calm. We were getting blown out, and there was nothing that stood out in my mind. I think anytime a quarterback gets in for the first time like that, as long as he doesn't just fumble the ball all over the place or not be able to call the play or get it off—if you don't do those things, then that's a success even if you throw an interception and you only throw three passes. It was still probably a marginal success.

The biggest compliment that I can give Tom is that he's the hardest working quarterback that I've ever played with. I've played with quite a few, and I've played with a couple that are awful big names. An example of that, and it was a pretty good story, he started getting a little bit comfortable. There was one day where we had to drive to practice. He and rookie tight end Chris Eitzmann, decide to hide my key and lock the car. Inside the car was my shoulder pad, jersey and helmet, and Bledsoe's shoulder pad, jersey and helmet. We had gone a couple of doors down to go visit with Adam Vinatieri for a minute. We get back and are hustling over to my car to get our stuff and jog out to the field 'cause it was time. It's locked. I said, "Drew, it's locked." He goes, "No." About once a year, I will lock my keys in the car—not that often, but too often really. I'm thinking 'no, this isn't the time or place to do that.' We're just starting to hit the panic button. About then, a hundred and twenty yards away, Brady's like, "Ha, ha, you idiots. It's up in that tree right there." So we grab the key and Bledsoe goes, "Hand me your phone." I go, "What?" He goes, "We're taking care of this right now." Cause Bledsoe's got a little 'phone tree' where he can just dial, and something gets done. I said, "No, we've got to do it right. We'll get them back later."

He proceeds to call a girl that has run errands for him and his wife and helped them out when they're out of town—that sort of contact. She ends up bringing up a vial of really fine glitter, so tiny you could hardly see it—like salt, but it was glitter. After practice they get Brady's car keys, and Bledsoe goes out and just jams all the air vents full of this glitter. He turns the vents so they all point to the driver and turns the air on full blast so that all it takes as soon as you start the car glitter's gonna be flying. We're all excited. We hustle out there. We're on the other side of the fence—it's Chad Eaton, myself, and Bledsoe in this car and we can't wait. This is going to be the funniest thing ever. Forty-five minutes goes by. It was our weight lift day—quarterback lift day, but Brady being a rookie, he has to get it done before the day begins and veterans can choose either before or after. So we knew that he was all done. He had already showered. That's when we had taken his car keys was when he was in the shower. Forty-five minutes goes by—nothing. We're sitting there in our car and starting to get a little bit irritated. We think that the prank's on him, and he's not coming out. So Drew gets on the phone again and proceeds to call and tries to track down where he's at and what he's doing. Come to find out, he was in watching film of himself of that day's practice. All that he had done was scout team work. I learned from scout team, but I could never learn anything from what I did watching the scout film. There were no rules to the play. You didn't even know what the play was. You were copying another team. You would learn in the physical fact of learning when you could get a ball into a certain coverage and when you couldn't and all that. But he spent his whole time in there after practice watching these things, watching himself on close-up copies, watching his footwork, trying to improve his ball faking, just his over-all drop, trying to learn if he's

We loved it. Tom probably thought his car was exploding.

giving the defense any tips with his head prior to the snap or during the snap—on and on and on. In a long roundabout way that's the other thing that I noticed is when he would do things like that, that I never saw other quarterbacks do. And the punch line to the story is eventually he did come out and start his car and glitter went everywhere. It was a pretty good deal. We loved it. Tom probably thought his car was exploding.

He ended up actually retaliating. It was a bad weather day and so we practiced inside our little practice bubble. It's sort of held up by air pressure. So the door you go in is a revolving door. When you kind of go in, it's a little bit of a 'whoosh.' So in that revolving door, he ends up finding, and I don't know where he found it, a life-size cardboard replica of Drew selling a product or something, and just stuck it in the door. No big deal, that's it. That's all he did. I think Drew's first comment was, "What an idiot. Does he have no clue?" Drew's a big practical joke guy. "Does he have no clue what he just did?" Because we were going to let him go with that one because we felt we got him back better. So then there was about five weeks left in the year and we decided that each week we would get him with something and escalate—each week would be a bigger and bigger thing. We talked about it a lot, because Drew's got an unlimited pocketbook obviously, so a prank that maybe costs a couple or three thousand dollars doesn't really matter to him.

The best one was Drew ended up calling another head coach. That coach had a contact at the FBI. In just a couple of days time, he ended up having some of the powder that banks would use in the event a robber took some money—where it would mark their hands. It's like invisible powder and it turns a real dark shade of purple.

> **…he'd say, "Check this out. What is this?" We were like, "I don't know— maybe leprosy."**

Drew and I put that stuff in Brady's bag and in the bottom of his socks. We opened up his bag and sprinkled it in, sealed it all back up, and put it in his socks. Once body heat gets going on that, that's what activates it. So about half way through practice, it's coming out of his shoes and up his leg. His legs are just the darkest purple, and he has no idea what it is. He doesn't even figure out at that moment that we've done this to him. He'd come over to us and he'd say, "Check this out. What is this?" We were like, "I don't know—maybe leprosy." And we're telling other people to look. Once we get in, now he's figured out that we got him because everybody's laughing. He was not a happy guy. He did not find any humor. The rest of the team thought it was hilarious. That was the best one I think that we got him back.

His locker was between Drew's and mine—all by uniform numbers—so he was sitting between us. Once he took his socks off and everybody saw how purple his feet were, he was pretty mad. He just grabbed his towel, put it around his waist and just started walking to the shower. Well, he was just leaving footprints on the floor—purple footprints on the carpet—ruining it. He didn't think twice about it. He was just trying to get dressed and get out of there. It was kind of a good thing that it happened with the new stadium on the horizon, as opposed to having it already been a new stadium. It would have been a different issue—ruining new carpet. The footprints are still there right now. There was no getting that out of the carpet. I don't think it was that big a deal. The first five or six footprints it was pretty profound. By the time he made it to the shower, I think it was pretty cleaned up already. He went to a Home Depot or someplace and bought every cleaning solution that God ever made. He just about rubbed his skin off at times because he just worked on it all night. He actually got it off pretty good. Inside the toenails and stuff it was impossible—time just had to happen.

I don't recall that he did anything else. He just realized that he couldn't compete. What else was he gonna do? If he does some little goofy thing again, we're gonna go back and get him bigger. One thing that I kept talking about was **He knew that it was just all part of being a rookie.** renting one of those portable electronic signs, like on a trailer. You see it when there's road work up ahead, and it'll have a blinking message on there. Drew and I talked about either renting one of those or literally renting a billboard on Route 1, going into the stadium and having it say 'whatever.' It wouldn't be what Brady would want. It was pretty amazing. We were impressed that he fought back as well as he did. At the same time, we were sorta scratching our heads as to why he would fight back. He knew that it was just all part of being a rookie. We made him bring in breakfast. We definitely broke him in. We weren't unkind or any different than we would respond to any other rookie.

I was released and then retired right after that season so I wasn't in camp last year. Season ended Christmas Eve, and I was released in January or February. I think it's sort of a pipe dream to think that having the quarterback roster as it was this past season—nothing changing this fall and having it work again I don't think is a possibility either.

I wouldn't say Brady is a stereotypical Californian. I've lived there off and on throughout my life. I know what it means to say that. He's just a good guy. He's very sincere. When we had the birth of our last child, he was the only single person to send us acknowledgement of that—he sent a gift. In a normal situation, if a single player like that even sent a card, it would be pretty much unheard of. My wife's gone around and around about other women, other wives who won't even acknowledge the birth of our child, and yet my wife has thrown them showers. She's like, "How rude of that girl to not even acknowledge our child when I did all that work for her and her family and friends." So when Tom did that, that tells a lot about a person. We had him over for dinner a couple of times our rookie year. Before and after dinner, we would talk in theory more than the actual X's and O's of a certain play because he would already have picked that up from the coaches. He was great with the kids. He's just a laid-back, very sincere person. When he is not taking full credit for the team doing what they did this past year it's because he truly understands that the coaches did a great job, that the defense scored a lot and gave the opportunity for the offense to score. Special teams did it. They had a running game for the first time in a number of years. He understands that it wasn't 'everybody got on my back and I carried the team to the Super Bowl.' He's very, I think, realistic to the fact that he played a big part in it, but he's not the total reason, and therefore he doesn't deserve or want all the credit.

> **I actually went to a sports bar for the first time in my life to watch an NFL game so I could see Tom...**

I live just outside of Seattle. I was real concerned all week about Drew's health when he got hurt. There was a lot of talk about how he was. I left him a very short message just saying that we're thinking about him. I did do some more determined calling to his other close circle that I knew would know what's going on. People who are out there. I was able to find out that he was gonna be okay. I was probably one of the first people to know how serious it really was. So my first concern was his health, and then all of a sudden I'm thinking, "Wow, Brady's starting already." I actually went to a sports bar for the first time in my life to watch an NFL game so I could see Tom because it wasn't on TV out here other than finding it on the satellite. I just wanted to see how he would do. When I made the team that year that Tom was there, my last year in New England, Charlie Weis pulled me in and said, "You're on the team. Your first job is to be the backup." He explained it to me about there would be times when Bishop will be the "two" and you'll be the "three," but for all intent and purposes you're the "two." "A job as big as that and as important as that is to teach Brady everything you know and get him ready to go." So when Tom got his first start, that was a pretty big day for me 'cause I wanted to see how he would do.

I figured that the game would probably be pretty uneventful game. I knew that Charlie Weis would protect him as much as possible. I caught a handful of games and that's sort of what I saw throughout the year. I did see them eventually give him a little bit more rope as he became more experienced but generally their plan didn't change a lot all year. There were a couple of games where they came out and featured the pass. That first game, I was a little bit surprised that they beat the Colts. Looking at how the game went with them running the ball like they did, and the defense stuffing Peyton Manning like they did, and how the Colts probably weren't as good as they'd been in the last couple of years—I think throughout the course of the year you eventually saw that. Looking back on it, 'No, I'm not surprised.' That day, yeah, I was surprised. There are not a lot of guys that win their first start.

When I was there in Foxboro that year, if someone had said to me, "Hey, in a year, this guy's going to be the Super Bowl MVP," I'd have said, "No." If someone would have said that the Patriots were going to win more than six games last year, I'd have bet about anything. And I've talked to a couple of guys that also left that year and their sentiment is exactly the same. They did get rid of a couple of guys that were kinda cancerous to the team and I think that goes as far in the direction of winning as anything does. That being said, I'm not that surprised that they were better, but—boy, we weren't very good the year before, a lot of problems. I didn't see any reason why it should change that much this year. I could see it maybe now for this upcoming year.

I loved Terry Glenn, and I think that he's a misunderstood person, but I think having him out of the offense now allows the quarterback, the coordinator and all those people involved to execute the offense and to attack the defense by what it's all dictating. In other words, you try to attack the weakness of a defense and you do that by design as opposed to trying to get your best player the ball. I think that when quarterbacks can just drop back and read the play out from what the defense is saying and from what the offense is trying to do, if he can do that, you're going to be better off than trying to get one guy the ball.

I was in Seattle for a couple of years with Joey Galloway and same thing—tremendous talent, but when you don't run the offense and you just try to get a guy touches, the offense doesn't work as well. But I can completely understand the coach's idea and argument of "This guy's got really unique

> Tony Dungy, Indianapolis Colts coach, is the last
> NFL player to throw and make an interception
> in the same NFL game. He was a defensive back
> and a backup quarterback for the Steelers.

abilities. We've got to get him the ball more." It doesn't take many games of your best player, one of the best players in the league, only getting three touches in a game, and you lose, and you go, "Wow, we've got a game breaker, and we're not getting him the ball. We've got to do it more." It kinda makes the whole thing work.

> **He understood those things from day one more than some guys ever figure it out.**

I know that Brady will improve. And I know that they will demand more of him as far as giving him more rope and more "check with me's—more audibles" those types of things. He's got a strong enough arm and he throws it with good accuracy so he can throw deep. He did throw deep on occasion. Generally, when he threw deep, it was warranted, from what I saw. There are times when you'll send two, or maybe even three, receivers deep. If a play is not there—you've got to check it down to your back. That's a credit to Brady. That goes back to understanding what the play is, understanding what the defense did to you on that play, and understanding what the prudent thing to do is. He understood that if it's third and thirteen, sometimes you have to complete it only for three yards and hope that he breaks a tackle and get a first down, and if he doesn't, well, then we punt, and it's a field-position game. He understood those things from day one more than some guys ever figure it out.

Even though Tom only suited up for two games that year he was very active. His job, because it worked out where he had really nice penmanship and when the play was called, was to chart the plays. He would write down which series it is, what play number in the series it is, the down and distance, the yard line and then the formation, movement and play. Then also, what the defense did. At the start of that year, he was probably getting the defense ten percent of the time. Then there were times where I would not be watching the defense either. In fact, I would tell him, "I'm not watching the defense this play. I'm not watching what the coverage is. I need to make sure what that backside defensive end does for a possible bootleg later," or something like that. I would really tell him, "I'm not gonna be helping you. You're on your own." It started out kinda average, maybe even above average, and that ten percent doesn't sound like a very good number, but it was average. Toward the end of the year, he had very high percentage, I would say—eighty to ninety percent accurate. There were times when, right when the play would happen, Charlie Weis would say something that the defense did and we'd look at each other, and we'd be shaking our head, 'No, that wasn't it.' Then the pictures come down from the press box and that tells you. It's a little bit hard with two still shots—one prior to the snap and one just into the snap. Then we would be confirmed as to what we saw. But those are things that you can't even hope to expect out of a rookie, let alone see it actually happen. He became more assertive because he was starting to be more accurate on what he was truly seeing. Therefore, he was stepping in on occasion, and you always had to watch that with Charlie 'cause he could turn on you and kinda make a scene. Tom would do a good job at times saying, "This is what they're doing. This is how we can attack it." And he was really able to help the team on occasion that year. I know that Drew did an awful lot of that last year. I talked to Vinatieri and he said this was unbelievable. I never envisioned following the Patriots nearly this close when I left because quite honestly I didn't get roots there like I did in other places that I played. I wasn't there that long. I was just ready to move on. But it was like a weekly soap opera. Katzenmoyer leaves training camp. Terry Glenn. And then Bledsoe. And Coach Rehbein dies. Every other problem was always Terry Glenn, but it was just one story after another.

Rehbein probably deserves as much credit as anybody because he put in that extra work with Brady. I'm sure that one of his big jobs on top of getting the whole quarterback staff ready was to bring Brady along. They met an awful lot together, one on one. That's really the person that got Brady going on the close-up videos of himself at practice. There's an awful lot of credit that he deserves. I really had sad feelings that he's not able to see what happened this year 'cause he deserves a lot of the credit for how Brady improved from year one to year two.

> **Rehbein probably deserves as much credit as anybody because he put in that extra work with Brady.**

Tom Brady is a great guy who works harder than anyone else. I'm happy for him.

REMEMBER WHEN THERE WAS THAT BIG RUN ON SUPER BOWL X CAPS?
KEN FLANDERS

Ken Flanders is Director of Retail Operations for the Patriots' Team Shops.

At this time last year, Tom was not a factor at all in any of our sales. We recognize the talent or popularity of the players by making their jersey, whether it be authentics or replicas. Tom was not even in the mix. Drew was obviously the guy. Then once Drew sustained his injury in the second game of the year, even though it was devastating, we had to start deciding whether we wanted to chase Tom Brady, not knowing how long Drew was going to be out. So we started chasing some part for him because he started playing well and the team started winning—he became an overnight phenomenal success. But it's a very tough situation because basically this is somewhat of an imported business. We have to book product weeks in advance. So it was tough to get some of his product on a timely basis, but we did pretty well.

He became popular particularly with women which means you sell smaller sizes in adult jerseys and definitely with youth sizes. Those were big. Shortly after we got in a reasonable stock of his jerseys—probably late October or early November—I saw Tom once as he was walking in the stadium door and told him that his jerseys were really selling well. Tom took the time to talk to me just briefly trying to understand the business. "What exactly does that mean?" I told him on the previous game, a home game against Buffalo on November 11, we set a record for selling the most jerseys of any player in one game. One reason was the fact that there was a shortage in the marketplace. He actually didn't even play that well but so what.

His father comes into the Pro Shop on a regular basis. He comes to most of the home games and we got to know him. He would usually come in the day before the game, obviously coming from the West Coast. He'd order product or pick up a product at the time. They were a very good family, and were extremely pleased. They were the biggest fans of anybody.

> Women buy 70 percent of all NFL merchandise and 44 percent of all major league baseball merchandise.

I remember before the Oakland game, that was later in the year obviously, but we knew there might be snow. And his father said, "Tom only played in one game," that he recalled, "in the snow at Michigan and had a poor game. I think Michigan had won six to nothing." Tom said to me afterward that he didn't want to go through that again." So it made me a little bit nervous going into that game. But obviously Tom played quite well, as you know.

I got to meet his sisters on numerous occasions, particularly on game days. They would talk about the Bledsoe-Brady situation. I said, "It's sometimes tough on me because I feel Drew was instrumental in the rebirth of this franchise." We had a lot of his jerseys on hand, even though he still sold well, don't get me wrong. He just wasn't playing. And they knew of his children and all about the Montana-Young controversy on the West Coast and they didn't want a situation like that. They knew how destructive it was for the team. I think they were encouraging Tom to keep it high profile and obviously Drew and Tom both did. But deep down, you could tell they were full of pride about how their brother was playing.

There were very few of his authentics at the time, just because they weren't available, so we were selling replicas. We were kinda caught in crossfire last year because we were still an Adidas team, and Adidas just kinda let the ball drop, knowing they wouldn't be involved in the NFL this year. And obviously Reebok authentics weren't available so it was a little bit tough in that respect, but we still did quite well.

So Brady set the record of a little over a hundred jerseys just in the pro shop for one game on a game day. That's a lot. It may not sound like a huge amount, but we probably had only about a hundred and forty-four so we sold the vast majority of them that one game.

Getting product was sporadic. It was one of those things, in the retail business, unfortunately, you always look back at situations and say you could have sold even more volume if you had the product. It's what we call a chase business, where you place orders and almost cross your fingers. "Can we get it in quickly?" Despite constantly selling out of his jersey, we still sold almost a thousand which was far and away our biggest seller of the year.

> In the 1983 Holiday Bowl, Brigham Young University quarterback Steve Young caught the winning touchdown pass in a 21-17 victory over Missouri.

> Adidas is named after its founder, Adi Dassler.

IF THE BRADYS WERE REALLY GOOD CUSTOMERS, THEY'D ORDER EVEN MORE
DEBBIE ROGERS

Debbie Rogers is the glue that holds Customer Service Relations together in the Patriots Commerce Department.

A few times walking into the stadium, Tom Brady would be at the door because it would be at the end of practice and he'd be icing down his shoulder. He'd just be out in the hallway on a sofa. He would get up and would open up the door for me—real nice gentleman and polite. "Yes, maam." He's got a lot of Southern qualities even though he's not really from the South.

When I saw the shoulder with the ice on it, I said, "I should be opening up the door for you." He said, "No maam, I'll be happy to do it for you." I seemed to run into him a lot up there. And he's walked into the Pro Shop many times, especially the week between the Oakland and the Pittsburgh game. A lot of the media were up at the stadium with TV cameras and he'd walk into the stadium, and even with the media cameras, they had no idea who he was. He'd walk into the Pro Shop and no one really knew who he was even during the playoffs.

Next day he came in, and it was a totally different story. He was bombarded, asked for autographs, and he actually stayed and signed every single autograph for everyone in the Pro Shop. There were probably fifty or sixty people there, and he probably spent about half an hour. He was really nice and generous and he always seemed to have a smile.

At the beginning of the season, he used to always come out every day after practice. He would walk out from the parking lot toward the Pro Shop where people would be standing and waiting. He'd actually sign autographs and then walk back into the stadium and watch film. Unreal! That would be like after Week Three when he first started playing to Week Twelve. He'd always come out every day and sign autographs.

At Christmas time we shipped a ton of merchandise for the whole entire family. We sent them out to California—just boxes and boxes of Brady jerseys for them. I've helped the family out many times in the store. They fly in for every game. His sisters fly in, too. Sometimes mom doesn't make every game. All the Bradys are nice.

WHEN IVANA AND MARLA PLAY BRIDGE, DO THEY BID NO TRUMP?

MARY HILLIARD McMILLAN

Mary Hilliard McMillan is the Public Relations Director for the Miss Universe Pageant Organization. She chose Tom Brady to be one of eight judges for the 2002 Miss USA Pageant. The pageant is owned by Donald Trump and CBS.

W e were so excited to book Tom as a judge. He's exactly what we look for especially for the Miss USA Pageant. I saw him for the first time in the Super Bowl. The next day I got on the phone with our talent booker and our judges' coordinator and said, "You guys have got to book him. He's perfect. He's the right age. He is obviously a man that has taste in beautiful women. And he's hot right now. He's on top of the world right now. We have to get him."

It ended up the same day, the day after the Super Bowl, our talent coordinator was listening to the radio and some DJ was saying how since the end of the game, Tom Brady had gotten over a thousand proposals of different kinds—most of them marriage proposals.

> **"He's on top of the world right now. We have to get him."**

We just sort of laughed and said, "Well, you know what? We're going to submit this proposal anyway because we really want him, and we'll see what happens." It might get buried in a pile of paperwork but who knows? It ended up coming back that he was very interested in being a judge. So that's how it all fell into place.

Obviously we were very excited for those exact reasons. Tom was super easy to work with as were his attorneys. Actually the only one I had any dealing with was Steve Dubin. He is phenomenal. It almost felt like you were working with some old buddies from college—that sort of thing. You would think that after Tom's experience this year and pretty much 'overnight fame,' his ego would be huge and he would have that 'celebrity' attitude that you run into a lot of times. He was the exact opposite, very approachable, very easy to work with. In our business when so many celebrities are involved, sometimes it does become an ego thing, and it makes working with those people extremely hard. In Tom's case it was not like that at all. Everyone was just so easy to work with. He's such a great guy. He actually brought Aaron Shea, one of his friends from college who now plays for the Browns, as his guest.

Aaron was super nice, too. They're football guys. They've never been to a beauty pageant. Also neither one of them had ever been flying on Mr. Trump's plane, sitting at a dinner table with all these major television and film stars and pop stars and recording stars. I think that at first maybe at least for Tom Brady—I'm not positive about this, you'd have to ask him yourself—he was sort of quict. I think it's just because he was sort of taking it all in.

> **The girls who were competing were so ecstatic to meet him.**

It's funny. The girls who were competing were so ecstatic to meet him. After the show, at the coronation ball, typically it can sometimes be a situation where a lot of these girls aren't so happy. They didn't win. Pageants are really competitive. These girls are basically going home without the prize, after three really long weeks. So they're not happy. And it can sometimes not be the most fun night for them but they were so excited to meet Tom. I remember there was one point at the Coronation Ball where Aaron and I grabbed a table back at the corner and put our chairs to blockade these girls from coming to take pictures and get autographs from him so that he could get something to eat. The great thing about Tom was—and we felt sorry for him—that's why we were doing it—he really didn't want us to do it. He wanted to meet all of them, of course, and take pictures and be the nice guy. He isn't at the point yet where fame has affected him in the way that he needs someone fending off people asking for autographs. He's still really excited to do it.

Tom Brady actually ended up taking a train from New England to catch a ride on Donald Trump's jet. That's what he wanted to do. We offered many different means of transportation but he wanted to take a train from Boston into New York. He was so cute. His attorney called and said, "Listen. Tom's really excited about this. He wants to get dressed up. He doesn't have a tux to wear. I'm wondering if you could hook him up." So I made some calls and set him up with an appointment at Calvin Klein here in New York at the Showroom for them to design a tuxedo for him to wear. He came in to New York. I think he ended up going to a hockey game or something that night with some buddies. We set him up with some parties to go out to take his buddies to after the hockey game. Then he went to Calvin Klein to get his tux fitted. Then Mr. Trump picked him up the following day, and they flew on Mr. Trump's plane to Gary, Indiana for the pageant. They stayed at the Coronation Ball all night. I think they partied even after the Coronation Ball with some of the girls and some of the delegates. He and Aaron then went into Chicago and met up with some more buddies from college who are now playing in various places. They had sort of a guys' weekend reunion, their first get-together thing since the Super Bowl.

Some of the other judges along with Tom were Willa Ford, a pop star who's on Atlantic; Dr. Joyce Brothers; Nikki Ziering, married to Ian Ziering from *Beverly Hills 90210*, and she is also a Barker's beauty; Victor Williams who is on the *King of Queens*; Jermaine Jackson; and Audrey Quock, a supermodel who was on the cover of the *Sports Illustrated* swimsuit edition.

It was clear that Tom did not really want any press surrounding this. He was sort of worn out from all of it. He wanted to be relatively low key. So with that direction, we didn't take many pictures. It's funny because then Tom gets there, and he's such a nice guy, and he's all about photos. The only one that we have that's really even usable is the one that was in *Sports Illustrated*.

I had dinner with Tom the night of the show. We were at the judge's dinner beforehand. I was sitting with him and Aaron. He was telling me that it was mostly sports talk on the plane, but that they had gotten along extremely well. Mr. Trump's a huge golfer so I know they talked about that for a while. I think they ended up in having a lot in common.

> **I work for Mr. Trump and I still get sort of overwhelmed by him at times.**

I work for Mr. Trump and I still get sort of overwhelmed by him at times. I think for your average twenty-four year old guy, being on a private plane with Donald Trump, is a big deal. Then knowing Tom and knowing that he is more shy than you would picture him to be, I think it was a cool thing for him.

I would be hesitant to mention any interest Tom might have had in any of the girls, but I think he did have his eye on one or two. Who knows?

Tom's scores were pretty high. He's such a nice guy that he didn't want to give a low score to any of them. I think Tom saw most of them to be beauty queens. As people were sitting at home and watching how he was scoring on TV and his buddies are watching, and you know, it can be a lot of pressure on a guy.

The whole night was just so chaotic and crazy, and I can't even remember as parting ways. I know Tom ended up having a good time. In fact, I know that he was supposed to go back to Chicago that night, and ended up staying longer to party and then going back to Chicago the next morning.

The amazing thing to me is how he is almost an average guy. He's great looking. He's extremely talented and athletic. He's got so much going for him. He's experienced this overnight fame, and he's still the same guy—or how I would have imagined him to be before being the MVP of the Super Bowl.

And it was the same way with his attorney, Steve. It's like you're on the phone with him, and it's just normal conversation. It's not that very, almost legal banter about what you're allowed to do, what you're not allowed to do, this is the access you can have—it was not like that. It was like, "Hey, Tom's coming to judge. Let's work out these details. Let's have a good time." He was excited. They were sitting at Steve's office on the website going through the girls with me prior to his coming to judge—telling me who they thought was hot, and who they thought had a good chance. They found the swimsuit photos online a few days later, and they were like, "Whoa!" They were like a couple of guys that I would have hung out with in college.

We typically have one to two athletes as judges on each panel every year. On the upcoming Miss Universe Pageant, we have Apolo Ohno booked. At last year's Miss USA Pageant, we had Roy Jones, Jr. There's always some athlete. We like to have a very well rounded panel that includes recording artists, TV stars, movie stars, athletes, people in other industries that would be considered celebrities, presidents of corporations to make it a really well rounded group because they have a really big job of choosing a winning girl. We like to go back to people to be judges again because they loved the experience and they know what to look for—so Tom could return. Past judges know what to look for, they've done the routine and they know the drill so it's easier. Next time—who knows? Shauntay Hinton from the District of Columbia was our winner this year and will represent our country in the Miss Universe Pageant.

Short Stories from Long Memories

The friendship between Brady and Drew Bledsoe did grow awkward at times last season. Bledsoe, Brady and three teammates went to one of the American League Championship Series games in New York last October. They took a limo bus down there, got great seats at the game. At that point, they were just hanging out. It was getting to the point where everybody knew Bledsoe would be healthy soon and it was going to become an issue. They had a private conversation at that game, and Brady said to him, "No matter what happens and what positions we get put in, I want you to know how I really feel about you. I want you to know I think you're a great player and you've been a great mentor." Brady recalls Bledsoe saying, "If you can do one thing for me: Don't do me any favors. Try to kick my butt. It would be an insult to me not to have you do that. The best thing you can do is try to be better than me every day." Was everything perfect for them from that point on? No. But they genuinely do like each other. Each genuinely believes that he is the guy to lead the team, which can't happen. I just think it was nice that Bledsoe could directly contribute to the Super Bowl win by playing so well in Pittsburgh in the AFC Championship game, but I believe that will prove to be his last game for the Patriots, and I think he's eager to explore all his options.

—— **MIKE SILVER**, Senior Writer at *Sports Illustrated*

The *METROWEST Daily News* is a smaller paper. I seriously doubt Brady even reads papers anyway. I did say to him one time in the locker room, "Hey, I knew you were gonna play like this. Congratulations." We had a good relationship just shooting the breeze in the locker room about his pickup truck and things like that." His truck is not that old, but at one time he did have a banana yellow Jeep. He got rid of it because Belichick's father, Steve, made fun of him. He is an eighty-four year old guy, long time coach at Navy, probably one of the greatest film and football strategist in the last fifty years. Steve Belichick was at a practice and saw Brady pull up in the yellow Jeep, and he said to him, "Where'd you get that Jeep?" He said, "I worked a deal out with a dealer." Steve said, "Oh yeah, good. He doesn't like you, huh?" "What do you mean?" "Why would he give you a yellow Jeep?" So Brady went back to the dealer and ended up with a pickup truck.

—— **TOM CURRAN**, *Providence Journal*, formerly of the METROWEST

You hear a lot around here, "Well, once teams get a book on Brady, he won't be as successful." That type of thing. And that's not true. He's got the right combination of football skills, the height, arm strength, certainly the intelligence. That's one of the things that by any standard he'd grade out in the highest percentile. I remember Belichick telling us a story one time about how, whether it be in practice or a game, sometimes Tom would walk off the field, and Belichick would ask him, "Tom why did you throw the ball there—to that guy?" And Tom would say, "Well, 'cause the linebacker was here, and the safety was there, and the receiver was here, etc." And Belichick would say to himself, "There's no way that can be true." Then he'd go look at the film afterwards and sure enough, everything that Tom described it was like an 'instamatic photo' or something. It was just exactly as Tom had described it. He has the ability that, for him, everything looks like it's in slow motion.

—— SEAN MCDONOUGH, Noted Network TV and Radio Analyst

Yesterday, Jermaine Wiggins said to all the guys, "Hey, did you guys see the shirtless wonder here on the cover of Sports Illustrated holding the ball like a baby?" They were just dying laughing, and Tom was like, "Whatever, man."

It was real funny—of all the pictures that they probably take, they would put that picture on the front. As far as the article went, of all the things they talked about, the thing that comes out is about how much he loves women. It's like they're bound and determined to write about or put on the cover whatever they initially had in mind anyway. They're trying to turn him into a character.

—— DAVID NUGENT, Close friend and roommate

Again, I've not known him that long. But you spend a round of golf with a guy, it's amazing how you feel like, in the course of four or four and a half hours, you can learn a lot about somebody. I left there thinking, "This is maybe the nicest, most unassuming professional athlete ever." Usually it doesn't matter whether you're a star or not, if you achieve the status of being a professional athlete and have people give things to you, even if you're the third-string quarterback, you develop a certain air about you. He was the antithesis of what I have gotten to know covering these guys and knowing some of them. Some of them are great guys, but they still take advantage of certain things that are bestowed upon them. He couldn't have been further from that prototypical professional athlete.

—— GARY WILLIAMS, Radio Talk Show Host

I was a little concerned the Wednesday, Thursday, and Friday before the Super Bowl when all the local news on radio and TV could talk about was where the victory parade would be, what time, whether to take off work—it was assumed that we would win. It wasn't win or lose, it was by how much would we win. I had a bad feeling in my gut based on that. Then watching the game first quarter, felt bad—second quarter, by half time, I'm nervous—everybody in St. Louis was scared to death. I think the better team won that day, but the Rams are the better team overall. We were "flat" and not prepared. I believe that Tom Brady's youth made him so naive under the pressure, that he didn't realize the significance of the event, because he certainly was rock-solid to the end.

—— TOM ROHLFING, Co-owner of the St. Louis-based company that printed the dust jacket and color inserts for this book.

Every team is set up for a big, gigantic party. Normally I go to the losers' party first, then I go to the winners' party. The reason for that is the losers' party is always over early, but the winners' party sometimes lasts all night. I was waiting to get a picture with Warner and Faulk both, but they never did show up. In fact, that happens a lot at the losers' party. The big stars don't even show up. A lot of the players don't even show up.

One time, we were crashing Pete Roselle's Friday night party. There were curtains. We pull the curtains apart, and the guy says, "You can't come in." I said, "Well, we're looking for a telephone." He said, "There's a telephone right there." The telephones were right in front of us, about three feet away. That's just an excuse you use when you're stopped "I'm looking for a phone." Or "I'm looking for the bathroom."

—— **DION RICH**, World-Famous Gatecrasher at Super Bowl XXXVI

I think Brady envisioned what was going to happen. I know that he was confused his rookie year—he would always talk to me "Why is there no emotion in the locker room?" "Why can't it be like college?" "Why can't guys get excited about playing the game?" I said, "It's a good question." It really doesn't come from the coach at this level, in my opinion. It's gotta be sincere. There's got to be a chemistry. Every team that I've ever been on we've always tried to create the chemistry. At times there was but nothing was ever generated like they had this year. I kept in contact with a handful of those guys. They just said it was different. It was just the belief that "we were going to do it, and we were going to do together." They totally bought into what the coaches had to say. How much credit Brady can be given to that—I don't know. I know that's how he felt that that's how he thought the game should be played. But, boy, to Drew's defense, I've seen the man cry in front of the team after a game so you can't tell me that Drew is definitely not one of those quarterbacks that said, "Oh well, there's next year." He fought every week as hard as I've ever seen a guy fight. I have nothing but praise for Drew; therefore it's hard for me to give all the credit to Brady. Somehow Brady got that mentality of, "Hey, let's go have fun. Why can't it be like it was?"

—— **JOHN FRIESZ**, Former NFL quarterback

We get over there, and have this phenomenal meal. Then we sat there, and I could tell the Bradys were both exhausted. It was almost midnight. We were listening to this old Irish guy singing tunes at the piano. I guarantee you they will remember that. It was a great evening. We went with four other fathers and sons. We sat around this big circle. Tom told stories, as a matter of fact, about Willie McGinest. McGinest was the guy who would go around to the rookies and tell you 'You're going to do this, and you're going to like it.' Tom said he was the one guy who scared him the most, and he had the entire table completely enthralled. McGinest told all the rookies that they had to go to this party one night during training camp. Tom looked at his calendar and said, "Oh my gosh. My sister's coming in." So he went up to one of the other guys and said, "Hey man, I'm not going to be able to be

Tom Brady's Junior High School had weird-shaped footballs.

COLLEGE BASKETBALL & NHL Midseason wakeup call

The Sporting News

SEE A DIFFERENT GA...

**NFL
CONFERENCE
CHAMPIONSHIP
PREVIEWS**

AFC:
Patriots vs. Steeler...

NFC:
Eagles vs. Rams

Four
TO THE
Front

*Patriots QB Tom Brady
must stay cool in the face
of the Steelers' torrid rush*

www.sportingnews.com

JANUARY 28, 2002

Celebrating during the Michigan days.

That's all folks!

Last minutes of
Tom Brady's
great career
at Michigan.

there because my sister's coming in, and I don't get to see her very much. You're gonna have to tell Willie that I can't be there." They were like, "We're not telling Willie. You can tell him. And if I was you, I would do everything you can to get out of whatever it is you've got to do with your sister, and you better be there." Tom said, "No, you're crazy. I'm not going. I'll tell Willie." So he went up to McGinest and said, "I'm not going to be able to go. My sister's coming into town." He was like, "I don't care who's coming into town. You'd better be there." Tom, at first, was like, "No, no, no you don't understand...." About the second time he tried to impress upon McGinest that, "Hey listen. You're not listening to me. I am not gonna be there." McGinest said, "You better be there." That's when Tom said, "Okay, I'll be there." So he backed down. Brady said he was the one guy on the team that he was fearful of, and when he had that little confrontation, he said there was never another time that he was ever gonna cross him. So one of the evenings that his sister was going to be in Boston, she was not going to be with him because Willie McGinest told him he had to be somewhere, and he was going to be there. He told that story and everybody loved it. All these fathers are sitting there listening. All the sons are loving it. There's nothing like hearing stories about 'inside the locker room' and Tommy was kinda holding court.

—— **GARY WILLIAMS**, Radio Talk Show Host

The first time I saw Brady at Bryant College during training camp his rookie year, he was wearing a baseball shirt, one of those three-quarter sleeve shirts, hat on backward and a backpack and baggy warm-up pants. He was walking through the campus and heading over to the cafeteria. I thought he was a young college student. Then, I got to thinking: Bryant College is not in summer session and it's not home to physical specimens, so who is this guy?

—— **TOM CURRAN**, *Providence Journal*

I think Tom Brady is terrific. I watched him during the course of the season. I don't know how you can get any more accolades than he's received. He earned the right, and he's excellent. I'm amazed at his poise and his confidence. He's got a good arm, and the nice thing about it along with that is he's got a great escape-ability skill. He can escape from the pocket and that's very, very important because he throws well on the run. I just think he's going to be fantastic. He's already outstanding and a great quarterback, but as he goes along, he's jut going to get better and better, so that's a big plus—really a big plus for New England.

—— **HANK STRAM**, Winningest Coach in AFL History

Over the years, Tom Brady worked hard. He was a slow kid who worked on his speed. He had slow feet, but he slaved away and now he has quick feet. He always had a pretty good arm. We had several kids who became big league players who worked their butts off to get where they were. Tommy was so bright. He was special. He would just take whatever you were trying to teach and he would work on it. His whole family would be at all the baseball games. Win, lose or draw, always a smile on their faces, and a very supportive family. When he was at Michigan, he didn't want to be recognized here at our games. He would sit in the stands at a baseball game, and someone would notice that he was here, but he just wanted to see the Serra Padres play. He would always come over and give the coaches hugs, but it would be after the game. He didn't want to interrupt the game. He was such a humble kid. Every year, he would come back and check on the old high school team. You don't have many guys do that, other than Tommy. At Serra, most of them come back here to work out 'cause we have a pretty good facility. They'll always stay in touch. The camaraderie and they'll come back to work out, to see the coaches, it's kinda like a second family.

—— **RICH JEFFERIES**, High School Hitting Coach

I was impressed only because he wanted to understand it, not just listen to me give him info, but to understand what it meant by replica, etc. Brady just wanted to understand our business, which is extremely unusual for a player. I told him we set a record for one game selling his replica jersey, and he just immediately said, "Well, I'm not sure what 'replica' means." So we talked about it. I explained to him that it is a screened version of the jersey, even though it looked the same as the screened jersey—it's a lower priced item, as opposed to the authentic. So he was pleased to hear that. Basically, being somewhat of a young kid, after we finished the conversation, he just said, "Well, that's cool." He's such an humble kid he just couldn't seem to understand why anyone would want his jersey…so he didn't buy any, but his family ordered numerous.

—— **KEN FLANDERS**, Patriots Team Shop

I would tell Tom on occasion—one was on a Monday night and the other was on a big home game that we had. It was getting late in the game, and the crowd is starting to go nuts. I looked at him and said, "You know what? I don't want to be here right now. I'd just as soon be in Idaho trying to chase down a white tail or something." He looked at me, and his jaw would just drop. He was like, "What?" He couldn't picture anything better than being out there—and me, too. If I was out there on the field that would have been one thing, but just standing there, it wasn't that great.

—— **JOHN FRIESZ**, Former Patriots Quarterback

I think people that say Tom Brady is the next coming of Christ are overreacting just a little bit. Anything can happen. He could get a serious injury. I think the kid has a lot of moxie. I enjoy watching him play, but it's gonna be very interesting to watch him next year when teams have really set out to watch how he plays.

—— **BOB MANNING**, Patriots and Drew Bledsoe fan

When I met them at the Super Bowl, I found the Bradys to be a really down-to-earth family, straight shooters. They told a funny story which really got me laughing. Tom's dad said, 'I had a call from Tom last night from the players' hotel." We said, "Okay?" Tommy said to me, "You have to meet me over by Hertz." His dad said, "Why do I have to meet you by Hertz?" He said, "Well, I'm trying to rent a car, and since I'm not twenty five, they're not gonna let me rent a car." He needed his father to go down to rent the car for him. He wasn't twenty-five years old yet so he couldn't rent a car. It made no difference that you're the star quarterback of one of the two Super Bowl teams or in a couple of days, the MVP of the Super Bowl. They just would not let him rent the car, which I think is ridiculous, but it's a legal thing. His dad went down and rented the car, and he was able to go on as a second driver. Tommy and some of the guys wanted to drive around, and there were a couple of places they had taken over for private parties, The Blues Brothers Café and others.

—— GARY ROTHSTEIN, *New York Times* Photographer

It was a lot more people than we are used to here. It's a real, real great community of people on this block, and they're very supportive of Tommy. I overheard a conversation between two little girls from the neighborhood as they walked upstairs in the house.

One girl said to the other, "This is where Tom Brady lives?" The other girl said, "Yeah. But he lives back East, too." Then the first girl said, "But you know, he has walked up and down these stairs a lot of times!"

—— PHIL BRADY, SR., Tom Brady's uncle on Super Bowl Party
at house where Tom was raised.

I never thought all athletes were jerks. The vast majority of them are at least decent guys. Unfortunately, too much of the attention goes to the guys who aren't doing the right thing or saying the right things. It's nice to know that people can be that way, especially when the spotlight gets bright. I kind of equate it to, and it's funny, he's been compared to this guy, Matt Damon, locally by some of the gossip columnists who think he looks like him. I've known Matt Damon since about 1991 when he was just a student at Harvard, and I happened to run into him at a place where he recognized me and came over and started talking about what a big Red Sox fan he was. He mentioned that his dad was a Syracuse graduate, as I am. Anyway we became friends and we've stayed friends. To see him when he literally didn't have five dollars in his pocket to now, having won the Academy Award and making millions of dollars a picture, he's exactly the same. He hasn't changed one bit. I look for any sign of ego or arrogance or self-absorption and there's none of it all these years later. Tom's the same way. Tom is one of those guys you just know is not gonna be the least bit affected by winning the Super Bowl, being in the Pro Bowl, being the Super Bowl MVP, doing national commercials. He's the kind of person who you just know wouldn't change at all. I admire him a lot. I really do. I think he's a terrific guy.

—— SEAN McDONOUGH, Noted Network TV and Radio Analyst

Figure it out. He's twenty-four years old, single and surrounded by fifty beautiful women. Furthermore, he's the nicest guy in the world and doesn't want to hurt any of the contestants' feelings so it seemed like the lowest score he gave while judging the Miss USA Pageant was like a 9.9.

—— A FORMER MICHIGAN TEAMMATE on Tom Brady's Judging Ability

Sometimes we do different travel things. Oftentimes they travel in private jets. They might have to go back to the team's city for parades and sometimes they have to leave for the Pro Bowl. Once we picked Tom Brady, we called the theme parks and told them to get ready for the parades. They make announcements in the theme parks about the parades. We had absolutely huge crowds on that Monday after the Super Bowl. There were tons of New England people here because obviously they're vacationing from the Northeast. It was kinda funny when you go, "Hey, anybody here from Boston or New England?" You hear a roar.

—— KEVIN YOUNG, Super Bowl MVP Coordinator, Disney World

While we were working out, the whole women's softball team was there watching us. And I think their eyes were more on him than me! I'm not bad looking myself, but he rolled up in a Lexus, and everybody kinda turned and looked. Then he got out of the car. He just had a regular t-shirt on, not like a tank top or anything. He had his hat on backward. I think I was out there in a tank top. The girls were just totally watching us. They had to be a little impressed with me because I was catching his balls.

—— PHIL GRATSINOPOULOS, Sacramento State Football Player

As a St. Louis resident—that's where the Sporting News is located— I had a higher than usual interest in the Super Bowl. Going into the Super Bowl, I think a lot people thought I that it might be kind of close. I don't think that anybody around here really expected the Rams to lose. A lot of Rams fans pretty much saw it as a done deal, I think, heading into that game—there was just no way the Rams were going to lose this game. A lot of people were already talking about the Rams in terms of some of the other so-called dynasties—would they be as good as the 49'ers and the Cowboys from the 90's, you know, and then to see them lose was just a huge shock to a lot of people. For several days after the game, I think there were a lot of people who were still kind of in disbelief about it and probably still are. It was pretty quiet around the office the next day.

—— MATT PITZER, *The Sporting News*

The defensive coordinator there with the Patriots is a Western Kentucky guy, Romeo Crennel, and he told me that Brady has such a maturity about him where he doesn't take anything but what they give him. He's very, very patient, understands things— just like in the Super Bowl game, those first two passes he threw on that last drive were check downs. Some quarterbacks would get greedy down there and feel you had to stick it someplace where you couldn't stick it and end up getting it picked and costing you the game. But he checked it down, and they ran out of bounds and stopped the clock and kept the drive going. That's maturity, I think, far beyond your years. In his interviews and things, Tom Brady just looks almost unbelievable. Is this guy for real? Then you realize after you see it four or five times, 'Yeah, he's for real.'

—— **JACK HARBAUGH**, Head Football Coach at Western Kentucky

I think Brady will continue to play very well. I think he reads defenses very well. He kinda reminds me—he does the shuffle step like Marino. Remember Marino used to step up. He'd move to the left, move to the right. He throws a different ball than Marino. Marino wasn't the fastest guy, but as a long-time Patriots' fan, I used to watch Marino with his footwork. Nobody would ever get him because he'd be able to move up. I think Brady has a great future. He's gonna be on commercials. He's gonna make a ton of money. He's like a poster boy for success. You know what it is I like about the kid—he's level-headed. That's why a lot of people say they hope success doesn't ruin him like it's ruined a lot of athletes. He's got great roots, and that's important.

—— **BOBBY SHEA**,Patriots Fan at the Super Bowl

Can he handle this type of attention? I broke into sports writing covering Joe Montana. I spent time with John Elway. I did a book with Kurt Warner whose situation is somewhat analogous. The great ones do handle it. We don't know if Brady's great yet. We do know that he has poise and the ability to block out pressure and perform. He believes he's not handling it very well. He believes he's overwhelmed, that he runs the risk of both alienating his teammates and detracting from his preparation by doing any of this. Obviously he's a work in progress.

—— **MIKE SILVER**, Senior Writer for *Sports Illustrated*

He's got everything you would want. He's smart. He's tough. He's got a good arm. He's a leader. He is a leader. You saw emotion displayed by him that was never displayed by Bledsoe. And I know you can have your silent-type leaders, Joe Montana certainly was one of them, but you see the difference. I do think it makes a difference on at least this particular team. Drew would walk off the field a lot of times after going three and out and making a bad play, head down, chin-strap off, kinda moping around. This kid would come off the field and wouldn't let it bother him. I think that filtered down into the team. I do think leadership, a lot of it in the NFL, comes from your quarterback.

—— **PETE SHEPPARD**, Boston Sports Radio Personality

There are other guys, but the thing that struck me about him—I know this is going to sound a little weird, was—how tough he was. I saw it one game, against Bellarmine, which is a really strong school. I believe he was sacked at least seven times, then hit after he threw at least another seven to ten times, and he never flinched. He never complained or whined. He just got back up and continued. That really, really struck me as to how tough he was under pressure. His offensive line wasn't anything special. I think that was obvious, at least in that ball game, and it was a hot day—it was dusty. It was pretty bad—it was warm, it was muggy, and he was getting punished and kept getting up and throwing the ball.

—— **JOHN HORGAN**, Sportswriter, *San Mateo County Times*

At New Orleans we did not get caught at all. That was really a black eye on the Secret Service. They came to my house on Valentine's Day. I invited them in. My house was a mess. I'd been on 'In Studio Radio' the night before for an hour, and I had pictures and articles all over. I was packing to leave for the Olympics in Salt Lake City so I had clothes all over. It was an absolute mess. They came in and read me my rights. They said it was going to be a federal offense if I crashed the security or Olympic events without a ticket, either one.

—— **DION RICH**, World-famous Gatecrasher at Super Bowl XXXVI

In the Penn State game, Tom was just poised. As a quarterback, you've got to worry about time. But it wasn't really like panicking, "We've got to do this. We've got to do this." It was more like, "Well take one play at a time and just try to get a first down. Try to get a couple of yards." That's how Tom was. The last drive, the one he threw to Marcus, it was just like yard after yard and that's all he was worried about. He wasn't worried about touchdowns, just yard after yard. Just do this first, and then let's do that. We practiced that 'fake limp' all week before the Penn State game. When Tom did it in the game, we were laughing on the sidelines because we knew what was going on but nobody else knew. I think he did a pretty good job of being an actor at the time.

—— **MARQUISE WALKER**, Michigan teammate of Brady

Obviously, everybody's aware of a family like that and they're a very classy family in the area. Not only were the girls successful, but the parents did a great job of exposing all of them to the right ways to go about things. They had them in camps and they had them in places that either would make them better or expose them to people to see. Tom was just kind of the youngest brother all along, and as it got going on, Maureen got more and more successful. I think for a while she held the strikeout record in the state of California for high school pitchers, which in and of itself is unbelievable. Softball out here is very, very big, and she held the strikeout record. She got a scholarship to Fresno State and Fresno State was in the nationals all the time, and so the Brady name was just rollin' along. When Tom was young, his dad and mom did an excellent, excellent job of continuously getting him to camps and clinics. He came one year and he was a catcher—and again everybody started to know him more for baseball because be played when he was younger. So they started to acquaint him with baseball. He was a lot like Nancy. They had similar body types and they were both catchers, and they even look a little alike. They were the two that were the closest in makeup. So then Tommy came along and then one year he came to our quarterback camp when he was around thirteen.

—— **TOM MARTINEZ**, Tom Brady's long-time quarterback coach

Also, another great example, which I thought characterized his whole year, was the Jets game, the second one. They're down thirteen to nothing, and he had a horrible first half, not so much his fault. The offensive line was not doing well. Antowain Smith was being stopped early and often. A couple of bad breaks here and there. The second half they're down thirteen to nothing, and he comes in the second half and I think he was thirteen of sixteen, or something, in the second half. He was just unbelievably poised leading that team down the field. The Patriots ended up wining that game 17-16. Just a phenomenal game he had there. Then in the Buffalo game, another play that stands out, and I'm surprised it never made the DVD video, is he took a hit that I still can't believe he got up from. It was one of the hardest hits I've ever seen in my life. He got tagged where his helmet went rolling down the field about twenty yards. He popped back up. There wasn't even a hesitation. He was right back up. I don't know if he knew where he was or whatever, but he was right back in there. That play didn't get a lot of national pub on the DVD or the VHS when the Super Bowl video came out, it was kind of a surprise...I couldn't believe it when we saw it. Fred Smerlas and I were watching it. My heart jumped out of my.... I said, 'He's dead." I thought he was dead. It was one of those hits   Jack Tatum on Darryl Stingley type of hit. I just couldn't believe it.

PETE SHEPPARD, Boston Sports Radio Personality

When Bledsoe went down, if anyone in the press box would have said, "This is gonna turn the season around, and I'll bet you guys a thousand dollars even up we win the Super Bowl," I'd have put them in the asylum. They'd have been laughed at. This team was dead. Well, you can't say they were dead, but 0 and 2 with everything that was going on, the best wide receiver in the midst of a four-game league suspension in a season which he was basically gonna contribute, as it unfolded, one game—period. Losing the guy that had taken every snap when healthy since 1993, for a kid who had thrown three passes all last year and completed one, a sixth-round pick who a lot of people wondered why he was even here in the year 2000 to lead this team that had never won anything. Had never won a league title before. Never won an AFL title back in those days. Had been to two Super Bowls, and got blown out of one. The other one ended up with them losing arguably the greatest coach they ever had. They called the '67 Red Sox '100 to 1 Odds, The Impossible Dream.' This was a pigskin version of it. There was no way it was going to happen. This team was going nowhere, absolutely nowhere. Again, one and three, on the verge of going one and four against San Diego—they were dead.

People my age want to fix up their daughters with him. He's definitely a guy who as time goes on he's gonna be more and more—it's already happening—appearing in gossip columns and stuff like that. 'Tom Brady was seen here, there or wherever.' He's supposedly got a twenty-four or twenty five years old girlfriend. It's happening already. He's looked at as a guy who 'Chicks dig Tom Brady.'

——— GLEN FARLEY, Brockton Enterprise

The family is fantastic. They are the salt of the earth. What a wonderful crowd that is, and they have wonderful neighbors. The whole neighborhood was galvanized for the playoffs and the Super Bowl. They literally shut down the block. The neighbors got the City's permission to shut the whole block down.

—— **JOHN HORGAN**, Sportswriter, *San Mateo County Times*

Tom and I have kept in touch, and my dad and Tom, Sr. have kept up. When the Patriots came down for their preseason game against the Panthers, we had lunch with Tom and his parents. We corresponded throughout the year. I had him on the show several times. Then when they came back down for that last regular season game, my folks went to dinner with Tom, Sr. and Galynn, but I had to do a college basketball game that evening so I wasn't able to go. Everybody stayed in touch. It's funny. Every time I see him, he's wearing the same thing he was wearing the day that we played. He has this Olympic Club black sweatshirt. He wore it the day we played at Ballybunion. I think there were four interviews he did during Super Bowl week, probably all done on the same day, and he was wearing that same sweatshirt. I thought his mom was great, too. Obviously that was the first time I had met her. I learned a lot more about his sisters from her. He talked a lot about his sisters. The thing that amazed me, in talking to his dad that day, was just the number of games he and Galynn went to throughout their kids' collegiate careers. The travel that he incurred just to be there to watch their kids play just amazed me.

—— **GARY WILLIAMS**, Radio Talk Show Host

The Brady visit was a pleasure from top to bottom. A kid who openly loved the game, supportive parents, with enough knowledge to really help their son, and a family with clarity in the direction they wanted to go. I remember him saying how playing in the big leagues was a dream of his, above playing football. His parents were kind and humble and it shows through Tom today. This was seven years ago, and I think he was wearing a University of Michigan hat backward. Even after seven years, this stands out more than most home visits. I'll remember bits and pieces of a lot of them, but I remember this one because they were just such humble people. They were just such great people. His father, you could tell, did his homework, but he wasn't going to sit there and act like the big shot. You get a whole range of fathers. Sometimes you get the father who has got the big ego, "And I'm my kid's representative, and he's not gonna sign for less then a bazillion dollars." The Bradys laid out exactly what they needed, and it was a lot of money. They were basically saying in order for their son not to go to Michigan, it's gonna cost you first or second-round money. But they weren't arrogant about it.

—— **MATT KING**, Major League Baseball Scout

I had a real interesting conversation with Tom after his first season in the NFL. He stopped by and he was here for over an hour. I was interested in a lot of different things, but there were a couple of things that really struck me that he had to say. He goes, "Coach, you know what? I know that I can play in this league." He said it with such confidence. It wasn't arrogance. It was just such self-confidence. He goes, "I know that, when I go in, I have to pay attention to detail. I know that when I drop back, whether it's a long pass down the field or whether it's just a swing pass, I know that I want to work on my technique. I want to do everything perfect, and I don't just go through the motions—ever. I'm not as good an athlete, and I'm not as good a passer as Drew Bledsoe, but I do know that because I pay attention to detail, when I get a chance and get an opportunity, I'm going to be able to make the most of it." Sure enough, the confidence, him saying, "this league's not too big for me, I can play at this level. I know that this is a very up and down game, and that anything can happen. I'm just going with the idea that whenever that opportunity presents itself, I'm gonna jump at it and I'm gonna be ready for it." The coaches back there had told him that at the end of the first season that they were real pleased with him and they were going to allow him to compete for the back-up job going into training camp last year. My first question was, "What's going to happen to Michael Bishop?" He goes, "Coach, I asked them the same question." They said, "Don't worry about Michael Bishop. Worry about yourself." Sure enough, he was given the chance. He was real excited about the prospect of going in and seeing that he was going to be able to compete for the back-up job.

——— TOM MACKENZIE, Tom Brady's head football coach at
Junipero Serra High School

As the Super Bowl went on, we were yelling a lot at each other and high-fiving each other. There were two guys next to me, Patriots' fans, and they had a few beers in them—they were loaded. During the game, I kept on jumping up. Our whole section was jumping up and down. There were only three lowly Rams fans three rows behind us, totally depressed. I look over to this kid next to me, and he wasn't getting up. I said to the kid, "What's the matter?" He goes, "I'm afraid of heights." They left after the first half, and we never saw them again. Since Bobby and I had been there before, we knew what to expect, but this guy was scared—he was like turning white. He was holding onto the seat. He was nervous. When we were high-fiving each other, he wouldn't even get up. He was very quiet.

——— BOBBY SHEA, Patriots Fan at the Super Bowl

Here's a kid where we're walking down the fairway, and I sort of just met Tom Senior, and got a handle that he was from San Fran and had his own consulting firm for ESOP deals. So then we kind of roamed over and caught up with young Tommy, and asked him where he was from. He said, "I'm up in Boston." I said, "Well, what do you do up there?" Just trying to catch up with him. He said, "I'm a fourth-string quarterback for the New England Patriots." After a few more holes, and getting to know him better and his disposition and his friendliness and saw that he was a quality young man. The professional athletes I know in Baltimore fortunately are kind of the good guys— Ripken, Brooks Robinson—those guys. You see so many of these guys that are just so very heady. Young Tommy was a gentleman. There's no question about that. We just had a good time with them. There was no special interest because of his involvement, and he certainly downplayed his position on the Patriots at the time.

During the Super Bowl we were very excited. We were rooting hard for New England, and we were rooting hard for him. It's funny you know, you kind of build up a support system for this. Suddenly some friends start to know about the relationship you have with him and other family members, and suddenly there's a support group just rooting and wishing this guy and his team well. My recall was that he said he was about a four or five handicap. I could certainly believe that. He hit the ball very well. I don't know how much time he gets to spend golfing, but I guess he might be getting a little more now. He'll probably get a few more invitations, too. He's just a regular guy.

—— P. DOUGLAS DOLLENBERG, Golf Partner in Ireland

I really didn't like Tom the first time I met him. But the last year, his senior year, I realized he was our captain and was the leader and you had to respect that. At the end of it, I thought he was a great guy. If you had any problems or needed to learn something, you could always go to Tom for it. Tom was an outgoing guy. He wasn't really in a clique or in a group. He could hang out with anybody and talk to anybody. That's the type of person he was. He was real sociable. He could socialize with anybody. Tom always seemed to be focused on whatever he was doing, especially in the game, just learning more and more about the game. If I had to pick one word, it would be 'focused,' just a real focused guy.

Tom used to talk about the coaches a little bit, just making fun of them, especially Coach Parish. How he yelled every five minutes, and Tom would just repeat what he said. I don't know how Tom did it, but he always was in the film room, more than anybody else. He could have watched film for everybody—that is how much he was in the film room. I remember days that I got up in the morning. I was down there at eight o'clock and you'd see Tom there with plays on a piece of paper giving it to Coach Carr. He was really into it. He'd have a game plan and have things he wanted to do. Nobody talked in the huddle. Only Tom could talk in the huddle. If you talked or interrupted him, he was quick to cut you off. When it's game time and serious, he's about business. He demands perfection, and that's what he got.

—— MARQUISE WALKER, Michigan teammate of Brady

Tom prepared very well. He would draw up plays himself. He would watch film and he would know what kind of game plan he wanted to see. Tom's success and his confidence definitely showed to the coaches and I think one of the reasons why Mike DeBord was a very good coordinator was that he listened to his players—particularly listening to a solid leader, a good intelligent quarterback. When your quarterback's leading your team, you want your quarterback to feel comfortable with what he's doing up there. I know Tom would go in there and would argue with DeBord for certain plays to get in. It was like, "Give me this play." Tom would always be wanting more check plays, little things that gave him more control. Tom's biggest frustration was to walk up to the line and look at the defense and know that the play is dead—that there's nothing he can do with the football, based on the defense and what's called. Tom always wanted as much options—he wanted to add as much of the thinking game and mental game and put as much of that into his control in a game because he can handle it. A lot of quarterbacks, the ones that are more afraid, just want something simple.

—— **JASON KAPSNER**, College teammate and friend

I think the competitiveness Tom got from his Mom, because his Mom's a tennis player and she refuses to let anybody beat her. Of course, his Dad used to beat Tom all the time in golf and then in the early stages of his collegiate career, we'd go out there and play with his Dad, and then he'd starting beating his Dad in the golf game. So his Dad was competitive in the golf and his Mom was competitive in tennis, and nobody wanted to play them because they weren't going to let you win. The other thing is that this is just the nicest family that you'd ever want to meet. You go and you greet them and like some people, they shake your hand. You greet the Bradys and you're going to get a hug, you're going to get a smile and "how are you doing." The one thing that did happen was that when I did leave Stanford to come back here to the Midwest, we had sold our house and so my wife was still out there working at Stanford. We were trying to figure out what she was going to do in terms of trying to find a place to stay before quitting work at Stanford and coming back here to the Midwest. The Bradys took her in and said she could have Tommy's old room because he's over in Michigan. So that even brought us closer to the family. This was a great bunch of people here. They're going to take the wife in and we really appreciated that.

—— **BILLY HARRIS**, Michigan coach who recruited Tom Brady

The main thing about being a Michigan quarterback is pressure. There is a mass amount of pressure on you compared to a lot of places. I remember Elvis Grbac coming back and telling us that it's harder to be a Michigan quarterback than it was to be a quarterback in the NFL. I never understood that, but actually going through this process and being here and being a part of watching Tommy and Brian go through what they did, it's hard. There's no doubt about it. The expectations here are unbelievable. That's probably part of the reason why Tommy is where he's at, is all of the struggles that he had to go through here at Michigan. He comments on this all the time as the reason that he's been able to accomplish the things he did outside of Michigan.

—— **SCOT LOEFFLER**, University of Michigan Quarterback Coach

The Bradys were 'regular' people. They weren't snobby or 'My son is the quarterback. And he might or might not win.' It was, 'Hey, wouldn't it great if they won—nobody's really counting on them win.' It was fun to sit and chat with them. His sisters tell stories. Now, he has a girlfriend who we did not meet. They told some funny stories where every time a girl called the house—he's a pretty good looking guy—they would screen the girls and check them out before they would let their baby brother go out with them, which we thought was quite cute.

—— GARY ROTHSTEIN, *New York Times* Photographer

As the season unfolded, I was really excited for Tom. I'm always excited for the underdog, and he's a great person so it happened to a really nice guy. He autographed pictures for the boys and sent them out right after the Super Bowl. Why? I called and asked him to, and told him to do it before he got too busy. He was very kind, and he wrote a little note and sent them off, and it was really nice.

I know of a couple of pranks they played on him, but I never really heard of him dating, and I never saw him with a girl at the times we were there. He may have had some girls after him, but I don't know. I never saw it. He's the type of man a woman wants her daughter to marry.

—— JULIE FRIESZ, wife of former Patriots quarterback, John Friesz

I was in a store here, and happened to pick up one of these publications that had John Wooden on the cover of it. He has always interested and fascinated me as regards to his philosophy and his approach to life and his approach to athletics. He has, what he calls, a 'pyramid for success' that took him fourteen years to develop. It's about fifteen building blocks, and the top block is 'competitive greatness'. Then along the edge, sort of that holds the blocks together in the form of a triangle, are different attributes. There are about fifteen of those. I think there is a total of thirty-one attributes.

Of course, this was after the Super Bowl, and in between the time when Tom came back to our school. My mind immediately went back to Tom Brady, and I asked myself, "Okay, you know what? I'm going to look at this thing and let's grade Tom Brady in each one of these areas." What I'm going to tell you is this: I couldn't give him less than an A minus in every single building block and attribute in the entire thing. To me, that's why Tom is who he is. That's why he's had the success of who he is because he has a tremendous degree of all these different attributes from industriousness, work ethic, loyalty, teamwork, unity and cooperation. There's a whole bunch of them. It would be hard not to give him the best grade available because of who he is and the way he acts. There are not many people that I can say that about. I think Tom can be as good as he wants to be.

—— TOM MACKENZIE, Tom Brady's head football coach at
Junipero Serra High School

If Brady had not decided to play football, I think he would have been drafted very high. A lot of it has to do with whether they'll sign. If you've got a top pick who's got a scholarship, let's say he was a baseball player, not football, but he had a scholarship to play baseball at Michigan. That would mean that we would have to be pretty darn sure that he was going to sign before we were going to commit a second or third or first-round pick on him. I can just tell you where I had Tom Brady rated. I had him rated as a second-third round pick. I thought he was good. From sitting and watching Brady from the stands, I felt he was very emotional, very driven. He's really matured. He was so cool. He was so confident. I just remember him being very emotional in a way that he really had high expectations for himself. I could tell that he was a team leader. When the team was losing or when they needed to get something going, he was a leader. He was a kid that really showed, 'Let's go. Come on. Let's get it going.' I remember him when he struck out. I just remember him when he struck out or made an out, he was kinda tough on himself. He's captured the respect of his teammates. You never know what a kid's gonna turn out to be from the standpoint of humbleness, but with Tom it has been no surprise at all. Just sitting in that house, watching him sit between his parents and he was just, "It's been my life-long dream to play major league baseball."

—— **MATT KING**, Major League Baseball Scout

We try to be low key when we have any celebrity on board. Something keyed in my brain when I was talking to Tom Brady, Sr. on the way down on the coach. I said, "I'm a Notre Dame fan myself. I remember working in my father's butcher shop every Saturday in the fall, and he would have the Notre Dame football game on the radio." There was a big rivalry between Notre Dame and Michigan. I don't think Tom, Sr. is thrilled with the way Notre Dame has conducted themselves over the past several years, and he's a big Michigan fan obviously. We kind of gave him a little bit of teasing back and forth there. Really we had two hundred and sixteen people in the event. It went very well, as it always does, but I didn't really get a chance to talk to them again until right after the final banquet. Wonderful, wonderful people.

—— **JERRY QUINLAN**, heads up an annual Father-Son Golf Tournament in Ireland each April.

"I knew Tom could do it." Coming out of Michigan, he'd had a lot of collegiate competition, and we knew he'd be able to do the same thing at the NFL level. He did some great things in Michigan, he just never got the credit he should have had. He also had a lot of confidence in himself that he could do it. I've always had a lot of confidence in him. The day before the Super Bowl, I called him up and said, "It's your time to shine, baby. Let's do it." And then he went and did it.

He said "I just can't believe all this is happening to me." That's one of the things that kind of surprised me—all this stuff that's going on. He's always been a laid-back guy, and now he's getting a lot of fame, a lot of things going on, a lot of people throwing stuff at him—he's still the same guy to me. We still will go out and do the same things. He's one of those guys that can be real fiery in the huddle. He's one of those guys that has a lot of confidence in what he can do and confidence in the team when he's around. So if he sees somebody slacking, he won't mind getting in their face once or twice even though he might be the smaller guy. He'll still try. He's just a great guy, and he was a great teammate.

—— **ANTHONY THOMAS**, Chicago Bears 2001 NFL Rookie of the Year

I watched him play in high school. You don't see his stress. I used to watch Tom Flores, the Raiders coach, when they were real bad, and he just stands there on the sideline. I'm just saying to myself, "If that was me, I'd be jumping up and down. I'd be choking the quarterback." And then they asked John Madden, "Well John, when you were coaching, you jumped up and down and you were running around." —and I have that Madden kind of a personality when I coach—by jumping up and down. John Madden said, "Well, have you ever seen a duck float across a pond on the top? He looks so cool and collected, but underneath he's paddling like heck." With Tommy, you never see that "paddling like heck." You never see the John Madden jumping up and down. You never see my boisterousness at the moment. He keeps it internal and whether he's "paddling like heck" underneath, we don't know, but you don't see that. You don't see that deviation from normal.

—— **TOM MARTINEZ**, Tom Brady's long-time Quarterback Coach

As time went on the first day or two, we didn't really talk together, but it became apparent that he was not your ordinary guy. I noticed people talking about him, "Well, what's the deal with this kid?" "He's a Patriots quarterback." "You're kidding me." Then they got more information about him and went up to him and said, "You didn't tell me you were a Patriots quarterback." From that there was a little tight-knit group of guys that hung out together—myself, Tom, Gary Williams, Doug Dollenberg, who was another young guy who was a scratch golfer from Maryland. It was matter of just having a great time. Even though here's a kid who was literally an NFL quarterback, which you don't run into every day, he was just another guy having a good time with his dad. They were just delightful. I never got to play with him. They played with the Buckleys, and we were in the foursome right behind him. There was one hole, I'll never forget this, and Tom is supposed to be about a five-handicap golfer. The eighteenth hole at Ballybunion is a very difficult hole, and you have to hit over a big dune. They hit, and we tee off. My father puts it on the top of a sixty-foot dune. Literally on the top of this thing. Lo and behold, about thirty feet away, there's Tom. His drive was up there, too, so I got a shot of both of them standing on the dune at Ballybunion.

—— **ROB CUNNINGHAM**, Golfing in Ireland with the Bradys

He was called 'Biscuits.' He used to be a little heavy, and we called him 'Biscuits' because he had the biggest butt in the world. He definitely had to get ripped on plenty—California surfer boy. He was a little bit of a 'pretty boy.' He would always be the last one ready to leave when we were going out because he definitely had to sit at the mirror and primped and got his gel on his hair and checked himself four times in the mirror. He was always perfect. Tom's the country club boy, so when we played golf, he always did better than we did. He was by far the best golfer. The guy that Tom always wanted to beat was Brian Griese. They're more at the same level. Tom's actually the one that introduced me to golf and got me into liking golf. When I got there as a freshman, I had never really played golf. That's kind of all there is to do in the summer, and we hung out. We had the same jobs. Tom and I had the same schedules for three years. We both had jobs at Merrill Lynch, where we interned and we would go from there to working out to playing golf—kind of our daily schedule. We would work three hours a week at the golf course and golf there every day so we were regular fixtures there. We had a pretty good time.

—— **JASON KAPSNER**, College teammate and friend

Tom Brady was a year younger than everybody in high school, the same age as my younger son. When they graduated, they had just barely turned seventeen. He was a late developer, skill-wise, very bright kid. Two things about Tommy that made him what he is today—in fact we just saw him this week. He came to our school and talked. I always kidded him that he made a real mistake: "When all this football joke is over with you get back to the sport you should be in, and you're gonna be an All-Star catcher." Two things Tom had—he was very bright, and he worked very hard in terms of learning what you're trying to teach. I don't care if it's just your basic 'where your feet should be' or 'your pre-swing waggle,' he would really work at it. Plus, he had some tremendous skill. He was a six foot, four kid that could throw, and a left-handed hitter.

—— **RICH JEFFERIES**, High School Hitting Coach

The biggest difference between us was in the bathroom. He was the primp, there's no doubt about it. He was always making himself look pretty. Every single thing that he does, he does it to the best of his ability. Whenever he goes and speaks in front of people, he's going to make sure it's the best that he can possibly speak. He's a perfectionist in every single thing he does and that's the reason why he's where he is now.

—— **SCOT LOEFFLER**, University of Michigan Quarterback Coach

I think Tom Brady is more of a gutsy guy. I think Tom Brady is the reason that team is here. I think Tom Brady is hungrier. I think they notice that and I think that's the reason they made the change when they made it. Bledsoe has all the talent in the world, but I like Brady's grit and dirt and bone. I'd love to play with the guy.

—— **CHI DI AHANOTU**, St. Louis Rams Defensive End

Tom had the worst possible first half of hitting in his Senior year. He couldn't even hit his way out of a paper bag. But at the end of the season he really came around and had a heck of a game against Saint Francis and he hit something like two home runs. As the catcher he instilled so much confidence in everyone else on the team. He was such a man behind the plate—the way he would catch the ball would make you feel like you're throwing the ball 50 mph when in reality you're throwing 85 mph.

Tom was fortunate enough to live close to school so he would always have his free time. He would go home and his mom would cook for him and he would play his video games and get ready for practice. He drove the worst car ever—a '75 Dodge. I think they got it for something like $200. But he didn't have to go far.

There was a time when we were over at the Taco Bell in San Mateo, and that was the place where people would usually hang out. We would go during summer time after bingo setup. Tom went to the Cal camp and he was telling us how he did against all these future major Division I players. It was interesting to hear what he was doing and he was telling us that he was the MVP of the camp, and it was so refreshing to hear that he was going to be on his way. And it was summer camp during the time that Mackenzie was coach, and that just really set the tempo. He was telling us that he might go to Cal, Illinois, USC, UCLA, or Michigan. And it was like 'MICHIGAN! What the heck is that?'

But talk about some good times. Every Thursday night, Tom, Steve Loerke and I would go to TGIF. We'd go there and just hang out for hours and totally BS the whole time. And it was a good thing because High School goes by so fast. It's nice to look back to the great times we had and we still go there and we sit for four hours. And we always end up getting the same thing and one guy would also put less in the pot than he owes. We'd just sit there and talk about anything and everything.

—— **KEVIN BRADY**, High School Teammate (No relation)

Pacific Trading Cards did a set with Brady. The March 1, 2002 issue of Sports Collectors Digest has Brady down as a kind of like the side-bar photo on the issue, but it's certainly not the dominant photo. To be honest with you, from a national news stand type publication, if we were to put something out with him on the cover right now, it would be too late, with football season over. His drawing power might be past from the standpoint of 'could we sell more with him versus right now maybe a baseball player, as that season gets started.' Or now when the season gets ready to go again in August and September, when we have issues ready to go out then, we have to ask ourselves, 'Will people recognize him?' On the magazine side of things from the newsstand, you generally only see the top portion of a magazine on a newsstand, so would people see someone in a Patriot's helmet and instantly 'Oh yeah, Tom Brady, I gotta get that.' Whereas a player such as Marshall Faulk, Brett Favre, those type players, you can put them on a cover and people know who they are without having to read the cut line. So that will be one of the internal debates we'll have, I'm sure, as we get into the summer months. Is Tom Brady national news stand for us, we're only doing twelve issues a year, will he be strong enough to sell a magazine versus a more veteran star? That's not to say we wouldn't do a story on him, but it's just a question of whether he'd be the cover feature.

—— **SCOTT KELNHOFFER**, *Sports Collectors Digest*

Tom Brady has made me a fan again of a player. At a certain age in your life, you stop really rooting for players. As a kid, you have your favorite players. I have a favorite player again. You may like certain guys. Now I root, unapologetically, for Tom Brady. He's my favorite player in the National Football League. That's something you feel like you'll lose once you become an adult. Having had the chance to be around him a little bit, I now have a favorite player in the NFL again. You know what—I'm not gonna apologize for it. That's something that he has added to that.

ary Williams, Tom Brady and Buck Williams preparing
to tee it up at Ballybunion.

Tom Brady with his Mom and Dad at Super Bowl XXXVI.

© Jim Mahoney

Tom Brady stretching during practice before Super Bowl XXXVI.

Tom Brady with the Most Valuable Player award from Super Bowl XXXVI

To the victors go the spoils...Judge Tom Brady at Miss USA Pageant.

MISS USA

It's thrilling to watch him play. It's more thrilling to know that he is a guy who is going to appreciate the success he's having. I'm thankful for that. That is something, that, even if he was a third-string quarterback, I'd root for him to get in and mop up. It is beyond my wildest dreams that I can root for a guy who a year ago, was trying to make the roster, and today he's the Super Bowl MVP. I've got a favorite player in the league again. As a thirty-five year old grown man, I love it 'cause I didn't think that would ever happen again in my life that I could want a guy's football card. That's very thrilling.

—— GARY WILLIAMS, Radio Talk Show Host

Several years ago, while playing football at Michigan, Tom Brady was a mentor to the fourth grade class I teach. He was the most unselfish, pleasant and hardworking young man you could ask for. The children and staff at Eberwhite Elementary in Ann Arbor are proud of him and wish him the best.

—— SHARON GREELY, Michigan fourth grade teacher

I don't think anybody's going to believe this, but right as we broke five hundred we were talking about the season and about how practice was going and he just interrupted and said, "We're going to the Super Bowl." I mean the way he said it and how he looked, I knew he wasn't just saying it. He was totally serious and confident. To me it seemed that he was going to just do everything in his power to get there. That made me want to do everything I could do and that's exactly what happened to our team this year. Everyone captured his enthusiasm and his desire to be the best that we could be. That's what ultimately happened.

I remember he made that remark real early in the season—too early for anyone to ever even think anything like that.

The way Tom said it, and the relationship I have with him, I know that he's not going to BS me. I believe him! He's our quarterback so obviously that's a key position if you're going to go to the Super Bowl. I knew that if he was going to do everything he could do, and if I could do everything I could do, and if everybody would do that—we had a chance.

—— DAVID NUGENT, Close friend and roommate

Chapter 8

Let's Get Technical, Technical

Let Me Hear the Coaches Talk, Coaches Talk

Tom Martinez

Matt King

Phil Gratsinopoulos

HE FOUND TOM BRADY DOWN AT THE CORNER OF WHAT AND IF
TOM MARTINEZ

Tom Martinez is a legend in California coaching circles. He is currently the softball coach at the College of San Mateo. He has also coached Women's basketball and football there, at one time serving as the head coach of all three at the same time. He has over twelve hundred and fifty wins at CSM.

CSM played a style of offensive football under Martinez that was cutting-edge for the time, a wide-open, sophisticated passing offense that is now used by teams all over the country.

Martinez wears half his lunch on his sweatshirt and works out of a narrow, cramped office overflowing with papers, equipment and video tapes. ("I know where everything is!")

Students approach Martinez with total respect and his love of teaching and coaching is evident in everything he does.

"Obviously, he's the guru of quarterbacks and softball," said Tom Brady, Sr., the quarterback's father. "Before Tommy's first start at Serra, he went into brainlock. We went up to see Tom Martinez and it took Tom about thirty seconds to relax Tommy, and get him ready to play

> **"Obviously, he's the guru of quarterbacks..."**

his first game. I remember he said, 'Let's go down and throw the ball a few minutes.' We did it and then everything was okay.

After Tommy's first year at Michigan, Martinez took him aside for an hour. Tommy was having a hard time throwing to his left. I filmed that session and Tommy must have played it back 200 times, literally, while he was at Michigan. Tom Martinez showed him how to take a drop and point his shoulder so the ball zips and doesn't spin. And that's just Tom Martinez doing for a kid what he's done for so many kids."

Tom Brady knows that there are no rest areas on the 'road to success,' but he may have found a secret short-cut with Coach Martinez.

It all started with the girls. Maureen is the oldest daughter. I coach softball and football at the College of San Mateo. I've run camps for as long as I've been here. So the girls came to the softball hitting camps. Maureen, the oldest one, was a phenom when she was very, very young—ten, maybe eleven—way before high school. So, she started coming to these softball camps and then she went into high school, and she was big for her age. So right away she was a phenom as a high school softball pitcher. Obviously, you're aware of them as they grow up 'cause everybody's talking about these young kids that are so good. Then came Julie, and then Nancy, and along came Tom. He was the only boy. All the local energy was going into the girls.

It all started with the Brady girls...

My camps are small. I don't do them to have 100 kids there. I do them so that the kids that come there get taught, so the camps are very small and personal, and I do all the teaching. There are people who work with me, but I don't hire them and then go sit and have a beer and watch everybody else coach them. Tom came up to camp. He didn't really stand out at the time. He was young. You can see that there is athleticism in the family in the sense of being able to catch and throw and all those kinds of things. He was never "Michael Vick" with feet—where you look up and you see a guy running all over the place and he just leaps out at you—that's not him.

There he was and he was going through it and he was going to the camps and then he came back. What was so amazing to me is just that he came back and he had grasped all the things that we do, even though I break it down in the utmost, finest detail. Most of it sails right over the head of a thirteen-year-old kid. I count on the fact that they will come back and that the next year they'll be more receptive to the things that they went away, tried and couldn't do. So, there he was, and had mastered for his age in the type of offenses that a high school frosh-soph team would run. He looked pretty good, and in the Brady way, he certainly wasn't going to be anywhere near the bottom of the barrel. He was still growing.

Then each year after that he came back. I'd never called him, never—not once. I'd leave it up to him, and he's always been very—I don't want to say the word "good"—that sounds like its good for me—but he's always been very honest when he needs something. He'd call me when he was in high school and he'd say, "It doesn't feel right. After you guys finish, would you spend a half hour, forty-five minutes with me?" So he'd come up with his dad and we'd spend whatever it was, half hour— forty-five minutes—

whatever. I could critique him very quickly and very accurately. I never sat down. I never try to tell a kid, "Hey, come to this camp because it's better than that other camp. I've worked a lot of big time college camps and I see what they do—the purpose and intent. The majority of those camps are not about mechanics. They am not about fundamentals. They are not about putting the kid through the camp and making money for coaches in the program. The kids play 7 on 7 and go home with a big smile on their faces.

Tom kept coming back to my quarterback camps. What's so amazing about Tom is he can assimilate what you tell him faster than anybody that I've ever coached. The next thing you know, within x number of throws, he's corrected what you tell him. I'm very detailed about what I tell him—the point of the ball and where it goes, and how do you make it go one way, and how do you make it go your way, and what happens if you're doing it the opposite way and how do you correct it, etc. One guy asked me—it might have been the guy at the Boston Globe, I don't remember, there's been so many now—he said, "Well how did you know when he was special?"

One day he came up to the school, and all of a sudden the ball started to come in like a man was throwing it instead of the high school boy.

One day he came up to the school, and all of a sudden the ball started to come in like a man was throwing it instead of the high school boy. Tom was still in high school at the time. There's a heavy ball and there's a light ball. The ball started coming in heavy, and if you throw it correctly, it should. The first two throws of the Super Bowl, he really put something on those. So, the ball started coming heavy and you can feel it. If you're catching it, all of a sudden you go "wow." It's one that will sting your hands a little bit. That's why when I keep hearing that Bledsoe has a better arm, you know that's a pile of crap. Bledsoe throws sidearm, and you can go get me anybody who throws sidearm, like Rich Gannon—go take Rich Gannon and get me a guy who throws overhand. The guy who throws overhand is going to throw the ball harder than the guy who throws sidearm, and I don't give a darn who you're talking about. So to me, Tom Brady—if you watch him—he's very, very mechanically good. The guys that do it that way are a heck of a lot better than the guys who don't. Anyway, to make a long story short, the ball all of a sudden—BANG—I mean the ball started to come in. At that time, Brady was not really a weight-trained, studly looking kid—all of a sudden the ball's coming in like a man's throwing it and you say "whooo."

What does the announcer mean when he says that the quarterback throws a "heavy" ball? From ball standpoint, there's two ways to look at it. Number one: if you caught it, there are balls that come in that are like somebody threw you a balloon and you catch it and it goes into your hand and it's accurate and right where it should be. There's not a lot of feeling—you have those little ribs on the end of them, and you catch it. Then there's the ball—and it feels like it's been sitting in water for three days—a leather ball sitting in water and it's heavy as heck, and it hits your hands and it feels like it weighs ten times what it weighs. There's a penetration. One of the terminologies—not "buzz" words—that I would use if I were teaching you is throw the ball *through* the receiver, not to him. Just like a horse. I can't ride a horse. I get on a horse and I know that darn horse says, "This guy's a city boy." Okay, you get the old cowboy on the horse and the horse knows that this guy knows how to ride. It's the same thing. If you're catching a ball and the guy throws it and it comes in kind of soft, you get one feeling, and when that guy comes with what appears to be a weighted ball and it hits your hands—it's a message that you don't have to say anything about...and a lot of that has to do with how the point of the ball approaches. If the point is up, the ball is softer, and if the point is down, the ball is harder.

...throw the ball through the receiver, not to him.

I use this example with young kids. I get frustrated. I stand behind them. If you drop back and you set your feet and you go to throw it, I'll say, "Now," and so you still have the ball in your hand. I had a couple of kids turn around and say, "Coach, don't do that." I said, "No, I'm gonna do it, because when the ball goes out of your hand when I say 'now,' then your ball's coming out at the correct time—if you still have it, then what? You're late." So, I'd get frustrated. It helps me to help with them. I tell kids: When the computers first came out, they came out with an Apple I, and Apple I went 8 times 6 equals 48. Then they came out with an Apple II, and it went 8 times 6 equals 48. Then they came out with Apple III: 8 times 6 equals 48. Now, is the answer correct in all three? They will say, "yes." What's the answer? "48." Okay, if you're athletic, two of those three are too slow. Now, I started to tell them, that was an Apple I decision—that was an Apple II decision—that was an Apple III decision, and it really made it much more understandable without getting on them.

The other thing—these are just coaching points from my end of it—arm speed tells you what a guy's thinking. One of the kids I had went back to Pitt and he played for Mike Gottfried. He got back there and Mike Gottfried filmed the scrimmage or whatever it is at the end of the Spring. So, he brought it and spoke at the clinic, and I went up to hear him. He showed it and he said, "What do you think?" I said, "He's confused." He said, "How do you know?" And I said, "His arm speed." The example being, that if some guy came by and took your wife's purse and he started to run and you had a rock, and you knew it was him, you'd fire that thing at him because you knew it was him right? You'd try to knock him down. Now, if three guys ran by and one guy picked it up and you had the rock and you weren't sure which guy had the purse, you don't fire it. You throw it slower because you're unsure. So, two things show you— one, their eyes, and two, their arm speed. So, getting back to those two combinations—I could tell a guy what he just did— that's an Apple I decision. The guy was open—the answer's 48—you're right. See, you'll get in an argument with the kid. He'll say, "Coach the guy was open, that's why I threw it." I said, "Yeah, but you threw it late—that ball should have gone Apple III."

> **Tom can feel it within a very few number of throws and that's the part that's kind of gratifying to me...**

Also that day, the point tip of the football wasn't quite doing what we wanted it to do, so we corrected it. Tom can feel it within a very few number of throws and that's the part that's kind of gratifying to me—not rewarding, it's gratifying—is to teach somebody something and then actually having them be able to use it and actually be able to feel what you're telling them and see it happen in front of you. That doesn't happen in coaching too fast. So, to do that is gratifying as a teacher. In that period of time, all of a sudden, yeah, you start saying, "Now he can start throwing those deeper outs. Now he can start throwing comebacks. Now he can start throwing the ball up the field a little bit further on routes that a typical high school, without a sophisticated passing game, can't do."

Of the twenty kids in my quarterback camp each year, very few would ever call me in the ensuing months, but Tom Brady always did. In twenty-seven years of doing camps, no one called like Tom Brady.

I used to work the John and Jack Elway football camp for Jack at Stanford. They would give me all their guys that were going to be seniors in high

> John Elway, Deion Sanders and Billy Cannon, Jr. were signed by George Steinbrenner for the Yankees and given $100,000+ bonuses. All three quit baseball for the NFL.

school that they wanted evaluated. So, the years that they were there when John was there for the camp, and he didn't do any teaching—he'd just watch, but Todd Marinovich went through it—Dan McGwire, Mark McGwire's brother went through it—Gino Torreta went through, Rob Johnson went through—there's ten or twelve very successful quarterbacks who went through those camps at that particular time. One of the kids who I had coached here at the College of San Mateo was the offensive coordinator at Stanford. When I would get to the Stanford camp, he'd give me those quarterbacks…so I'd get a pack of them—eight or ten of them and then I'd give my opinion of their arm strength, mechanics and decision-making ability, and a lot of things that I've broken down into smaller detail that I think are important other than watching how many miles per hour the guy can throw it. Then a lot of parents started to come up and say, "Hey, you ought to run a camp yourself, then I'd get my kid into your group." So that's when I started the Tom Martinez Quarterback and Receiver Camp at the College of San Mateo.

It's all about what you're about. For me, I've never been about taking money and going and buying something and getting gratification from that. The gratification has come from watching a kid, from putting a smile on their face, you know, teaching them the fundamentals. There's a "feel" that when you start to throw the ball correctly and you know you are in control of the ball. It gives you confidence, because you know now you are in control. You deal with periods of times where there were twenty-eight NFL teams and there were twelve quarterback coaches. If you look now at the major universities, there's a lot of guys that are young quarterback coaches that are there because they were quarterbacks, not necessarily because they really understand it. I grew up with Mike Holmgren, I've listened to Paul Hackett and there's a series of fifty greatest buzzwords to be a quarterback coach. If you just walk around, you can hear them everywhere. They're undisputed because nobody asks any question, yet most of them are nothing but cliché words. They're words that you don't know what the heck you're talking about, and you throw one of them out and you look around and everybody kinda… "Hey," and nobody asks a question and, "Hey, that sounds good." I hear a couple of these guys speak at clinics and they're throwing buzz words around. Everybody walks out. They've got the same

> Mark McGwire's brother, Dan McGwire, a former #1 pick of the Seahawks, is the tallest NFL QB ever at 6'8".
> Former Celtic and Toronto Blue Jay Danny Ainge is the tallest second baseman in Major League history.

fifty down and they go back home and they don't know what the heck they mean. But somebody in 1943 started saying that, and it might have been somebody very prominent, so he spoke at a clinic and some guy copies it and he carries it on and you get a vocabulary that is acceptable to your environment. It all sounds good…and up you go and the next thing you know, you're a Nostrodamus. I mean, I'm an old-timer and I always say, "Tell it like you smell it." When you see me, you get what you get.

All of a sudden, who's the guy who always came back here? Tommy. You know why? Made sense to him. I don't throw buzz words out that I can't explain. I have a vocabulary to teach, but it teaches you words that will get your muscles to do what they need to do. It's not a word you yell out at a camp so when everybody hears it, it sounds like, "Jeepers, well, this guy's a genius." There's some people that people give a whole lot of credit to, and I've listened and I've asked questions and, to be honest with you, they can't teach it. So, I think Tom felt comfortable that I knew what the heck I was talking about and that I could explain it to him in terms that he both understood and could very quickly assimilate. He was smart enough to know when it didn't, and then when it didn't, he'd come up and—he'd never say, "You know, I've got about ninety percent of this down. It's just this last ten percent here that I have to…" You could see he went and worked on it. So those he was fine and comfortable with, and then the ones that he wasn't— he had an extra dime to call up.

Before Tom's Senior year, he went to the Cal camp and they were really hurting at the time. They had gone through a series of coaching changes. They were on their way south. He was the Most Valuable Player in the camp. A lot of times, what college camps do is they'll pick out a kid they want to recruit and all of a sudden the guy's the Most Valuable Player in the camp. I'm not suggesting that he wasn't. I'm just saying that I've sat in on meetings where, "What do you think of this guy?" "I like that guy better" "Well, we want this guy so we're going to give him a certificate," so that he walks away from Cal with a certificate. He became their number one recruit. I think it was Cal Coach Keith Gilbertson, but I'm not sure whether it was Gilbertson on his way out or Gilbertson going into his last year. It was before Steve Mariucci arrived as head coach at Cal. Once you hit it in a

Steve Mariucci, 49ers coach, and Tom Izzo, Michigan State Basketball coach, were childhood and high school best friends in Iron Mountain, Michigan.

camp like that and somebody really wants you—it's true of every kid that's been here—once somebody "legitimate" lays it on you, they want you. Then all of a sudden everybody wants you because now you're were good enough for them. That labels you as being okay. Anyway, then all of sudden Tom jumped up in the ratings. I don't know anything about how Michigan got in on the deal—and then he went to Michigan. That was surprising because we had not had a lot of Midwest or East Coast contacts out here.

Obviously, the first part of Michigan was frustrating. I think he may have expected it at the beginning, but then as time wore on his dad called and we'd talked a couple of times about, "Would it be a good thing if Tommy transferred?" I said, "You don't want to start jumping around." It's hardly ever worked for the people that have done that. You've made a decision and now you've just got to go and battle. The other thing is, who's to know even at that point—that any of this was possible. So, I just said, "You picked it..." And I always ask, "If you got hurt, would you transfer from that school?" "Well, yeah I would." "Well then, that's not a good decision when you're going there for football." A lot of people say "No, I really like it." They have a "Major." To go through all that is whatever it is that they like about it, and I say, "Okay, good, because you're liable to get hurt. You're liable to blow your knee out and your career is over with, and now is it a good decision?" So, the Bradys went through those thought processes of maybe moving him, and he stayed. To me, his Michigan experience was really a great foundation to build on, although it probably didn't seem that way at the time. I think, number one: playing before that many people prepared him for the big crowds in the NFL; number two: I think the fact that he had to compete, especially with Drew Henson, gave him the experience of not necessarily just being handed something; and number three: I think the offense of Michigan was probably very similar to what Belichick was

> The Rose Bowl Parade originally had nothing to do with the Rose Bowl football game. It was a celebration in Pasadena for the ripening of the oranges.

> Gatorade is named after the mascot for the University of Florida. It was developed by a professor there under a grant from Stokeley-VanCamp.

> Steve Spurrier was the only quarterback to go 0-14 in one NFL season, with the '76 Buccaneers.

trying to do, especially at the beginning, with him at New England. I think he couldn't have gone to a better place to prepare him. Now he could have gone to Florida and thrown it more times, and he could have gone to some other places that you might say, "Hey, he got to throw it twenty five more times a game." But, playing in the Rose Bowl and in the Orange Bowl and all the things that happened at Michigan, I think really took him from possibly a young man to a man.

Did I ever think he'd be able to start at Michigan? Probably, the answer is "no." I could say, "Yeah, oh yeah, geez," but they can pick from the top thirty quarterbacks in the United States, and in high school he never was given a situation where he was able to throw the ball enough times in games that you could really say, "Well, he's throwing it fifty times a game and completing thirty five. He's a shoo-in." I mean, he was throwing it sixteen times and completing ten. So for me to stand here and say, "Yeah, I thought he could go to Michigan and win the Rose Bowl,"—I'd be BS'ing. On the other hand, as I've stepped back and watched him, Tom Brady is a person who has all the attributes that it took to make this thing happen, and his parents who gave him and put him, and all the girls too, in situations to succeed. I think when you stir that around—his parents guiding him into very, very good environmental situations and the experience of Michigan from crowd to ballgames to offense to competition against other quarterbacks, when maybe the coaches weren't pulling for you. I think all of those things led to this wonderful season, and he's the guy that's been able to put it all together in just a frightening quick hurry.

He's never had a camp where he was the "guy." I don't care what anybody says, he's never prepared to be the starting quarterback of the New England Patriots. You let a guy go into a camp as a starter, and he's throwing to the number one receiver, not the guy that's going to be cut the next day. So, he's never had a camp to prepare for this.

How many times is an NFL quarterback going to complete five out of five on third down?

Belichick didn't want a guy that wanted to throw it forty times. I don't think Bledsoe would be happy going back with Belichick and hearing "Okay, we're going to run it seventy percent of the time." Like they said, "Well, he completed sixty-four percent of his passes." I said, "You know what? He completed most of them on third down early in the year." What's the ratio on third down? It's not throwing like Montana used to throw on first down and complete seventy-five percent, and then third down maybe he's completing forty-five percent, and you put those two together and he averages sixty four percent. Through DirecTV, I watched Tom play some games, and it was run first down, run second down—it was third and seven. Then he had to throw it third and seven— first down. They got eight yards. Then they came back—run the first down, run second down—now it's third and 5. He completes another one—well, he's two for two on third downs, and in any given drive, how many times is an NFL quarterback going to complete five out of five on third down? He might complete five of five on a drive, but he's not going to complete five of five on third down. So, to me, you look at the statistics and say that the Patriot's point and purpose was to run the ball, use the clock and let Belichick win the game with his defenses. Tom Brady is the perfect quarterback for Belichick. I said that a long time ago. Brady didn't care if he threw it—he was playing—number one, and they were winning— number two, and so he's like a "pig in poop." He's happy. Now you take the other guy—I'm not picking on Bledsoe—I'm just saying, you take that kind of a quarterback who's made money and his name and fame from throwing four touchdowns a game—they don't like that. They don't want to play for a coach that runs the ball seventy five percent of the time. They're the ones in talking to the owner begging to get an offensive coach in here.

When Tom got drafted in the sixth round by the Patriots in 2000, I was just hoping that he would make the team. Many of Tom's friends were particularly worried about Michael Bishop of Kansas State, a mobile, strong-armed quarterback who was ahead of Tom on the Patriots depth chart. Bishop is a great scrambler, but scramblers don't win titles in the NFL. Fran Tarkenton started off as a scrambler, but didn't end up that way.

Do you know why Steve Young ran so much in the beginning? He'd drop back and his eyes were up the field for about a second and a half. As soon as the first guy was covered, his eyes went down and he's trying to figure what all he could run through. After a couple of years, he stays in the pocket and wins the Super Bowl. If you throw on the run, your percentage goes down big time and your interceptions go through the roof. If you put Michael Bishop third down and six and you tell him to convert five balls on third down—there's no way! I mean, I'd go borrow from the bank at fifty percent.

During the Super Bowl, the announcers said Brady was sacked forty-one times. Someone asked me, "What do you think about that?" Well, if you're a coach who has a good defense, you demand that the quarterback takes the

> The Packers have sold out every game since 1960 and at $40 have the lowest average ticket price in the NFL.

sack rather than throw it up for grabs. A few years ago, I went back to Green Bay to see my childhood friends, Mike Holmgren and Gil Haskell, who were, of course, coaching there. We were looking at Packer film after Brett Favre's second year. Favre had thrown twenty-six interceptions and eighteen happened when he was on the run. When a play broke down timing-wise, he started to run around. All of a sudden he looked across the field and he saw a guy that was five yards away from his corner, and he threw it across the field to the other side. Then the defensive back just goes back and "signals for a fair catch." Almost all the interceptions were scrambling around when he really wasn't sure where to go. Well, Brady didn't do that, he stays in the pocket, and he hangs in there until the last second.

Things in the Bowl of Life are in there for a reason, now who knows why?

There's a couple of plays on that last Super Bowl drive where he threw it at the last possible moment. I think the first two plays where he hit the back right over the middle—he held onto that ball as long as he possibly could.

Things in the Bowl of Life are in there for a reason, now who knows why? There's fate, there's luck, there's whatever you want to say. Tom Brady would be Superman if he had just had all these things himself. That's why I trace it back. His parents have put him in situations, not for this to happen, because who the heck knew that this would happen, but wherever he was going, he would be prepared when he got there. I'm sitting there watching the fourth quarter of the Super Bowl and saying, "I hope the world doesn't come tumbling down because it could get as ugly as it is positive in a fast hurry." But, I'm looking at him and saying, "He's making great decisions." There are at least three plays on that last drive against the Raiders where he looks right and it's covered or it's too close—he goes all the way back to the left. Well, show me a fifth year guy that does that. They look and the guy's covered, and that's when Steve Young ducked his head and ran with it—got three yards, used up 30 seconds on the clock, and you know why? He didn't know where to go with it. You look at this guy—first year starting—he's looking one way—it's not there— then he looks the other way, picks up the first down and away they go. You say, "Where the heck did that come from?" Well, you know what?

It is true that NBA Coach Pat Riley never played college football, but was drafted by the Dallas Cowboys. His brother, Lee, played seven years in the NFL. It is not true that Pat Riley combs his hair with a pork chop.

That's what I said, I think Michigan was just an unbelievable decision for him. People are tracing it back to me. Here's my feeling with that: number one, I think I'm the first person that ever made sense to him mechanically, and it wasn't "buzz" words. There are teaching, coaching, terms that teach certain things, but they're not that cliché 'doesn't mean crap' kind of word if you know what I'm saying. So all of a sudden, off he goes. It's kind of why I'm uncomfortable with speaking on his behalf because I've never called him. I've never called his dad. I've never called his mom. I'm so happy for all of them and they're class people and everything else, but I don't want to ever say anything that makes it sound like I'm standing up and running down the middle of the Michigan band being leader of the band— "Look what I did"—because that's not me—never been me. Yet, I think where he goes back to me is I think I broke it down for him in finer detail than it's ever happened for him. I think when he comes back and it doesn't feel right then I can correct him. When I correct him, then he has the ability to correct it, and he'll say in front of me, "Now that feels good." So when he came last year in March or April, right before their minicamp, he said, "I always like to come back and get a little tuned up." So we worked on throwing deep, on how to throw deep and those kinds of things. He wasn't throwing to Brown and Patten and Glenn—he wasn't throwing to those guys. He might in a drill someplace, but he isn't doing a scrimmage or anything that means anything—that's Bledsoe.

So, it's hard—that's why I was trying to tell him that when you work with people longer, you will understand their bursts. You'll understand certain things, but as a generality. I'd say, "Here's what I would do if I were you. What you're asking me— here's how you make it look better. Here's how you make it succeed given certain unknowns or certain situations." Now, if you've played with a guy for a year and a half or two years, you're going to complete it eighty percent of the time—not in the beginning. So, that's kind of what we did and then he just threw. We've got a kid that once played here to catch…and we worked on it, and all of a sudden, right away—not very long—there he goes and the ball's right there. He says, "See, I feel it. I got it." We did some other things and then he turns around and walks over to the kid who's been catching his deep throws. We were out there an hour, I guess, and he gives this kid an NFL football. You should have seen the kid's eyes. All of our softball girls are sitting there. I can't get them to a softball game on time or to leave for a game on time, and they're there an hour early

> Former astronaut and Senator John Glenn was
> Ted Williams' squadron leader in Korea.
> Ted Williams was John Glenn's wing man.

to see Tom Brady. They're looking—and this kid's eyes—he just saw Santa Claus. He did that, and then after the Indianapolis game, through his dad, he sent the game ball. There's a class in there. Even at the end of the Super Bowl in the interview, when they're giving the Most Valuable Player things—he gives Bledsoe credit—"If he hadn't have done it last week, we wouldn't be standing here today." Those are things that are well beyond twenty four years of maturity. It separates—that's why he's there and a whole lot of guys are drinking beer and watching it on television.

You know the thing that's so impressive about Tom Brady? This is my observation and I could be wrong. I think because of the supervision of his parents, he would have transferred this ability to finalize, detail and prepare his mind for anything he did. Therefore, those are the self-directed people. To me, it's like going into a class, maybe from a grade professor, and he's talking about how to plant tomatoes, and you come out and you plant cucumbers, and your cucumbers turn out just as good as his tomatoes because you were able to take the process and apply it to a different situation. So many kids that I see in today's deal—they can't even simulate anything that you taught them because they are not good listeners. I sense that with him, whatever direction he goes in, he's going to approach it with the same professionalism and intensity—none of which is self-centered.

Let's say that somebody says, "You know what, he went to your camp—I'm going to send my kid to your camp." Now what do you think they think? They think they're going to pay whatever the fee is and then in six years the guy is going to be standing up there getting a Super Bowl trophy. The point is that there is so much more to it than just going to a camp. You have to have the ability to assimilate whatever somebody teaches you. You have to be able to pay attention to detail—you can't get caught up in "hoopla." Belichick, as great a game plan as he did, which was awesome, the greatest thing he did was to keep that team together because it could have split in a "New York" hurry. If I'm one of those big tackles who's been in the NFL for fourteen years, I don't give a crap if it's Tom Brady or Drew Bledsoe—I want a ring. When it comes down to the end, I don't care who plays and all the sentiment and that kind of stuff—that's for after the game and that's to talk about when you're fifty years old. I want to win that dang game!

To have that leadership quality—it's like "cat hairs"—there are a lot of people that walk by and don't get any "cat hairs" on them. I think he walks by people and he gets all the cat hairs on him. I mean, he's picking up cat

> The rings for the Super Bowl winners cost
> twice as much as the rings for the losers.

hairs from everybody he's ever been around. So ultimately who's responsible? Everybody is. Yet I personally think not enough credit is given to the mom and dad because they put him in a situation where there were cat hairs to be rubbed off on, and then he just walked by and they rubbed off on him and I think he's been able to take advantage. He's not trying to get earrings in every orifice, and he's not trying to get lucky. I mean, that's not his one and two goal. And you know what? That's probably the goal of ninety five percent of the rest of them. So when you get so caught up in what you're trying to become that you are not what you really are, then I think you waste a whole lot of opportunity because your nose is going in the wrong direction.

> **He's not trying to get earrings in every orifice, and he's not trying to get lucky.**

All I can say is that he's been in good situations. Even the ones that aren't as good as they could be—I think he turned them around and made them positive. It would be a heck of a thing to figure out what the heck he's all about, but you know what? I don't think many people understand that these factors go into it, and they think that you walk up and down the line and you get an injection of mechanics, and therefore you're pretty damn good. It goes way beyond that. And it's what it turned out to be. You put him up with those other guys, and he's probably the best second quarterback in the NFL. I think he did way better than Drew Bledsoe would have done. If Drew Bledsoe played, I don't think they would have gotten to the Super Bowl. I'm not a big Bledsoe mechanics guy. I think he's an interception or a sidearm throw away from losing a game. You're paying a hundred million to Bledsoe and three hundred thousand to Brady. You can't expect the guy for three hundred thousand to give you what a guy for one hundred million is going to give you. But you know what you don't want? You don't want a guy to come in and lose the game. To me, if you look at him, and he was playing behind Warner, just as an example, he would never lose a game for the Rams. He's going to get the ball to the guy that he needs to get it to and he's going to figure out how to not turn it over. If you look at Tom Brady, he looks like he's been out there since he was born. But the greatest number is winning, and that's the part where somebody said to me, "Do you know what his record was at Michigan and what his record was at New England…put it together? Holy cow, it's something like 34-8.

To be honest with you, and this is going to sound phony and it really isn't, I've been doing this long enough now that the two things that meant the most to me, that I was really rooting for, was for his class, number one. And I do that whether I've been around someone or not. There are just certain people in athletics that you know, Cal Ripken—maybe he's the extreme at one end of it, but you're rooting for him—John Elway to win the Super Bowl—you root for John Elway 'cause John's got a lot of everything else going for him, but you know what? He was a heck of a quarterback and he went all those years and he didn't win it. You say, "Hey, he's a good guy—I want him to win it and I hope he wins it for his legacy." So, Tommy Brady is as nice a person as you're ever going to meet in your whole I life so, number one, from that perspective—that jumps up at me. If he was a jerk and he had gone through here, you'd still say, "Well yeah, you know….", but you'd be a fan of his if you ever just saw him and talked with him for five minutes. So, that makes it easy to do that. The other part of it is that I'm big on values. I'm old-fashioned and my parents raised me that way. Respect is a word that has disappeared from our society. Respect of young kids

> **Tommy Brady is as nice a person as you're ever going to meet in your whole I life**

to older people—respect from me to my parents—respect from people to police officers, respect from kids to teachers—I mean, you go down the line and the word is gone. They found every other way to tear it apart. Like I said, I've never made one phone call to Tom—ever, and my wife kept telling me, "Call him, call him—wish him well in the Super Bowl." There are a couple things I saw that he was doing, and if he chooses to call, then I'll show him. I'll say, "These are things I saw." I'm not going to call him up and give him, you know… "Hey Tom, guess what?" I don't do that—that's not me. I might have when I was younger, but I'm older now and I don't do that. Even though it's happened, he'll call, and he'll call in good time. And if he doesn't call, he's got a whole lot of stuff going on that's more important. I know him well enough that it meant something to him, and the greatest thing he could ever have done was to take that game ball from the Indianapolis game, his first NFL start, and sign it and send it to me. He played the game and obviously we knew he was going to play and everything so I watched it.

His sisters were at the game. The telecast kept showing them in the stands. The next thing you know, the next week his dad came up to the school one day and said, "Here, Tommy wants you to have this." It was the game ball from the Indianapolis game. He wrote the date and the score. I'm going to misquote it, but he said something like, "The first one of many," and then he signed it. To me, that spoke volumes. It gets back to what I'm saying and I'm not trying to be a jerk, but I want everything that happens to come from him. He doesn't owe me a penny, and if he calls up, and he wanted to do it weekly, I'd be there for him. To me, people start taking advantage of other people and I'm just of the feeling that if he felt in his own mind that he didn't need to do anything, then he shouldn't—then God bless him for doing it. I've never been around a person who would have ever done anything like that—getting your first start in the NFL and then sending somebody else the game ball. I think I could live another hundred years and—I couldn't believe it. Our Board members at the school were talking about it and a couple of people started to cry—saying they got tears in their eyes. I wasn't there. I said, "This is unbelievable." I don't want to say this because he doesn't want it to be that way and I think it would ruin him with his teammates, but

> **...and I think it would ruin him with his teammates, but he's darn near the perfect guy.**

he's darn near the perfect guy. If that starts coming out, then I think it's going to hurt him more than help him—all this generosity and all this good guy stuff he's going to take crap for. But that's who he is, and to sit there on national television and say, "Hey, we wouldn't be here if it wasn't for Bledsoe last week." It's always somebody else and it's always in an appropriate manner.

I'll tell you one thing—he's something else! The things I try to tell the kids—if all we're talking about is how to hit an outside drop to right field, we've all wasted our time. How do you apply what we're trying to show you to any frustration you have in your life? How do you apply preparation to success? Is any of it lucky? Is any of it planned for? Even the best laid plans—are they ever going to fail? And, how do you deal with it? To me, the more I get to read those kinds of books about successful people, the more I appreciate them, because you can read statistics, and obviously, statistics are deceiving because if you played every game in your life in Foxboro in the snow, and another guy played in St. Louis in the Dome, you can't look at numbers and say this guy completed two hundred and the other guy completed eighty, so the guy that complete two hundred is better than the guy that completed eighty. It's the human part of it. That's where I think he's still a "virgin in the bushes." I think as people get to know him, they'll learn it's not phony—it's not made up. There are too many circumstances where the quality of a person arises for it to be programmed.

I would never want the Bradys to think that I'm running out to be the "leader of the band" because of what happened. That's the furthest thing from the truth. Yet I've spent my whole life coaching and in the state of California. I've won more games than any coach in the history of community college athletics. This year I think I'm going to pass fourteen hundred, and no coach has ever won a thousand games in the state of California in combined or any one sport or anything, so it's not like I'm looking out of a peep hole at somebody and trying to manifest goodness for political correctness. You know how many games I've coached? I've coached in college alone, probably close to 2,000. I've coached softball and then I coached women's basketball. And I was the winningest women's basketball coach in state's history, and I'm going on 800-plus wins in softball. So, the point being, is that this is coming from a crap-load of experience. It's coming from watching a whole lot of kids compete. It's coming from all different kinds of personalities. It's coming from all different kinds of ethnicities. It's coming from all different kind of...whatever. Is he the finest, as a kid that went through a camp? He's probably, obviously, the finest that ever went through anything. But at this time—at twenty-four years old—are you kidding me? He's more mature than guys that are in their mid-thirties in the NFL and yet he's never had a camp of his "own." So I just hope that all of this is so opposite of what he is that that he comes out of this

> **...he's exactly what the corporate market is looking for as a representative of quality human being and intelligence.**

off-season of endorsements, etc., because when they see him and hear him, he's exactly what the corporate market is looking for as a representative of quality human being and intelligence. Like I said, I think he's still—a little "virgin in the bushes," but when they see him and see who he represents and who he is, he's going to be one of the best ever for "put him out in front."

Watch a football game. Watch the quarterback's decision-making. If you look at a lot of quarterbacks' arm speed and quickness of decision—you're going to throw up. Serious? It's pathetic. When I watched some of the Bowl games this year, I'm saying, "You've got to be kidding me—who the heck is coaching these guys?" It's brutal. I guess we've been fortunate out here because Cal and Stanford—they've had some good quarterbacks and coaches. I always talk about yellow socks cause it's like a dog when he pees on himself. When you get scared, you start peeing, and I'll tell him, "You had yellow socks on that one." Now instead of having to get on his dignity, there's a couple of little things that you say to him that, "Man, yellow socks ran that decision," and the other kids will start laughing. I'm really saying, "Hold onto it longer—be tougher."

As for the Super Bowl, I was so happy when that field goal went through because, what I was fearful of is that he's a private person, and that's why I felt somewhat uncomfortable about saying things about the family or him, or whatever. Who knows where he would have set his own boundary, and I'm certainly the last one to want to cross that. You look at it and you say,

"You've got to start...twelve and three...won the AFC, beat the Raiders who everybody out here thought was the next thing to God...go back and beat Pittsburgh, and everybody thought Pittsburgh was going to bury him, and then to have a line of 16 points in a Super Bowl tells you what the intelligent money people thought. You know, there's no chance in this thing, and then get selected to the Pro Bowl, and then be given—and in any particular order put those in, but get to start the rest of the year, even though Bledsoe comes back healthy and then gets hurt, but recover enough to play, and then play, but not only play but play well, and then have the last drive and then the field goal go through and then the MVP—I mean, you could have stopped a long time ago and that would have been a great season for anyone. So, when you put it together, it's almost like you are really watching Disneyland, because there is too much to it. That was a funny commercial that they had—an interview with Brady and Bledsoe. Bradshaw interviewed them and they were contrasting the two, and he said, "One hundred million dollar contract," he said, "Drew, what do you drive, Mercedes?" "Yeah, Mercedes." "Tom, what do you drive?" "Ram truck." So they went through all this stuff, and they're laughing back and forth on the contrast. Then at the end of the game when they gave him the car, it was kind of funny because the whole pre-game was "Brady drives a Ram truck." That' s what made it funnier. It was well done. You just hope that all of this leaves another place to go down the trail without Tom being deemed unsuccessful if he can't re-achieve. He's so down-to-earth that I just hope it doesn't ruin him.

Definitely, football aside, Tom Brady is as fine a kid as I've had in my camp—no question.

What Heisman Trophy winner has made the most money?
The 1959 winner, Billy Cannon of LSU, was arrested
for counterfeiting in the early '80s and spent almost
three years in jail. Technically, he is the only
Heisman Trophy winner to ever "make" money.

In the 1979 baseball draft, the Kansas City Royals
drafted high school baseball standouts
Dan Marino and John Elway.

The Los Angeles Rams were the first NFL team
to wear helmets with a logo. The Cleveland Browns
are the only team with no logo. Shouldn't the
Cleveland helmets be brown instead of orange?

THESE TEN THINGS ARE THE SEVEN SIGNS YOU'RE HOOKED ON BRADY
MATT KING

Matt King is a baseball scout in Northern California. During Tom Brady's final two years of high school, King was hot on his trail for the Florida Marlins.

This was back in '95 when I scouted him for the Marlins. In '93 we're about the third club to go on computers so we actually could type our reports into laptops and download it onto a system. Everything is typed and Gary Hughes was one of those Scouting Directors, who was a great teacher. Gary's a pretty much 'keep it simple,' 'cut out the B.S.' kind of stuff. What you'll see in my report. It's very succinct. It's very to the point. I have all of Tom Brady's ratings from hitting, to throwing, to power, to fielding, to running. Running was not as important—he was a catcher at that time. Then in the column to the right, I have all my hand-written notes because we would have a conference call at which time we would have to "sell" our players. It's interesting to say the least. I was covering northern California for the Marlins. That was a good time, because at that time—in fact, I have all my reports for 1995. I was lucky enough that year to get a second-round pick, Randy Winn who is now with the Tampa Bay Devil Rays.

Pat Burrell, the Phillies young star, was in that draft class, and he was not even on my draft list whereas Tom Brady was high on that list. Burrell got drafted in something like the fifty-something round. If you talk to any scout that's honest—great kid, great body. You looked at him as a senior in high school and said this kid has got to got to go to college. He just doesn't have the actions—you know the quick-twitch actions you need to play in the big leagues. That's what we're doing. We're not scouting for minor league ball players—we're looking for big leaguers. This kid in one year just completely—his freshman year—my mouth just fell open when I saw him playing in Miami. He was incredible. Within one summer, this kid was like— 'this isn't the kid I scouted. This isn't the kid I saw.' Any honest scout would tell you that they probably didn't have him very high, if at all, in their draft list. He was a guy that had good ability, but when you looked to project him to the big leagues, you just didn't see the actions. He just didn't have those quick-twitch actions.

I saw him one night, about the fourth time I came into for the seniors and thought 'okay, this is it. I'm gonna make my decision on Pat Burrell tonight.' He played in a high school tournament night game. Brady's team had played earlier that day. The kid pitching was throwing about eighty four miles an hour, and Burrell struck out twice off this guy. This kid was throwing the old proverbial puffs up there. He didn't hit, so I thought, "Okay, he's off my draft." I'd seen him all the way through high school, and this was his senior year, and I've got to either go out on a limb or not. I had no doubt—he fell off my draft list. Then as a freshman, he broke almost every record as a freshman in NCAA history. He hit five hundred as a freshman at the University of Miami. I have no idea what happened. The kid had some qualities that were hard to overlook—good kid, hard worker, but I don't know how many home runs he hit his senior year in high school. Let's just say for example, he hit eight or nine. He hit thirty-something at the University of Miami.

Serra High School is a pretty good hotbed for athletes.

Serra High School is a pretty good hotbed for athletes. It's not gonna be very hard to find a guy like Brady. It was already known that he was a top area quarterback, and that he was going to Michigan. He had signed an early letter of intent to play at Michigan. On top of that, his team that year had another pretty good player. In fact, the other player, Gregory Millichap was also on my draft list, ranked just behind Brady. He never amounted to any kind of professional athlete. He went to the University of Hawaii. He could hit—he had bat speed. If I was to compare a guy like Millichap or Brady to Burrell, and you were to just ask me point blank, "Which player is going to go further?" I would have said, "Oh, Brady's gonna play, Millichap's gonna play. They have a chance to play in the big leagues." Burrell—no way. He doesn't have the quick twitch. He doesn't have quick enough bat speed or quick enough arm speed.

When you're scouting Serra, you may even be scouting the team they're going to play against because they play in a very, very good league, so just by default you'd see a player three to five times a year. So a guy like Brady isn't a guy you'd just kinda say, "Hey, I've found a diamond in the rough." He was six-four, two ten is what we had him at. He swung from the left side, threw from the right side.

It's amazing when reading his scouting report how I flash back to the home visit." That's the visit when we go in the house, and I actually remember what we discussed and exactly where we were sitting. This six foot, four inch kid sitting in the middle seat of the sofa with his dad on one side and his mom on the other, his shoulders somewhat slumped as if embarrassed to be bigger than his parents, but genuinely close to his family. He was a tireless worker, having just returned from the gym where he'd gone after baseball practice at Serra High School.

Brady was a guy I saw quite a lot. He wasn't one of those guys where it's like 'okay, this guy's just an average player, maybe I'll see him one time.' I probably saw Brady and his teammate, Greg Millichap play six, seven times his senior year. I also saw him as a junior. Brady was a guy who moved up my list. He started off low on my list because he hadn't grown into his body, and he was big, and catchers typically aren't six feet four. I don't know

> **So I ranked Brady's arm strength as a senior in high school at a fifty-two so he had an average major league arm as a high school senior.**

what he's listed at now on the Patriots roster, but if he's six-four, and he's not grown fully, how are you going to project the guy? Who's the tallest catcher you ever saw—Bob Melvin maybe? The average major league player is ranked a fifty—as a high school player, most of your numbers are gonna be in the forties and thirties. They're gonna be below average, well below average, but our job is to project them in the future. So I ranked Brady's arm strength as a senior in high school at a fifty-two so he had an average major league arm as a high school senior. Our ranking system was present and future so his future ranking was sixty-two. Sixty is above average, so I ranked his arm above average. Very few players get above—the ranking system goes to seventy, then eighty. I would say, in six, seven years of scouting with the Marlins, very rarely did a guy ever, ever get to seventy or eighty. Seventies and eighties are your Barry Bonds, your power numbers, guy that are just— there's not very many of those guys. You are rarely going to get sixty. Most average major league players are fifty. For him to get a sixty meant that he was going to get bigger and stronger. That was his biggest asset of all the ratings. I had his hitting ability as a thirty as a high school player, which is well below average. I projected him as forty-five so I projected him as a below-average hitting catcher. He's not gonna be your Mike Piazza or someone like that. I had him listed as a thirty with power, which is well below average in high school, to a future power of fifty-five.

So I had him above-average power so he's a guy that's gonna hit fifteen to twenty five home runs or something of that nature. Running speed—they didn't require us to get a running speed on catchers back then so I didn't even have a running speed on him. Arm accuracy was a forty-four, which is below average, and then later on projected as a fifty-seven just below the above-average ranking. That would be excellent, a guy who would hit every day in the big leagues. He could hit two sixty. He could catch a little, and he could throw—that would be your every-day catcher. He'd be an every-day catcher. He might even be a guy that doesn't hit that well, but he's an above-average catcher. He might even find himself on an All-Star team. I think he'd kind of have to back his way in a little bit. He is gonna be restricted on a few of his areas of his agility, catching-wise, 'cause of his height. I wrote down in my notes—this is the important part, the numbers, 'cause you won't understand the numbers unless I explain them to you.

This is my summation: "Physical description—big, tall, strong, lanky athlete. Large hands. No known injuries. Abilities—arm strength, loose easy arm, athletic ability, left-hand hitter with occasional pop in his bat and power potential. Shows good agility behind the play for a big guy. Weakness: Inexperience behind the plate. Just learning the position. Hand and footwork behind the plate just need work. He crouches at the plate, and it takes away from his power and his selection at the plate needs work." He really was a free swinger. He swung at a lot of bad pitches.

Summation: Big Boy, signed as a quarterback to attend the University of Michigan on a football scholarship. Has shown excellent arm strength throwing behind runners, easy actions. (Easy actions means that he just does it easily, smooth. It's almost like when you watch Barry Bonds hit a homerun, it's like—'there's no way that ball went that far.' Here's a guy that swings with just such pure—his stroke is so pure and so 'in the groove.' It's easy for him. The ball just pops off his bat. It's almost like he can tell you where he's gonna hit the ball.) Throwing was easy for Brady. He's not grunting and straining to throw the ball. It left his hand, and you think "This guy's not gonna get much velocity on it." But the ball just exploded out of his hand. That's what easy action is. If he continued to grow, catching may have been prohibitive, and he had potential arm strength to pitch. I think that was a very high likelihood.

Brady was the type of young athlete that just brings real joy to my job.

Ricky Nelson and John DeLorean married daughters of 1940 Heisman Trophy Winner Tom Harmon of Michigan.

I'm not surprised at all by what he has done. I always wondered whether his emotions would ever end up being a negative for him. Obviously, he grew emotionally. I remember him making outs or striking out or grounding out, I just remember him looking like he wanted to throw his helmet a hundred yards. You could tell he just had very, very high expectations of himself. You always wonder if a someone would be able to get their emotions together. You think of some players in the big leagues that their emotions have kinda hindered them.

But that's not really my job. My job is to rate his tools and that's one of those intangibles you really don't worry about but you wonder about. In my notes here I say, 'It'll take high second-round money to sign him and forego University of Michigan. Five hundred thousand dollars is in the ballpark.

We'd have a conference call meeting. They'd call and say, "Okay, talk about your players. Start with the bottom and go up." That year Brady was, on my list for northern Cal, number four. I drafted one of them and he didn't do much. The other one, Darren Hooper, a great talent, went to Arizona on a football scholarship I believe. The top one on my list was Randy Winn and he ended up getting to the big leagues. I was lucky enough to get him. So I got the top two out of five guys on my list, which was good.

Here are my notes, "Will take high second-round money to sign to forego the University of Michigan. Five hundred thousand dollars in the ballpark. Fierce competitor with a super arm and no fear. Hitting has improved immensely from the beginning to the end of the season. Incredible work ethic. I like this guy. He has drive. He works out every day at the gym. He'd love to play before a hundred thousand plus fans at Michigan but knows that baseball is, in his words 'the sport.' Above all, an alternative Serra Padre perspective (MY boss, Gary Hughes, is a Serra grad.) may strengthen the Marlin organization. Round is not important. If he slides, we should still draft him."

As soon as you rank a prospect in the top five or six rounds area, once I, as a scout think that he's good enough to go in the upper part of the draft, that's when I need to notify others. I think Brady was probably seen by five of our scouts. He was seen by Gary, the big boss. I know Orrin Freeman saw him. I know that Jax Robertson saw him. I know that Dick Eagan saw him. I would guess that Keith Snider saw him because he had an area close to mine, and he

The revenue from one home football game at schools like Michigan and Tennessee pays for all the scholarships for all their athletes in all their sports for the entire school year.

probably saw him, and I'll bet Tim Schmidt saw him. So he probably was seen by even more than five guys, just from my organization.

Gary never told you what he thought about a prospect after watching him. He didn't want his opinion to influence the area scout. When it came down to it, it didn't matter what he thought until the very end anyway. So if he said, "Yeah, I think he's not a guy that I would...." And I say, "Okay." And I don't have the guts to keep him on my list—I drop him down to the thirtieth guy on my list, that's not my job. My job is to be a free-thinker. There were always a lot of scouts at Brady's games. I think that was the year when there were quite a few players there to see—Brady, Millichap, Burrell and Randy Winn.

If I were to run into Brady out somewhere today, I would congratulate him for his accomplishments, I would tell him, "I know you've worked hard to get where you're at, and I know you've stuck to your guns as far as the beliefs you've had in yourself. The way you carry yourself and the way you come across is real. It's what we need more of in professional athletics."

I just remember always waiting to hear his name...

I just know this is a guy, I'm sure that accepting money is going to change him. Very few people are immune from changing from those things. But I can tell you, I think he was seventeen years when I saw him, and now seven years later—here's a guy who knows his roots. He knows who he is. If you remember seeing some of his interviews, he'd say, "I want to say hello to my sisters." You know he loves his family. I didn't hear all of his interviews, but I hear that stuff and I go, "That's the guy I met seven years ago."

Michigan is one of those teams that is going to be on national TV four or five times a year. I just remember always waiting to hear his name, and I don't think he played much until his junior year, his fourth year. He hung in there. I wish I had a bug in his ear knowing what he was thinking during all that time. He split time his senior year. He had to have just been working his butt off trying to prove himself. I just remember even seeing him as a senior and going, "This is great. Here's a guy that's really hung in there, he was a fifth year senior at that point, and I'm thinking he's not really gonna go anywhere. He's not gonna really do anything."

> In 1941, Buff Donelli was the head football coach for the Pittsburgh Steelers and Duquesne University.

PHIL OFTEN REMINISCES ABOUT THE GOOD OLD DAY!

PHIL GRATSINOPOULOS

A year ago Phil Gratsinopoulos was working out with Tom Brady catching passes at College of San Mateo (CA). Little did he know the only other guy on the field with him would be Super Bowl MVP just nine months later.

I played two years of football at College of San Mateo for Coach Martinez. Then I got a full scholarship to Sacramento State, and that's where I'm now playing football as a junior. Last spring following my sophomore year, I was working out with other quarterbacks at CSM. Coach Martinez and I are pretty close. I was just always working out up there at the gym getting ready for spring ball. Coach Martinez told me to be at school at a certain time one day because Tom Brady was going to be up there. Brady goes back to Coach Martinez every summer and spring. Coach Martinez had taught him how to throw a ball.

I had heard of Tom Brady but did not know the guy personally. He was pretty much kind of like big talk around San Mateo because he made it to the pros. Actually I had met him before because I had met a girl friend, Kelly, who was real close with his family. Coach just called me and told me to be up there to catch passes. I was totally excited because I had never caught passes from an NFL quarterback before so I was there early. I think I went in the weight room for a little while before so I could look bigger when I went out on the field—I pumped some iron! We just went out there, and I was warming up with him. Then I started running some patterns for him.

Coach Martinez and Tom would decide what patterns we would run. He's got a tight spiral. His ball comes in good. He throws harder than the quarterbacks I had caught before. You can tell he's got a strong arm. I wasn't really looking at his drop-back. I was the guy that was running the routes and stuff. When I turned, he had already released it. He leads you good. He does everything perfect. What can I say—eye contact. When I run a curl route and turn around, the ball's right there, and it's on the money like to the point where I'm gonna turn to the outside, the ball's on the outside right at the shoulder. I think he can throw deep, but we didn't see him throw deep that much this year. I don't think it's a question of his arm strength. I think it's just the offense that he's running there in New England and what they want to do with the ball. He's a young quarterback, and I think as he gets more confidence and gets older, he'll start going down the field more.

I will regret one thing for the rest of my life. He had brought an NFL ball to the workout. At the end of the workout, Tom goes, "Here, you can keep this." Coach Martinez said, "Why don't you have him sign it?" I go, "Maybe next time," and kind of blew him off. Then this year, he got NFL Super Bowl MVP. I still have the ball today that he gave me but missing the Tom Brady John Hancock.

I asked him how he thought my hands looked. I might have dropped one ball. He said I looked good and had good height. He said if I wanted to go to the pros I'd have to bulk up a little more. He said height and hands look pretty good. He said speed was pretty good.

I'm really looking forward, if he comes back and throws again, to going and catching balls from him. That'll be an honor to go do that again.

My college buddies and I watched him all during the season, and I'd go, "You know what, I caught balls with that guy." A lot of people believed me 'cause they knew that I was from the same area as him. A couple of guys knew my coach, Tom Martinez, so they believed me. Then when the Super Bowl came out, I told them I couldn't believe it. It was a shock.

> **He went out there with me as humble as a jayvee quarterback, but he was in the pros.**

Tom Brady is a real class act. He went out there with me as humble as a jayvee quarterback, but he was in the pros. He just listened to Tom Martinez and what he said. Talking to me, it was like he was just another guy that was throwing me the balls and I was catching them. He was a real nice guy, and he thanked me for catching his balls, like I was doing him a favor.

When I watched the Super Bowl, I was just sitting there, and my eyes were glued on Tom. It was like watching, not a movie star, but I've never really met somebody and been close to somebody like that who has gone on to do something like that. He would be like my first guy that I would know and have actually caught passes from and bonded with him in a way that he would recognize me, and it was just amazing to see him do that. The part that I was really intrigued by was afterward when he had the hat on, and he said, "I'm going to Disney World." That was what really got me. Not so much the game, but afterwards, and the media comes in, and all that stuff, I was just like, "Oh my God. I don't believe that's him." And I was thinking, 'Not too long ago, I was catching his passes.'

I wasn't that surprised to see how well he did when he got the chance. He did the same thing at Michigan. He wasn't the guy right off the bat, but it just seems that he really steps up and makes big plays when the team needs him to do that. He doesn't let the team down. At Michigan, he wasn't the first guy, but I'm sure he was a great student of the game, and as soon as his number got called, he just answered to that. That's exactly what he did in New England.

Tom Brady at Junipero Serra High School

Final Page

There are some enduring mysteries of life:
What exactly does George Hamilton do for a living?
Why is Peter Gammons' picture on the twenty-dollar bill?
Why would anyone for any reason hire Buck Showalter to
work for them before he has a charisma bypass?
Why is George Karl the highest paid coach
in the history of sports?
When will George Steinbrenner realize that "BOSS"
spelled backwards is "Double SOB?
Where do they find artificial lawn mowers for artificial turf?
And why can't every man conduct his affairs
like Tom Brady?

Go now.

Help

The publisher is working on a series of books called *Fandemonium.* Fans of over eighty professional and collegiate teams will tell their favorite stories about going to a game, watching on television or listening on the radio.

The first two books in the series, *Fighting Irish Fandemonium* (Notre Dame) and (Green Bay) *Packers Fandemonium* are being released in late summer 2002. If you have a funny, poignant or interesting story on the Red Sox, Bruins, Wolverines, Yankees, and so on, contact us at our website: www.fandemonium.net.

Appendix

Tom Brady had an appendectomy in
October 1997 in Ann Arbor, Michigan.

Kurt Warner had his appendix removed on May 16, 2000
at Missouri Baptist Medical Center in St. Louis, MO.